Shakespeare's
Comedy of
Love

Shakespeare's Comedy of Love

Alexander Leggatt

Methuen & Co Ltd

First published 1974
by Methuen & Co Ltd
11 New Fetter Lane, London EC4
© 1973 Alexander Leggatt
Printed in Great Britain by
Richard Clay (The Chaucer Press) Ltd
Bungay, Suffolk

SBN 416 79120 4 (hardbound)
SBN 416 79130 1 (paperback)

Distributed in the USA by
Harper & Row Publishers Inc
Barnes & Noble Import Division

For Anna

Contents

	Acknowledgements	viii
	Preface	xi
1	The Comedy of Errors	1
2	The Two Gentlemen of Verona	21
3	The Taming of the Shrew	41
4	Love's Labour's Lost	63
5	A Midsummer Night's Dream	89
6	The Merchant of Venice	117
7	Much Ado About Nothing	151
8	As You Like It	185
9	Twelfth Night	221
10	Conclusion: beyond Twelfth Night	255

Acknowledgements

I am grateful for the help and encouragement of J. Leeds Barroll, William Blissett, Clifford Leech, and Peter Marinelli, all of whom commented on various early stages of this work; and I am particularly grateful to Professor Blissett, who read the final draft and saved me from many errors and infelicities. The imperfections that remain are my own responsibility.

Papers arising directly or indirectly from this work were read at various times at the Shakespeare Institute and at the University of Caen, and I wish to thank those concerned for their hospitality, and for the opportunity to send up a few trial balloons.

I am glad to acknowledge the help of the Canada Council, which provided a research grant allowing me to spend a summer in preliminary work. And I am particularly grateful to the Department of English of University College, and to the Canada Council, for providing, respectively, the time and the money for a year's leave of absence during which most of this book was written.

Alexander Leggatt
University College
University of Toronto
June 1973

Note

All references to Shakespeare are to Peter Alexander's edition of the *Complete Works* (London, 1968).

In the afternoon
We will with some strange pastime solace them,
Such as the shortness of the time can shape;
For revels, dances, masks, and merry hours,
Forerun fair Love, strewing her way with flowers.
Love's Labour's Lost

No masque to-night; the wind is come about.
The Merchant of Venice

Preface

The complaint that there is not enough criticism of Shakespeare's comedies is now heard less often than it used to be. We have come to take these plays quite seriously, hunting through them for central themes, archetypal patterns and other features that make a work of art respectable; and a substantial body of criticism, much of it sensitive and interesting, has been the result. But comedy is notoriously dangerous for the critic. On the one hand, the solemnity of his manner as he probes the inner seriousness of a comedy may contrast disconcertingly with the tone of the play itself; on the other hand, if he tries to make us appreciate the fun of the play, he may be like the sort of host who makes his guests acutely uncomfortable by asking every five minutes if they are enjoying themselves. These are familiar dangers, easier to acknowledge than to avoid. But in dealing with Shakespeare's comedies there is a third danger, more insidious and perhaps more serious: the normal, understandable desire of the critic to seek the inner unity of a work of art. This aim, reasonable in itself, can have unfortunate effects. 'Unity' can be too narrowly defined, and when everything is seen as contributing to a central idea, a single pattern of images, or a particular kind of story, then individual scenes or characters may be understood from that point of view alone, and thus denied their full life. By the same token, since so many of Shakespeare's comedies use the same devices, there has been an understandable tendency among critics to seek the unity of the series as a whole, with a corresponding neglect of the individuality of particular plays.

Of course this can happen in the criticism of any work; but it is especially unfortunate when it happens with Shakespeare's comedies, since so much of their fascination stems from their unpredictability. The critic must be always alert, always prepared to change his line of inquiry. To seek for subtle psychological realism among, say, the lovers of *A Midsummer Night's Dream* is to court frustration; to neglect it in *Much Ado About Nothing* is to miss half the play. Even within particular plays the ground keeps changing: much of the dramatic life of a play like *As You Like It* (as I will try to show in a later chapter) depends on swift, unpredictable shifts in idiom, from casual naturalism to high artifice. The criticism that tries to make a work of art stand still will be in serious difficulties here.

What I have tried to do in this study, then, is to reverse one of criticism's normal interests, to seek not the internal unity of each play but its internal variety. The starting-point, usually, is some instance of tension between different kinds of style or dramatic idiom within the play. This can lead in a variety of directions: to discussions not so much of theme, character or archetypal pattern, as of how thematic interests are qualified by other factors; how different kinds of characterization interact; or how the level of fantasy or the closeness of the story to familiar folk tales can shift from scene to scene. In short, instead of freezing the plays in order to demonstrate one particular thing about them, I have tried to see them as dynamic and constantly changing. The same applies to the series as a whole: each play will be seen to a great extent as a reaction against the one that preceded it.

But of course certain issues do recur. The advantage of selecting for this kind of study a group of plays like the so-called 'romantic' comedies from *The Comedy of Errors* to *Twelfth Night* is that the recurring plot situations, and the recurring interest in one experience, romantic love, provide a basis of common material that helps to control the discussion. The variety of Shakespeare's comic art is more striking when we set it against the apparent uniformity of the material he begins with. Plot devices such as disguises and journeys, thematic interests such as language, convention and above all romantic love itself – all these topics will confront us in play after play; but never in quite the same way twice. Shakespeare may begin by examining romantic love; but he ends by examining the materials of his own art, and each play is a fresh experiment, a fresh interplay of opposing styles and visions. It is this sense of a dynamic art – growing, changing, self-questioning – that I have tried to capture here.[1]

[1] A word should be said about the omission of *The Merry Wives of Windsor* from this study. I think more highly of the play than do many critics, but I feel the best way of approaching it is not to group it with the romantic comedies (it is a very different kind of play) but to compare it with other specimens of citizen comedy. I have approached the play from this angle in a forthcoming study of citizen comedy.

The Comedy of Errors

In the second scene of *The Comedy of Errors*, Dromio of Ephesus meets Antipholus of Syracuse for the first time, and rebukes him for not coming home to dinner. Antipholus ignores the rebuke (which means nothing to him) and turns to a more urgent matter:

ANTIPHOLUS S: Stop in your wind, sir; tell me this, I pray:
Where have you left the money that I gave
you?

DROMIO E: O – sixpence that I had a Wednesday last
To pay the saddler for my mistress' crupper?
The saddler had it, sir; I kept it not.

(I. ii. 53–7)

We settle ourselves for a couple of hours of farce. The confusion seems to be on a purely material level – mistaken persons and mislaid goods. Shakespeare is keeping to the spirit of his source, the *Menaechmi* of Plautus, where the action takes place in a hard southern daylight and the issues are all practical ones.

But at the end of this first scene of confusion, Shakespeare introduces a new note. In Plautus, Epidamnum is seen as a place of danger, but danger of a prosaic and familiar kind:

For assure your selfe, this towne *Epidamnum*, is a place of outragious expenses, exceeding in all ryot and lasciviousness: and (I heare) as full of Ribaulds, Parasites, Drunkards, Catch-

poles, Cony-catchers, and Sycophants, as it can hold: then for
Curtizans, why here's the currantest stamp of them in the world.
Ye may not thinke here to scape with as light cost as in other
places.

(II. i. p. 17)[1]

Antipholus of Syracuse sees Ephesus in quite a different way:

They say this town is full of cozenage;
As, nimble jugglers that deceive the eye,
Dark-working sorcerers that change the mind,
Soul-killing witches that deform the body,
Disguised cheaters, prating mountebanks,
And many such-like liberties of sin.

(I. ii. 97–102)

The sleight of hand that deceives the eye, the cunning of the confidence trick, shades into something deeper and more sinister,
deception and shape-shifting that attack not merely the purse but
the body and soul. There are no such overtones in Plautus. Nor is
there much sense of wonder in the characters; only a temporary
bewilderment that is easily explained away. Shakespeare's Antipholus of Syracuse, addressed by name by a woman he has never
seen before, asks, 'How can she thus, then, call us by our names, /
Unless it be by inspiration?' (II. ii. 165–6). In the parallel incident
in *Menaechmi*, the courtesan's cook addresses Menaechmus by
name, and an explanation (wrong, but reasonable) is immediately
forthcoming:

These Courtizans as soone as anie straunge shippe arrive at
the Haven, they send a boye or a wench to enquire what they
be, what their names be, whence they come, wherefore they
come, &c. If they can by any meanes strike acquaintance with
him, or allure him to their houses, he is their owne.

(II. i. p. 19)

No such reassuring explanations are offered to Shakespeare's
characters. At times even the audience is left in the dark, for

[1] References to *Menaechmi* are to William Warner's translation, in Geoffrey
Bullough, *Narrative and Dramatic Sources of Shakespeare*, I (London, 1957). On the
likelihood that Shakespeare knew and used this version, see Bullough's introduction, pp. 3–4.

Shakespeare takes fewer pains than Plautus to give a logical under-propping to his comic fantasy. There is nothing improbable in identical twins, but identical twins with the same name take some explaining, and Plautus is ready with the answer: 'When it was tolde us that you and our father were both dead, our Graundsire (in memorie of my fathers name) chaunged mine to Menechmus' (v. i. p. 38). Shakespeare provides *two* sets of twins with the same name, and not a word of explanation.

The Roman comedy of confusion takes place in a practical world, where nothing is inexplicable, and where the issues at stake are largely the material ones of who owns what and where the next meal is coming from. The play has a single vision and a uniform texture. But Shakespeare gives us a play in a more mixed dramatic idiom. The market-place atmosphere of Plautus is still present, but it no longer monopolizes the play; it is varied by suggestions of fantasy and mystery, and the result is a mixture of styles that goes much deeper than changes from prose to verse, or the varying of metres. It is a mixture of different ways of viewing the world, of which different dramatic styles are ultimately a reflection. Nor is the decision to mix idioms in this way artificially imposed; it springs from Shakespeare's own fresh and imaginative meditation on the central idea of Plautus, the idea of confusion. *The Comedy of Errors* is unusual in that mistaken identity is itself the primary motif, not (as in *As You Like It* or *Twelfth Night*) a technical device to aid the presentation of some other issue. Perhaps Shakespeare, before he could use mistaken identity as an instrument, had to give it a thorough examination. And in exploiting the situations arising from it, Shakespeare demonstrates that confusion, the gap of understanding between one mind and another, can exist at a deeper level than who's-got-the-chain or which-twin-is-it-*this*-time. These questions are important to the action, and much of the play's immediate comic life depends on them; but they are also signals of a deeper breakdown of understanding; the characters seem at times to inhabit different worlds, different orders of experience.

Some of this effect is created by the mingling – and, at times, the collision – of dramatic styles. In II. ii Adriana, meeting the man she thinks is her husband, attacks him passionately for straying from her, urging him to recognize that as husband and wife they are bound together in a single being, and that consequently she shares in his corruption. Taken out of context, the speech is passionate and earnest, idealistic in its view of marriage and urgent in its emotional response to the breaking of that ideal. But the context is all-important. Adriana's speech follows immediately – with no transition whatever – a racy comic turn between Dromio and Antipholus on time, falling hair and syphilis; she breaks in on two characters who are operating in quite a different dramatic world. And any chance we might have of making the transition from one mode to another and taking Adriana's speech seriously is killed by the fact that all her high talk about the closeness of the marriage bond is directed at the wrong Antipholus, who – after listening to about forty lines on how closely he and Adriana are bound together – asks innocently, 'Plead you to me, fair dame?' (II. ii. 146). Or consider the following passage:

ANTIPHOLUS S: The fellow is distract, and so am I;
                And here we wander in illusions.
                Some blessed power deliver us from hence!
                                    [*Enter a* Courtezan.
COURTEZAN: Well met, well met, Master Antipholus.
                I see, sir, you have found the goldsmith now.
                Is that the chain you promis'd me to-day?
ANTIPHOLUS S: Satan, avoid! I charge thee, tempt me not.
DROMIO S: Master, is this Mistress Satan?
ANTIPHOLUS S: It is the devil.
                                    (IV. iii. 37–45)

Here, the attitude of each character is comically dislocated. The courtesan is simply living her casual, material life, while Antipholus is struggling between heaven and hell, in a metaphysical nightmare where even a call for 'some blessed power' is met by (for him) a fresh appearance of evil, and (for the audience) a comic anticlimax. The contrast is driven home, once again, by the different styles of speech – the casual chatter of the courtesan, the explosive horror of Antipholus and, on the side, Dromio's more familiar recognition of the powers of evil. This introduces us to a device we will see Shakespeare using throughout his comedies: a speech is comically dislocated by being placed in the wrong context, usually through being addressed to an unsympathetic or uncomprehending listener. The comic value of this device is obvious, and is exploited throughout the play. Yet, as with many such devices, it requires only a twist of emphasis, or a new situation, to make the effect pathetic or disturbing. The gaps of understanding between us are not always amusing. While we laugh easily enough when Adriana fires a long, emotional speech at the wrong Antipholus, it is not so funny when, later in the play, Aegeon pleads with his son to save his life, and his son refuses to acknowledge him.

The effect is to show how frail and vulnerable our attitudes and assumptions are, to bring into sharp focus the incompleteness of anything we may say or do, the fact that, however serious or important it may seem to us, there is always another viewpoint from which it is wrong, or trivial, or incomprehensible. The collisions of different minds that take place throughout *The Comedy of Errors* help to suggest this. When, for example, Adriana strikes a posture of languishing grief, Luciana's sharp comment deflates it immediately:

> Since that my beauty cannot please his eye,
> I'll weep what's left away, and weeping die.
> LUCIANA: How many fond fools serve mad jealousy!
>
> (II. i. 114–16)

The triple rhyme clinches the point: Adriana is not even allowed the neat finality of a concluding couplet. But one might say that Luciana is getting her revenge, for earlier in the same scene she had delivered a lecture to Adriana on the necessity of order in marriage, urging that a wife should submit patiently to her husband, only to receive this reply:

> A wretched soul, bruis'd with adversity,
> We bid be patient when we hear it cry;
> But were we burd'ned with like weight of pain,
> As much, or more, we should ourselves complain.
> So thou, that hast no unkind mate to grieve thee,
> With urging helpless patience would relieve me;

But if thou live to see like right bereft,
This fool-begg'd patience in thee will be left.

(II. i. 34–41)

One of the most persistent comic points in Shakespeare is the disparity between theory and reality, the breakdown of philosophy in the face of experience – particularly when the experience is yours and the philosophy is someone else's. Throughout the play, Antipholus of Ephesus is (like his wife) the recipient of much good advice about the necessity of patience – from his friends (III. i. 85–106), from the officer who arrests him (IV. iv. 18) – in short, from people who do not really share his problems. He obviously hears this good advice once too often, and retaliates by giving Pinch an object lesson in the difficulties of philosophy: 'My master preaches patience to him, and the while / His man with scissors nicks him like a fool' (v. i. 174–5).

The gap between different understandings of the world is centred on the two Antipholus brothers. In *Menaechmi* the twin brothers inhabit the same prosaic, domestic world and undergo basically the same kind of experience; in *The Comedy of Errors* not only are their characters more sharply distinguished,[2] but the difference between their experiences is more emphasized. In the words of A. C. Hamilton, Antipholus of Ephesus 'endures a nightmare' while his brother 'enjoys a delightful dream'.[3] One is showered with gifts, money and women; the other is locked out of his house, arrested for debt and tied up as a lunatic. The difference in their experiences is signalled by a difference in style. The scene in which Antipholus of Ephesus is locked out of his house (III. i) is noisy, raucous and farcical, full of spluttering threats and bawdy insults; it is immediately followed (III. ii) by his brother's courtship of Luciana, a quiet scene of romantic feeling shot through with more subtle comic irony, a scene in which the focus is on

---

[2] The difference between the characters is summarized by Marion Bodwell Smith, *Dualities in Shakespeare* (Toronto, 1966):

> Antipholus of Syracuse is the milder and less rash, the more courteous and considerate of the two. Where Antipholus of Ephesus meets obstacles head-on and is with difficulty persuaded by his friends to make the best of a bad situation, Antipholus of Syracuse is more inclined to go with the tide rather than fight against it (p. 22).

[3] *The Early Shakespeare* (San Marino, 1967), p. 96.

emotional rather than on physical problems. The contrast is not rigid throughout, for Antipholus of Syracuse is involved in a good deal of knockabout farce, but it is significant that as soon as his brother appears (III. i is the latter's first scene) we are made aware of this disparity between them.

They seem to inhabit two different towns. For Antipholus of Ephesus, as for the rest of the native population (and initially for the audience) Ephesus is the familiar seaport town of Plautine comedy, a small world of commerce and domesticity, where, as E. M. W. Tillyard puts it, 'everyone knows everyone else's business, where merchants predominate, and where dinner is a serious matter'.[4] Shakespeare even sharpens the commercial interests of the town, giving them a distinctly unflattering emphasis. A dispute over the Duke of Syracuse's treatment of Ephesian merchants has led to 'mortal and intestine jars' (I. i. 11), and to a sentence of death on any merchant from one town who visits the other. This is the predicament in which Aegeon stands in the first scene. According to the Duke, he is condemned

> Unless a thousand marks be levied,
> To quit the penalty and to ransom him.
> Thy substance, valued at the highest rate,
> Cannot amount unto a hundred marks;
> Therefore by law thou art condemn'd to die.

> (I. i. 22–6)

Though the point is not much developed, this crude measuring of human life in financial terms anticipates the inhuman legalism of Shylock;[5] and throughout the play there are several small touches conveying the Ephesians' narrow concern with money. The merchant who talks with Antipholus of Syracuse in the second scene is kind enough to warn him against the law; but he refuses an invitation to keep him company and join him for dinner, on the grounds that he is already engaged 'to certain merchants, / Of whom I hope to make much benefit' (I. ii. 24–5). The officer who arrests Antipholus of Ephesus refuses to release him, even when told he is mad and needs treatment:

[4] *Shakespeare's Early Comedies* (London, 1965), pp. 54–5.
[5] See Smith, *Dualities in Shakespeare*, p. 24.

ADRIANA: What wilt thou do, thou peevish officer?
Hast thou delight to see a wretched man
Do outrage and displeasure to himself?
OFFICER: He is my prisoner; if I let him go,
The debt he owes will be requir'd of me.

(IV. iv. 111–15)

In this commercial world, Antipholus of Ephesus appears to have occupied, when the action begins, a solid and respectable place. Angelo the goldsmith describes him as 'Of very reverent reputation . . . / Of credit infinite, highly belov'd' (v. i. 5–6). His marriage, whatever its internal difficulties, is eminently respectable, having been arranged by the Duke himself (v. i. 137–8, 198). In the commercial and domestic spheres he inhabits, disruption may be fun for the audience, but it is unsettling and unpleasant for the victim. As we see throughout Shakespeare's comedies, love seems to thrive on irrationality and confusion, and emerges from it strengthened, renewed and satisfied: the experience of Antipholus of Syracuse is roughly parallel to that of Demetrius, Orlando and Sebastian. But the world of commerce simply goes crazy when an irrational factor is introduced, and the only satisfaction is for chains and ducats to be restored to their original owners, as though the confusion had never taken place. Nothing is gained in the process, for the transactions of business are barren and limited, incapable of the sudden, spontaneous enrichment that we see in the transactions of love. What is enchantment and enrichment for one brother is simply confusion for the other, a confusion that must be put right. The only party to gain something is the audience: since commercial life has been depicted in such unflattering terms, we are bound to take a special, mischievous delight in seeing it disrupted.

One may even question whether the disruption of Antipholus's marriage leads to any good result for the characters. The disorder produced by mistaken identity is linked to a more familiar disorder, a longstanding unhappiness between husband and wife. Adriana tells the Abbess that her husband has not been himself all week, though his rage has only broken out that afternoon (v. i. 45–8). And when she confesses that her nagging has disrupted the normal rhythms of his life, the Abbess lectures her:

In food, in sport, and life-preserving rest,
To be disturb'd would mad or man or beast.
The consequence is, then, thy jealous fits
Hath scar'd thy husband from the use of wits.

(v. i. 83–6)

We know, of course, that his 'madness' depends more on the mistaken-identity confusion than anything else (we have seen him cheated of a meal for reasons other than his wife's scolding tongue). But the Abbess's speech reminds us there are other, more familiar ways a man's life can be disrupted, and with similar results. It is clear enough that not all of Antipholus's problems stem from the fact that his brother is in town, and we may wonder if these problems can all be cured by the discovery of his brother. One curious feature of the ending is that, while the problems of the marriage have been thoroughly aired, there is no explicit reconciliation between husband and wife. The director may contrive a forgiving embrace, but nothing in the text requires it. At the end of *Menaechmi*, the wife is curtly dismissed as one more piece of household goods to be auctioned off as her husband leaves town to live with his brother (v. i. p. 39). Shakespeare does not give us that, either; he leaves us, instead, with a silence that the performers have to fill by some decision of their own.[6] For the critic, with only the text before him, the final state of this marriage must remain an open question. But we may suggest that in the domestic, commercial world of Ephesus there are no miracles.

No miracles, at least, for the native population. For the outsider, Antipholus of Syracuse, Ephesus is a different kind of town altogether, a place of magic and enchantment. His wonder and bewilderment remind us of the town's reputation as a centre of magic,[7] a reputation to which none of the native population ever refers. And while – if we shake ourselves – we may remember that nothing supernatural actually takes place, we see the town to a great extent through the eyes of the outsiders, for they are given

[6] There is a similar silence at the end of *Measure for Measure*, when Isabella says nothing to Claudio, and is given no chance to reply to the Duke's proposal of marriage.
[7] See R. A. Foakes, introduction to his Arden edition of *The Comedy of Errors* (London, 1962), p. xxix.

more dramatic prominence than the natives, and treated, on the whole, more sympathetically. Viewed from the special angle of the outsider, even the normal intercourse of life becomes bizarre and unsettling:

> There's not a man I meet but doth salute me
> As if I were their well-acquainted friend;
> And every one doth call me by my name.
> Some tender money to me, some invite me,
> Some other give me thanks for kindnesses,
> Some offer me commodities to buy;
> Even now a tailor call'd me in his shop,
> And show'd me silks that he had bought for me,
> And therewithal took measure of my body.
> Sure these are but imaginary wiles,
> And Lapland sorcerers inhabit here.
>
> (IV. iii. 1–11)

The prosaic, day-to-day business of a commercial town becomes something strange and dreamlike, because it is all happening to the wrong man.

Each brother's experience of the confusion of mistaken identity is matched by the more familiar experience of being unsettled by a woman. Antipholus of Ephesus has his domestic routine disrupted by an unseen brother and a nagging wife; Antipholus of Syracuse is enchanted by a strange town, and suddenly bewitched by love (the curious name given him in the Folio, 'Antipholus Erotes', suggests both wandering and love). Even when addressed by Adriana, he sees himself as in a dream, a dream to which he is willing to surrender:

> Am I in earth, in heaven, or in hell?
> Sleeping or waking, mad or well-advis'd?
> Known unto these, and to myself disguis'd!
> I'll say as they say, and persever so,
> And in this mist at all adventures go.
>
> (II. ii. 211–15)

But this surrender is still somewhat tentative; he offers himself to Luciana more recklessly: 'Are you a god? Would you create me

new? / Transform me, then, and to your pow'r I'll yield' (III. ii.
39–40). Earlier in the play, there was discontent in his words, 'So
I, to find a mother and a brother, / In quest of them, unhappy,
lose myself' (I. ii. 39–40). But now he is eager to lose himself in a
more profound way, transformed by love.[8]

There is certainly a transformation in his understanding. As the
market-place and the tailor's shop acquire an aura of mystery for
him, so too does Luciana. Here the special perspective of the outsider fuses with the special perspective of the lover, whose view of
his lady is a transforming vision, comically at odds with reality.
In their scene together, we note the practical, worldly manner of
Luciana's advice:

> If you did wed my sister for her wealth,
> Then for her wealth's sake use her with more kindness;
> Or, if you like elsewhere, do it by stealth;
> Muffle your false love with some show of blindness . . .
> Then, gentle brother, get you in again;
> Comfort my sister, cheer her, call her wife.
> 'Tis holy sport to be a little vain
> When the sweet breath of flattery conquers strife.
>
> (III. ii. 5–8, 25–8)

Her words appear cynical; but there is an undercurrent of sadness
in them, as she tries to make the best of a difficult situation. Above
all, she is realistic: there are no appeals to higher feelings, and she
does not attempt to revive a dead love. But for Antipholus this
rueful, worldly, but perfectly clear advice is transformed into a
divine, oracular pronouncement, veiled in mystery:

> Sweet mistress – what your name is else, I know not,
> Nor by what wonder you do hit of mine –
> Less in your knowledge and your grace you show not
> Than our earth's wonder – more than earth, divine.
> Teach me, dear creature, how to think and speak;
> Lay open to my earthy-gross conceit,

[8] For a detailed discussion of the loss of identity as a theme in the play, see
Harold Brooks, 'Themes and structure in *The Comedy of Errors*', in John Russell
Brown and Bernard Harris (eds.), *Early Shakespeare* (London, 1961), pp. 55–71.

> Smother'd in errors, feeble, shallow, weak,
> The folded meaning of your words' deceit.
>
> (III. ii. 29–36)

But the comic disparity between Luciana as we see her and the lover's special vision, though clear enough, is less drastic than it might have been. The alternate rhyme they both use gives a heightened, formal quality to her speech. Despite its worldly content there *is* something oracular in its manner, and the result is a subtler comic effect than we might have expected. The double vision of Luciana is not just a matter of contrasting our reactions with the lover's; it is built into the presentation of Luciana herself – so that, while laughing at the lover, we can see his point of view. Though romantic love is a secondary motif in this play, the balance between mockery and sympathy, characteristic of later comedies, has already been struck.

This surrender to a special vision is placed ironically against Adriana's very different view of the transformations of love as they occur in marriage. Here the woman surrenders to the man (in courtship it is the other way round) and the surrender can be not life-enhancing but ruinous:

> Do their gay vestments his affections bait?
> That's not my fault; he's master of my state.
> What ruins are in me that can be found
> Not by him ruin'd? Then is he the ground
> Of my defeatures. My decayed fair
> A sunny look of his would soon repair.
>
> (II. i. 94–9)

And she later insists that her husband's corruption will spread inevitably to her (II. ii. 118–45). In the speeches of the lover, the idea of surrender is still innocent and uncomplicated, unbruised by reality. In the speeches of the wife, it has become tinged with self-pity and resentment, as we move from the idealism of courtship to the tensions of the sex war.[9]

[9] The contrast between lover-and-mistress and wife-and-husband is reviewed by Charles Brooks, 'Shakespeare's romantic shrews', *Shakespeare Quarterly*, XI (summer 1960), p. 355. He takes a more sanguine view of Adriana's marriage than I have.

The idea of enchantment and transformation – including surrender in love – is seen from a third angle, that of Dromio of Syracuse, and there is a contrast between master and servant, as there is between brother and brother. What is normal life for the Ephesians and a dream for Antipholus of Syracuse is a folktale horror story come true for Dromio: 'This is the fairy land. O spite of spites! / We talk with goblins, owls, and sprites!' (II. ii. 188–9). In place of his master's exotic 'Lapland sorcerers', Dromio imagines Ephesus as a town full of more familiar bugbears – fairies and devils. When his master (as he thinks) is arrested for debt, he spins elaborate fantasies about the sergeant as a devil (IV. ii. 31–46; IV. iii. 12–18). (His brother, characteristically, spins smaller fantasies out of the more prosaic business of being beaten – II. i. 82–5; IV. iv. 26–37.) And while Antipholus is eager to surrender himself to a woman and be transformed by her, Dromio's view of this surrender is (like the woman) radically different, and expressed in a comically contrasting style. A few lines after Antipholus has addressed Luciana as 'mine own self's better part; / Mine eye's clear eye, my dear heart's dearer heart' (III. ii. 61–2), Dromio enters, fleeing in panic from the fat kitchen wench, and exclaiming, 'Do you know me, sir? Am I Dromio? Am I your man? Am I myself? . . . I am an ass, I am a woman's man, and besides myself' (III. ii. 73–8). He fears that she would have 'transform'd me to a curtal dog, and made me turn i'th'wheel' (III. ii. 144). The transformations of love can be comically humiliating as well as exalting.

One of the touching minor effects in the play is the way Antipholus and Dromio of Syracuse listen to each other, and sympathize with each other's point of view. When he hears what his servant has endured in the kitchen, Antipholus concludes, 'There's none but witches do inhabit here' (III. ii. 154) and decides, despite his love for Luciana, to 'stop mine ears against the mermaid's song' (III. ii. 162). (He had addressed her, earlier in the scene, as 'sweet mermaid' – III. ii. 45.) He yields to Dromio's pleas, and decides to leave town that night. But Dromio can also sink his own fears and recognize how his master is profiting from Ephesus:

Faith, stay here this night; they will surely do us no harm;

you saw they speak us fair, give us gold; methinks they are such
a gentle nation that, but for the mountain of mad flesh that
claims marriage of me, I could find in my heart to stay here still
and turn witch.

(IV. iv. 149–53)

To be cast adrift in a town of magic is both exhilarating and
frightening; and the interplay between Dromio and Antipholus
on this point conveys this dual quality subtly and even movingly.
The interest of the play goes deeper than the farcical one of
wondering what will happen next; we do wonder that, of course,
but we also watch to see how the characters will *react* to what
happens.

At the centre of the play, then, is a farcical comedy of situations
that gives rise to a more subtle comedy based on contrasting the
characters' responses to their situations. The interest springs from
a series of immediate, *ad hoc* effects – collisions of style, confrontations of character – and we live from moment to moment, unconcerned, for the most part, with the larger sweep of the story.
But there *is* a larger story in the background, and a very different
kind of story from the farcical tale of confusion that occupies our
attention for most of the play. The story of Aegeon is a tale of
wandering, shipwreck and separation, more in the tradition of
romance than the tradition of drama.[10]

Aegeon represents yet another area of experience, isolated from
the other characters – an isolation signalled dramatically by the
fact that after his long opening scene he is virtually forgotten until
the end of the play. Even in that first scene, we seem curiously
detached from him. His long account of his misfortunes is literary,
clever and rhetorical in a way that prevents a full emotional
engagement:[11]

---

[10] Bullough, in *Narrative and Dramatic Sources*, includes a passage from Gower's
Confessio Amantis as a probable source for Aegeon's story.

[11] Here I take issue with the frequently expressed view that Aegeon's account of
his misfortunes carries a nearly tragic emotional impact. See, for example, H. B.
Charlton, *Shakespearian Comedy* (London, 1966), p. 71; and Derek Traversi,
William Shakespeare: The Early Comedies (revised edition: London, 1964),
p. 12.

In Syracusa was I born, and wed
Unto a woman, happy but for me,
And by me, had not our hap been bad.

(I. i. 36–8)

So that, in this unjust divorce of us,
Fortune had left to both of us alike
What to delight in, what to sorrow for.
Her part, poor soul, seeming as burdened
With lesser weight, though not with lesser woe,
Was carried with speed before the wind . . .   (I. i. 105–10)

Shakespeare restrains our interest in Aegeon's problems in order to focus more sharply on the problems of his children, thereby reversing what might be the natural response – to feel greater concern for loss and suffering than for the confusion of mistaken identity. He keeps the story of wandering very much at a distance, as something faintly literary, related rather than experienced; and concentrates instead on the more obviously dramatic material of immediate confrontations between characters. Later, in *Pericles*, *Cymbeline* and *The Winter's Tale*, stories like Aegeon's will be made fully dramatic; but in *The Tempest* Shakespeare returns to the method of *The Comedy of Errors*.

At the end of the play, however, Aegeon returns – as it were, bringing his story with him – and as the characters come together for the traditional comic denouement the barriers between them dissolve and the different worlds they inhabit begin to fuse. A stage image and a joke connect the sufferings of Aegeon, condemned by the laws of Ephesus, to the more comic sufferings of his son:

AEGEON: I am sure you both of you remember me.
DROMIO E: Ourselves we do remember, sir, by you;
          For lately we were bound as you are now.
          You are not Pinch's patient, are you, sir?

(v. i. 291–4)

And as the knots are (figuratively and literally) untied, some of the wonder experienced by Antipholus of Syracuse begins to touch the more practical Ephesians. When the Duke sees the twins together he exclaims:

> One of these men is genius to the other;
> And so of these. Which is the natural man,
> And which the spirit? Who deciphers them?
>
> (v. i. 331–3)

To some extent the denouement is a practical, Plautine unravelling of the knots: the right people finally come together in the same place, and the various Ephesians who have lost money and property have it restored to them. But there are also strong suggestions that the denouement is an act of destiny (picking up Aegeon's concern with Fortune) and a miracle (recalling Antipholus of Syracuse's view that Ephesus is a town of magic). Certainly it cannot be brought about by institutional authority: the cry of 'justice' with which the Ephesians appeal to their Duke is a confused babble that produces no result, since everyone's idea of 'justice' is different and the Duke has no idea what the problem is.[12] In the last scene the Abbess, not the Duke, is the real figure of authority, remaining calm and clear-headed while he struggles to make sense of the matter. She alone registers no surprise, accepting the strange events as easily as if she had expected them to happen all along. And she presides over the final feast, suggesting in her invitation that what has taken place is a new birth – thus linking the miracle of the ending with the normal processes of life:

> Thirty-three years have I but gone in travail
> Of you, my sons; and till this present hour
> My heavy burden ne'er delivered.
> The Duke, my husband, and my children both,
> And you, the calendars of their nativity,
> Go to a gossip's feast, and joy with me;
> After so long grief, such nativity!
>
> (v. i. 399–405)[13]

---

[12] According to Marion Bodwell Smith, 'In Shakespeare's plays the cry for "Justice!" is seldom heard without the accompaniment of some sort of irony' (*Dualities in Shakespeare*, p. 23). Cf. also R. A. Foakes, Arden introduction, p. xlviii.

[13] This idea is taken up in the final romances. Pericles refers to his newfound daughter as 'Thou that beget'st him that did thee beget' (v. i. 194) and Cymbeline, reunited with his children, exclaims 'O, what am I? / A mother to the birth of three?' (v. v. 238–9).

As the Abbess takes centre stage away from the Duke, so the fussy legalism he has represented is swept away by a deeper authority, the spontaneous force of life. The Duke himself brushes aside the Ephesian law, on being offered the ransom for Aegeon: 'It shall not need; thy father hath his life' (v. i. 389). And at the end the Dromios, after debating the question of precedence, conclude that the question is irrelevant: 'We came into the world like brother and brother, / And now let's go hand in hand, not one before another' (v. i. 423-4).

The emphasis, at the end, is not on the creation of a 'new social unit' (as in Northrop Frye's theory of comedy)[14] but on the renewal of an old family unit. Shakespeare is silent about the marriage of Adriana and Antipholus of Ephesus; and Antipholus of Syracuse's (presumably) approaching marriage is politely but firmly put to one side, as something to be discussed later. He says to Luciana:

> What I told you then,
> I hope I shall have leisure to make good;
> If this be not a dream I see and hear.
>
> (v. i. 373-5)

He is still caught up in the wonder of the family reunion. In Plautus, Menaechmus of Epidamnum sells all his household and returns to Syracuse with his brother; Shakespeare softens the emphasis considerably, but the point is the same: the final image of security is not a wedding dance but a christening feast, a *family* celebration. This may be because of the play's concern with identity: identity is surrendered in love and marriage, but when the original family is recreated, the characters join a comforting social group which asks only that they be their old selves. After the challenges to identity throughout the play the characters – and perhaps the audience – need this kind of comfort, a return to the old and familiar, rather than the start of something new which marriage symbolizes.[15] Even at the end, the characters'

---

[14] 'The argument of comedy', *English Institute Essays, 1948* (New York, 1949), p. 60.

[15] Stanley Wells has pointed out the importance of non-sexual love as a 'driving force' in the play: see 'Shakespeare and romance', in John Russell Brown and Bernard Harris (eds.), *Later Shakespeare* (London, 1966), p. 60.

disparate lives and experiences are not brought into a total harmony: security is achieved – and this is characteristic of Shakespeare's comedies – by selecting one experience, and fixing on that. Marriage is not brutally dismissed, as in Plautus; but it is quietly placed in the background, and no great hopes are pinned on it.

In the rejoining of the broken family, there is – as in most comic endings – a clear element of wish fulfilment. The play itself is a special, artificial ordering of experience, and, while we are not given the sort of distancing epilogue we find at the end of *A Midsummer Night's Dream* or *As You Like It*, the manner of the play throughout is sufficiently stylized to remind us that it is a work of literary and theatrical artifice.[16] The play is, even for a Shakespearian comedy, unusually full of rhyme, of jingling verse and of comic turns and set pieces – such as the debates on time and falling hair (II. ii. 63–107), and on the respective merits of cheer and welcome (III. i. 19–29); or Dromio of Syracuse's grand description of the fat kitchen wench in terms of European geography (III. ii. 113–37). And the play presents a story starting from a fantastic premise and moving to an almost equally fantastic conclusion. But at the same time, for all its artificiality, it deals with the most normal and intimate relations of life – wives and husbands, parents and children. In comparing the different worlds the Antipholus brothers inhabit, we saw an intersection of the special and fantastic with the normal and everyday – Ephesus as a town of sorcerers, and as a town of merchants. The same intersection of the fantastic and the normal becomes part of the audience's own experience as it watches the play – a strange and stylized fable built out of the most familiar relationships of life. The result of this interweaving of the fantastic and the everyday is to make us see each kind of experience from the perspective of the other – just as Antipholus of Syracuse is brought to see ordinary tradesmen as 'Lapland sorcerers', or the Abbess sees the coincidental rejoining of a long-sundered family as an event as natural as childbirth. The comic strategy of the play is one of dislocation, forcing us to see

---

[16] As Clifford Leech points out, 'the multiplication of farcical incident' also achieves a sense of distance. See the introduction to his Arden edition of *The Two Gentlemen of Verona* (London, 1969), p. lxix.

experiences from a fresh perspective, reminding us that no one understanding of life is final. The mixed dramatic mode gives shading and variety to what could have been a one-note, mechanical farce; but it also embodies a comic vision of the instability of life itself.

2

The Two Gentlemen of Verona

The dating of Shakespeare's earliest comedies is uncertain, and it may be that *The Two Gentlemen of Verona*, rather than *The Comedy of Errors*, was his first venture in the genre. It would be difficult to argue that either play developed out of the other; rather, they seem to lie side by side. Certainly *The Two Gentlemen* shows quite a different use of the technique I examined in the last chapter. Instead of setting a variety of different kinds of experience against each other in a swift and flashing interplay, Shakespeare takes one particular experience – that of being in love – and sets it against a background that varies between hostility and indifference.[1] The technique of dislocation is the same, but the concentration is steadier, and we are allowed more time to examine and explore the central experience. Being in love dominates the mind of the victim; it is a private, enclosed and very special state, and our awareness of how special it is is sharpened when we see the lovers against the indifference, or the sardonic detachment, of an outside world full of people who are not in love.[2] The breakdown of understanding between the Syracusans and the Ephesians in *The Comedy of Errors* depended partly on the external situation of

[1] See Donald A. Stauffer, *Shakespeare's World of Images* (New York, 1949), p. 36; and Norman Sanders, introduction to his New Penguin edition of *The Two Gentlemen* (Harmondsworth, 1968), pp. 34, 36.
[2] Stauffer and Sanders, cited in note above, both point to the host's contribution to the scene where Julia discovers Proteus's treachery: 'By my halidom, I was fast asleep' (IV. ii. 131).

mistaken identity; here, we are more aware of an essential gap between different minds: there is less bustle on the stage, more attention to the interplay of personalities. It is worth remarking that this play has the smallest cast in Shakespeare, and consists to an unusual degree of scenes involving only two or three speakers.

The most obvious device, and the one that (properly enough) has received the most thorough critical attention, is the use of the clowns to provide a satiric perspective on the lovers.[3] While it would be forcing the issue to claim that the parallels between the lovers and the clowns are sustained and systematic, there are many touches here and there to show the clowns mirroring, in a comic way, the events of the love plot. Proteus's farewell to Julia is followed by Launce's account of his parting with his family, and small touches tighten the connection: Julia cannot speak, Crab will not weep; there are plays on the word 'tide' in both scenes (II. ii. 14–15; II. iii. 34–7). The reunion of the friends in Milan is followed by the reunion of the servants. Proteus's trick on Valentine, leading to his banishment, is followed by a scene in which Launce (Proteus's servant) tricks Speed (Valentine's servant) into delaying an errand, and the scene concludes with Launce's boast, 'I'll after, to rejoice in the boy's correction' (III. i. 373). With the leisure provided by reading, as opposed to watching, the play, one could go on accumulating such parallels for a long time, and it would be easy to exaggerate their importance. In the theatre, one is sufficiently aware of them to keep the lovers in mind while watching the clowns, and this is what matters. To watch similar events causing emotional crises in one case, and casual laughter in the other, trivializes the events by removing their uniqueness. It also reminds us how far apart the characters really are. But there are many moments which do that more sharply and directly. We see Proteus worrying about the reception of his love letter, and Speed simply concerned with being paid for delivering it (I. i. 92–143). Valentine, satisfied in love, declares, 'I have din'd', but Speed insists, 'though the chameleon Love can feed on the air, I

---

[3] See, for example, E. C. Pettet, *Shakespeare and the Romance Tradition* (London, 1949), pp. 101–4; and Harold F. Brooks, 'Two clowns in a comedy (to say nothing of the dog): Speed, Launce (and Crab) in *The Two Gentlemen of Verona*', *Essays and Studies*, XVI (1963), pp. 91–100.

am one that am nourish'd by my victuals, and would fain have meat' (ii. i. 159–62). Launce speaks less directly to the lovers, but his own courtship, in which wealth becomes the deciding factor (iii. i. 293–360), reminds us of the practical side of marriage, hardly touched on by the lovers; and he reminds us too, as they do not, of the practical side of love: 'when it stands well with him, it stands well with her' (ii. v. 19–20).

For Speed, especially, the lovers have become strange creatures, hardly recognizable as normal human beings. From his point of view – as for Dromio of Syracuse – the transformations wrought by love are comically degrading:

> you have learn'd, like Sir Proteus, to wreath your arms like a malcontent; to relish a love-song, like a robin redbreast; to walk alone, like one that had the pestilence; to sigh, like a school-boy that had lost his ABC; to weep, like a young wench that had buried her grandam; to fast, like one that takes diet; to watch, like one that fears robbing; to speak puling, like a beggar at Hallowmas. You were wont, when you laughed, to crow like a cock; when you walk'd, to walk like one of the lions; when you fasted, it was presently after dinner; when you look'd sadly, it was for want of money. And now you are metamorphis'd with a mistress, that, when I look on you, I can hardly think you my master.
>
> (ii. i. 16–28)

Not only is the lover 'metamorphis'd', but his view of his lady is a vision the ordinary eye cannot recognize:

> SPEED: You never saw her since she was deform'd.
> VALENTINE: How long hath she been deform'd?
> SPEED: Ever since you lov'd her.
>
> (ii. i. 56–8)

Love is a chameleon in more than its capacity to feed on air. At moments like this, the clowns have something like a choric function, a special authority to comment. And this authority is increased by their special relationship with the audience: they are partly characters in the story, but partly also Elizabethan stage clowns, half outside the borders of the play, belonging to a world not only larger than that of the lovers, but larger than the play itself.[4] Launce addresses the audience directly, even intimately; and the business with his shoes may perhaps remind us that he is also Will Kemp, famous for his comic footwear.[5] Speed not only speaks in rhyme but *knows* he is speaking in rhyme:

VALENTINE: How now, sir! What are you reasoning with
                                                        yourself?
      SPEED: Nay, I was rhyming: 'tis you that have the reason.
                                      (II. i. 130–3)

And a few lines later, when he remarks 'All this I speak in print, for in print I found it' (II. i. 157), we see him stepping back from one of his own speeches. At moments like this the clowns put us at a distance not only from the lovers, but from the play itself.

But Shakespeare is not content simply to set lovers against clowns, amusing though that exercise may be; within the play, there are other devices to make us see the lovers' experience as special and limited. The outside world is constantly impinging on them, interrupting their private contemplations, jarring them loose from their absorption in love. The play opens with a dialogue between a man who is in love and a man who is not, and the outside world has an awkward habit of breaking in, even on the lovers' soliloquies. Julia, reassembling Proteus's letter, indulges in a romantic fantasy of coupling their names together:

> Thus will I fold them one upon another;
> Now kiss, embrace, contend, do what you will.
>   [*Re-enter* Lucetta.

LUCETTA: Madam,
               Dinner is ready, and your father stays.
                                      (I. ii. 128–31)

---

[4] See M. M. Mahood, *Shakespeare's Wordplay* (London, 1968), p. 28; and Robert Weismann, 'Laughing with the audience: *The Two Gentlemen of Verona* and the popular tradition of comedy', *Shakespeare Survey*, XXII (1969), p. 37.
[5] See John Alan Beaufort Somerset, 'The comic turn in English drama 1470–1616' (unpublished Ph.D. dissertation, University of Birmingham, 1966), pp. 402–3. The suggestion must be made tentatively, since the play may have been written before the founding of the Lord Chamberlain's Men, and we have no means of knowing if Shakespeare had Kemp in mind.

As the fantasy reaches its climax, mundane reality breaks in, and Julia suddenly looks as foolish as someone caught delivering a speech to the bathroom mirror. The effect is echoed, and the challenge to love is sharper, in the following scene. We have just heard of Antonio's plans to send his son away when Proteus enters, rapt in the contemplation of a letter from Julia:

> Sweet love! sweet lines! sweet life!
> Here is her hand, the agent of her heart;
> Here is her oath for love, her honour's pawn.
> O that our fathers would applaud our loves,
> To seal our happiness with their consents!
> O heavenly Julia!
>
> ANTONIO: How now! What letter are you reading there?
>
> (I. iii. 45–51)

Again, a private fantasy of love is broken, and with more damaging results: far from applauding their love, Antonio is about to separate the lovers. And while Proteus is left alone to contemplate the insubstantiality of love, the scene ends not with his soliloquy but with the entrance of the servant Panthino: 'Sir Proteus, your father calls for you; / He is in haste; therefore, I pray you, go' (I. iii. 88–9). Jolted out of the narrow, enclosed world of love, Proteus is being sent away – significantly – to broaden his education.

Even when there are no direct interruptions, the lovers' statements about love are often placed in a context that dislocates them. Seen in isolation, Proteus's speech on the power of music is serious and eloquent:

> For Orpheus' lute was strung with poets' sinews,
> Whose golden touch would soften steel and stones,
> Make tigers tame, and huge leviathans
> Forsake unsounded deeps to dance on sands.
>
> (III. ii. 76–81)

But Proteus is advising the clownish Thurio on the winning of a woman whom he fully intends to court for himself; at least in part, the eloquence is the eloquence of a confidence trickster dazzling his victim. And for all the beauty of the serenade, no Orphean magic hypnotizes Silvia, who remains stubbornly hostile to both men. 'Who is Silvia?' is, like Proteus's celebration of Orpheus, easy to quote out of context as a gem from Shakespeare, a rare touch of beauty in an otherwise unsatisfying play. But seen against its proper background the beauty is edged with irony. Nor is romantic beauty the only effect to be dislocated in this way: Valentine's advice to the Duke on courting a lady makes him sound like a very clever, worldly wise young man; but gradually, as the Duke turns the conversation towards the subject of rope ladders, we realize how much the glib-sounding lecture is actually being manipulated by its listener; however blasé Valentine may sound, he is really playing into the hands of a man more clever and worldly wise than he is. Proteus as a romantic, and Valentine as a cynic, both sound like confident and experienced spokesmen of love. But each is comically out of his depth. The realization of this strikes us more slowly, with less explosive laughter, than when Adriana addresses a serious and eloquent appeal to the wrong Antipholus – but the basic comic technique is the same.

With the later comedies in mind, we might expect these devices to be counterbalanced by a defiant acceptance of love, like Orlando's 'I would not be cured, youth' (III. ii. 389). But when we look for this counterbalance here, it is curiously difficult to find. In the opening debate on love, Valentine (the non-lover) gets most of the dialogue, describing love as foolish and destructive. Proteus hardly fights back at all, and admits in soliloquy:

> Thou, Julia, thou hast metamorphis'd me,
> Made me neglect my studies, lose my time,
> War with good counsel, set the world at nought;
> Made wit with musing weak, heart sick with thought.
>
> (I. i. 66–9)

Thus Speed's point of view is introduced early in the play, by one of the lovers themselves. And as Dromio of Syracuse feared to be transformed into a curtal-dog, Proteus sees himself undergoing a similar metamorphosis: 'Yet, spaniel-like, the more she spurns my love / The more it grows, and fawneth on her still' (IV. ii. 14–15). Even Valentine, who is happier in love, sees it, not – as

Berowne does in *Love's Labour's Lost* – as a new faculty for the lover, that 'adds a precious seeing to the eye' (IV. iii. 329), but rather as a power imposed on the lover from outside, something which demands service rather than giving strength:

> O gentle Proteus, Love's a mighty lord,
> And hath so humbled me as I confess
> There is no woe to his correction,
> Nor to his service no such joy on earth.

(II. iv. 132–5)

There are touches of the Berowne point of view: arguably in the last line of the speech just quoted, and certainly when Valentine defends love against the traditional charge of blindness: 'Why, lady, Love hath twenty pair of eyes' (II. iv. 91). But for the most part, love is embraced with a rueful awareness of the burdens it imposes, and of how insubstantial its satisfactions are:

> O, how this spring of love resembleth
> The uncertain glory of an April day,
> Which now shows all the beauty of the sun,
> And by and by a cloud takes all away.

(I. iii. 84–7)

The idea of lovers as victims is conventional enough, and is present throughout Shakespeare's comedies; but normally it is played off against other views of them. Here, to an unusual degree, it is the dominant impression. Scenes are juxtaposed in such a way as to show the lovers ironically trapped in situations they do not understand. As Proteus celebrates his success with Julia, the audience knows he is about to be sent away from her; as Julia prepares to journey to Proteus, looking forward eagerly to their reunion, the audience knows he has already betrayed her. Pushed hither and thither by awkward parents, dependent on cheeky and unreliable servants, victimized by the workings of the plot, the lovers appear helpless and vulnerable. They have the pains of love, but few opportunities to indulge in its satisfactions. Thus the comic distancing of love, instead of contributing to a doubleness of vision, seems to be in itself the play's main function.

But a comic interplay of perspectives is maintained through the presentation of the lovers themselves. They may not struggle against the indifferent outside world with any great conviction or success; but there are struggles within their own natures that give them tension, life and dramatic interest. Much of this tension is centred on the way they feel and express their love. Since love has been established as such a special, peculiar experience, it is natural that its expression should also be special and peculiar. The play is full of formal set pieces on love. As Norman Sanders remarks, it 'is almost a complete anthology of the practices of the doctrine of romantic love which inspired the poetic and prose Romances of the period',[6] and the literary, slightly academic quality that this suggests is borne out in the speeches of the lovers. Valentine and Proteus are revealed in their first dialogue as two bookish young men:

> PROTEUS: Yet writers say, as in the sweetest bud
> The eating canker dwells, so eating love
> Inhabits in the finest wits of all.
> VALENTINE: And writers say, as the most forward bud
> Is eaten by the canker ere it blow . . .
>
> (I. i. 42–6)

– and so forth. Throughout the dialogue Proteus seems at least as concerned with matching Valentine's puns as with defending love (I. i. 19–27, for example). The whole passage is something between a formal debate and a verbal game; it reminds John W. Draper of a *conversazione*.[7] The same quality can be seen on Julia's first appearance, in her dialogue with Lucetta:

> JULIA: But say, Lucetta, now we are alone,
> Wouldst thou then counsel me to fall in love?
> LUCETTA: Ay, madam; so you stumble not unheedfully.
> JULIA: Of all the fair resort of gentlemen
> That every day with parle encounter me,
> In thy opinion which is worthiest love?
> LUCETTA: Please you, repeat their names; I'll show my mind
> According to my shallow simple skill.
>
> (I. ii. 1–8)

---

[6] Penguin introduction, p. 8.
[7] *Stratford to Dogberry* (Pittsburgh, 1961), p. 52. Draper lists a number of scenes in the comedies as belonging to the *conversazione* tradition.

Passages like this, in which love is not so much an experience as an announced subject of debate, show the lovers as having a detachment from their feelings, and consequently a self-control, that contrast interestingly with the more emotional absorption in love they express at other times, especially when they are alone. One of the play's fundamental patterns, in fact, is an alternation between dialogues on love, which are clever, detached and frequently satiric, and soliloquies in which love is expressed in a straightforward, serious way. In Proteus's altercation with Speed over his letter to Julia, for example, the lover is distracted from his concern with the letter by the temptation to play verbal games with the servant. He becomes fully serious about it only at the end of the scene, when he is alone. It is as though the very privateness of love makes it difficult, even for a lover, to be fully serious about it in company.

But love cannot remain private if it is to communicate to the beloved. Despite what Proteus says of Julia's silence at their parting – 'so true love should do: it cannot speak; / For truth hath better deeds than words to grace it' (II. ii. 17–18)[8] – words are vitally important to the lovers of this play. Major declarations are made by letter, and the men especially display their love by displaying their verbal wit: Valentine and Thurio fight for Silvia, not with sword or lance, but with (to quote Silvia herself) 'a fine volley of words' (II. iv. 30); in applauding the skill of the players, she underlines the artificial, set-piece quality of their dialogue. But the clowns also engage in wit matches, in which puns are prominent: as Speed remarks, 'Well, your old vice still: mistake the word' (III. i. 279). This points to a central problem. The fact that verbal cleverness comes so easily to lovers and clowns alike shows how far it is from the essence of love; anybody can play with words. Yet even when love is seriously expressed, the expression is likely to be formal, literary, self-consciously eloquent:

> And I as rich in having such a jewel
> As twenty seas, if all their sand were pearl,
> The water nectar, and the rocks pure gold.

> (II. iv. 165–7)

8 There may be a comic echo of this in Launce's 'To be slow in words is a woman's only virtue' (III. i. 326).

John F. Danby has remarked that in this play the lovers' feelings 'are never lived through, only announced – often in long, beautifully formal passages of verse',[9] and for Howard Nemerov 'so ideal is the nature of their worship, that it fixes itself repeatedly on word or image rather than on what they represent, on names rather than on things'.[10] Love depends for its expression, in fact, on the sort of verbal cleverness that can actually detach the speaker from his feelings. It depends on words, and words are (like Launce and Speed) unreliable servants.[11]

With this in mind, it seems appropriate that the character most thoroughly dependent on appearances, conventions and verbal surfaces is Proteus.[12] He thinks cleverly, and he thinks in images, describing his change of heart: 'Even as one heat another heat expels / Or as one nail by strength drives out another' (II. iv. 188–9). From description he goes to justification, invoking the power of love to provide him with some convenient rationalizations:

> O sweet-suggesting love, if thou hast sinn'd,
> Teach me, thy tempted subject, to excuse it!
> At first I did adore a twinkling star,
> But now I worship a celestial sun.
> Unheedful vows may heedfully be broken;
> And he wants wit that wants resolved will
> To learn his wit t'exchange the bad for better.

> (II. vi. 7–13)

The fact that he can talk cleverly about his betrayal seems to make it acceptable to him; he literally talks himself into it. The air of self-conscious calculation with which he does this begins to affect all his relations with the others. He treats affections as commodities to be weighed and measured:

---

[9] 'Shakespeare criticism and *The Two Gentlemen of Verona*', *Critical Quarterly*, II (winter 1960), p. 316.

[10] *Poetry and Fiction: Essays* (New Brunswick, NJ, 1963), p. 30.

[11] William Leigh Godshalk has pointed out the importance of love letters in the play's design; and he adds, 'the letters always miss their mark, are involved in some confusion, or fail in their communication'. See 'The structural unity of *The Two Gentlemen of Verona*', *Studies in Philology*, LXVI (April 1969), pp. 168–81. The device of the comically misdirected letter is used for a similar purpose in *Love's Labour's Lost*.

[12] See Sanders, Penguin introduction, pp. 16, 23–4.

> Methinks my zeal to Valentine is cold,
> And that I love him not as I was wont.
> O! but I love his lady too too much,
> And that's the reason I love him so little.
>
> (II. iv. 199–202)

There is a touch here of the cold legalism of Ephesus. And as he calculates gain and loss, the logic of his argument slowly reveals his essential selfishness:

> Julia I lose, and Valentine I lose;
> If I keep them, I needs must lose myself;
> If I lose them, thus find I by their loss:
> For Valentine, myself; for Julia, Silvia.
> I to myself am dearer than a friend;
> For love is still most precious in itself.
>
> (II. vi. 19–24)

The clever rhetorical balancing reveals a coldness at the heart. We are firmly prepared for the ironic distancing of his eloquence in the later scenes. Even in his later role as a spurned lover there is an element of pose, of calculation. He says to Julia, 'Your message done, hie home unto my chamber, / Where you shall find me sad and solitary' (IV. iv. 84–5). His feelings may be real enough, but he cannot express them without striking attitudes. Proteus seems at first glance the most introspective and self-aware of the lovers; yet he is the one with the smallest mind, and the narrowest sense of the possibilities of love.

Valentine, in conversation, can be as glib and clever as Proteus, and seemingly as cold. There is a cynical detachment in his advice to the Duke, with its calculating assessment of female behaviour and its jingling, artificial style:

> If she do frown, 'tis not in hate of you,
> But rather to beget more love in you;
> If she do chide, 'tis not to have you gone,
> For why the fools are mad, if left alone.
> Take no repulse, whatever she doth say;
> For 'Get you gone' she doth not mean 'Away!'
>
> (III. i. 96–101)

But, as I have argued, this attempt at worldliness (like Proteus's attempt at romantic eloquence) is comically dislocated. And shortly afterwards, when he is banished, he speaks in a different voice, revealing what we may take to be private feeling, wrung from him by grief, rather than social pose:[13]

> To die is to be banish'd from myself,
> And Silvia is myself; banish'd from her
> Is self from self, a deadly banishment.
> What light is light, if Silvia be not seen?
> What joy is joy, if Silvia be not by?
> Unless it be to think that she is by,
> And feed upon the shadow of perfection.
> Except I be by Silvia in the night,
> There is no music in the nightingale;
> Unless I look on Silvia in the day,
> There is no day for me to look upon.
> She is my essence, and I leave to be
> If I be not by her fair influence
> Foster'd, illumin'd, cherish'd, kept alive.
>
> (III. i. 171–84)

The rhetorical balance is still there; it is the only language he has; but the contrast in tone and content is striking. Like Antipholus of Syracuse – and unlike Proteus – he is willing to lose himself in love: so much so that when Proteus calls him, he refuses the name 'Valentine' and calls himself 'nothing' (III. i. 193–8). Launce makes a joke of it, offering to strike at 'nothing' (III. i. 199–201); and the rhetorical balancing of Valentine's speech still keeps us somewhat detached from it; but we may feel that for once an ideal has been expressed that can fight against the distancing devices, and restore some of the balance between serious assertion and mockery. Yet Valentine's innocence can also cause laughter, as when he fails to understand Silvia's transparent device for declaring her love, or when he seems astonished that Speed has noticed he is in love (II. i. 37–9). He seems curiously inept at defending or

---

[13] A different view is expressed by Clifford Leech in the introduction to his Arden edition of the play (London, 1969), p. lxiv. Leech regards the element of rhetorical posturing as uppermost, even here.

protecting himself, and he himself describes Proteus as more experienced and sophisticated (II. iv. 60–70). Like Proteus, he is
comically limited and subject to irony, though his helpless innocence and his capacity for self-surrender rouse a more indulgent
kind of laughter.

Silvia's function in the play is comparatively simple: to receive
adoration, accepting or rejecting it as the case may be. She shows
a modicum of calculation in her first appearance, and a certain
degree of initiative towards the end. She can display both wit and
feeling, but in the last analysis her role is a passive one, dependent
on the actions of the men, as her curious silence in the final stages
of the denouement may indicate. But Julia is another matter. She
has generally been regarded as the most fully realized character in
the play,[14] and one reason for this may be that she presents the
most complex interplay of form and feeling, of engagement and
detachment. In her first scene she veers back and forth between
treating love as a game of flirtation (in which her role is to pretend
indifference) and being angry with herself for doing so. In conversation with Lucetta, she rejects Proteus's letter, and then in
soliloquy admits ruefully that she is simply playing a game:

> What fool is she, that knows I am a maid
> And would not force the letter to my view!
> Since maids, in modesty, say 'No' to that
> Which they would have the profferer construe 'Ay.'
> Fie, fie, how wayward is this foolish love,
> That like a testy babe will scratch the nurse,
> And presently, all humbled, kiss the rod!
>
> (I. ii. 53–9)

In displaying her feelings, she also displays a refreshing capacity
for wry, satiric self-criticism. And yet the pretence of which she
accuses herself is not so easily thrown away, for despite her intention of playing straight, as soon as Lucetta returns Julia puts the
mask back on:

---

[14] Madeleine Doran suggests that 'too much "character" in Julia has fouled up
the conventional lines of Shakespeare's story'. See *Endeavors of Art* (Madison,
1964), p. 325. The remark is characteristic of the way Julia has been regarded.

> My penance is to call Lucetta back
> And ask remission for my folly past.
> What ho! Lucetta!

[*Re-enter* Lucetta.

LUCETTA: What would your ladyship?
   JULIA: Is't near dinner time?

(I. ii. 64–7)

– and once more she pretends indifference to the letter, to the
point of tearing it up. But even this apparently final gesture is not
so final as it looks, for once Lucetta is offstage again, Julia quickly
reassembles the fragments. In doing so, she reveals how much
even the frank expression of love depends on forms. She now plays
another and more earnest game, in which the words on a sheet of
paper acquire a special reality in the eyes of love:

> I'll kiss each several paper for amends.
> Look, here is writ 'kind Julia.' Unkind Julia,
> As in revenge of thy ingratitude,
> I throw thy name against the bruising stones,
> Trampling contemptuously on thy disdain.
> And here is writ 'love-wounded Proteus.'
> Poor wounded name! my bosom, as a bed,
> Shall lodge thee till thy wound be throughly heal'd;
> And thus I search it with a sovereign kiss.

(I. ii. 108–16)

– until once again the appearance of Lucetta (in a passage quoted
earlier) jolts Julia from her fantasy, and restores the pose of indifference. Throughout this sequence Lucetta – like Speed and
Launce – provides a sardonic background commentary, knowing
perfectly well that Julia's indifference is pretence; but the effect is
different from, say, the dialogues of Valentine and Speed, in
which the master's innocence and the servant's shrewdness are
placed in simple opposition. Here the contrast is between the
rapid, volatile shifting of Julia's mind and the steady honesty of
Lucetta's – and Julia, once Lucetta is offstage, can express
Lucetta's point of view. In the interplay between social pose and
private feeling, Julia can be both a player in the game and a

looker-on, commenting on her own play. And even in her frankest
expressions of feeling there is still a certain playful irony.

At this point, Julia is to a great extent immune from the irony
that affects Valentine and Proteus, since she is capable of being
ironic about herself in a way that they are not. But after Proteus's
betrayal, she is placed by the plot in an ironic state of ignorance,
and this is reflected in her behaviour in the scene where she
decides to journey to Proteus, disguised as a boy. She has lost
some of her balance, expressing her devotion to Proteus – and her
misplaced faith in his constancy – with passionate extravagance,
and leaving the practical side to Lucetta:

LUCETTA: Alas, the way is wearisome and long!
  JULIA: A true-devoted pilgrim is not weary
            To measure kingdoms with his feeble steps;
            Much less shall she that hath love's wings to fly,
            And when the flight is made to one so dear,
            Of such divine perfection, as Sir Proteus.
LUCETTA: Rather forbear till Proteus make return.

(II. vii. 8–14)

And she appears shocked by Lucetta's practical reminder that she
must wear a codpiece (II. vii. 53–4). But once Julia has arrived in
Milan and realized the truth about Proteus, not only is her
balance restored but (as happens to other disguised characters in
the comedies) her capacities are extended. Her disguise is a
pretence, but unlike the falsehood of Proteus it is a pretence that
reveals truth: her disguised role as a servant to Proteus reflects
her genuine dependence on his favour. The same idea is reflected
in a more complex way in the much discussed account of how she,
dressed in Julia's gown, depicted the forsaken Ariadne and moved
Julia to tears with the truth of her performance (IV. iv. 154–68).
In the words of Anne Righter (Barton), 'The passage sets up a
series of illusions receding into depth of which the most remote,
the tears wrung from Julia by the stage presentation of a lover's
perfidy, in fact represents reality.'[15] Like Valentine she is now one
of the victims of love; but unlike Valentine she can look after herself, and the disguise suggests that too. It gives her the masculine

[15] *Shakespeare and the Idea of the Play* (Harmondsworth, 1967), p. 94.

freedom of action that Silvia lacks (and that results in her dependence on the unreliable Sir Eglamour). In serving as the messenger of Proteus's love, she decides – like Proteus – to keep her
own interests first. But her feelings are more complex, less calculated, and she comes to her declaration of practical self-interest
with some of the shifting and hesitation that marked her earlier
behaviour:

> How many women would do such a message?
> Alas, poor Proteus, thou hast entertained
> A fox to be the shepherd of thy lambs.
> Alas, poor fool, why do I pity him
> That with his very heart despiseth me?
> Because he loves her, he despiseth me;
> Because I love him, I must pity him . . .
> I am my master's true confirmed love,
> But cannot be true servant to my master
> Unless I prove false traitor to myself.
> Yet will I woo for him, but yet so coldly
> As, heaven it knows, I would not have him speed.
>
> (IV. iv. 86–92, 99–104)

The different styles and points of view present throughout the
play begin to come together in the figure of Julia, a woman in
male attire, a lover disguised as a servant. We now hear from her
the sort of sardonic, joking asides that we heard from Speed,
Launce and Lucetta earlier in the play – as in v. ii, when she
heckles Thurio from the sidelines, exposing his own worthlessness
and Proteus's hypocritical flattery of him. She is even capable of
wry jokes about her own situation, as when Proteus claims his
former love is dead: ''Twere false, if I should speak it; / For I am
sure she is not buried' (IV. ii. 102–3). In the first shock of seeing
Proteus courting Silvia, she expresses her grief in a series of rueful
puns on musical terms: the reticence and detachment enforced by
her conversation with the host forbid a passionate soliloquy, and
there is something touching in the way the play's characteristic
verbal juggling is adapted to an expression of feeling. She appreci-
ates Silvia's rejection of Proteus's courtship, and her sympathy for
his first love; even across the barrier imposed by the disguise, a

bond of sympathy is established between the two women. Yet
when she is given Silvia's picture to take to Proteus, this sympathy
is combined with an awareness of her own injuries, a certain
natural resentment and, at the end, a brief, refreshing touch of
vulgarity:

> Come, shadow, come, and take this shadow up,
> For 'tis thy rival. O thou senseless form,
> Thou shalt be worshipp'd, kiss'd, lov'd, and ador'd!
> And were there sense in his idolatry
> My substance should be statue in thy stead.
> I'll use thee kindly for thy mistress' sake,
> That us'd me so; or else, by Jove I vow,
> I should have scratch'd out your unseeing eyes,
> To make my master out of love with thee.
>
> (IV. iv. 192–201)

Julia's position in these later scenes could have called forth
nothing more than a self-indulgent display of grief; but she is
given a wider range of feeling, and consequently of style – the
widest range, in fact, displayed by any character in the play –
including tart exasperation and sardonic detachment. Clifford
Leech has even suggested that her faint in the last scene is deliberate and calculated;[16] this, like the more celebrated collapse of
Lady Macbeth, can be argued both ways, and a final decision
must rest with the performer; but the mere fact that the debate
can take place shows how much Julia's role in the play has been
opened out.

By this time she has taken the dramatic focus away from the two
gentlemen, who dominated the early scenes, but who in the process were revealed as inadequate spokesmen for love – Proteus
being too calculating, Valentine too helpless, and both of them
too vulnerable to mockery. The growing dominance of Julia,
capable of both suffering and action, prepares us for the fulfilment
of love in the final scenes. We are also prepared for it in other
ways. Little has been said in the play of the positive value of love
but, towards the end, the persistent playing on the idea of
'shadows' suggests that without fulfilment in love, the lovers are

[16] Arden introduction, p. lxvii.

incomplete beings, worshipping only the images of one another.
As Proteus says, begging Silvia's picture:

> For since the substance of your perfect self
> Is else devoted, I am but a shadow;
> And to your shadow will I make true love.
>
> JULIA (*aside*): If 'twere a substance, you would, sure, deceive it,
> And make it but a shadow, as I am.
>
> (IV. ii. 121-5)

There are several such passages, and they carry the implication
that only fulfilment in love can restore the lovers to wholeness of
being.[17] It is characteristic of the play, however, that the positive
side of the idea is implied, not directly stated, and we are more
aware of the hunger than the satisfaction. Equally characteristic,
and more striking, is the way the triumph of love is prepared by
the comic dislocation of another value. I refer, of course, to the
most hotly debated moment of the play. The speaker is Valentine:

> Who by repentance is not satisfied
> Is nor of heaven nor of earth, for these are pleas'd;
> By penitence th'Eternal's wrath's appeas'd;
> And, that my love may appear plain and free,
> All that was mine in Silvia I give thee.
>
> JULIA: O me unhappy!   [*Swoons.*
>
> (V. iv. 79-84)

The ideals of friendship and forgiveness, bound together in this
passage, are initially quite serious, but Valentine's expression of
them quickly becomes overblown, as he identifies himself with the
Almighty, grandly dispensing forgiveness and handing over Silvia
as though she had no say in the matter. More important, he treats
what is happening as a private affair between the two men, and
Julia's swoon (real or pretended) is a sharp, comic theatrical
reminder that there are other interests at stake. The value of
friendship is subjected to the dislocating technique that was used
on love in the earlier scenes – the sudden intrusion of a new perspective.

But this still does not provide a positive assertion of the right-

[17] See John Vyvyan, *Shakespeare and Platonic Beauty* (London, 1961), p. 72.

ness of love; rather, we are made to feel that other ideals are just as vulnerable to mockery (this may apply not only to friendship but to the virginal chivalry of Sir Eglamour, whose response to a real crisis is to run away). We have to be content with the somewhat narrower satisfaction of seeing the lovers get what they want. Even the positive side of Julia's nature is directed more towards winning Proteus than understanding why the effort is worthwhile. And in the final scene, love's dependence on surfaces, on forms and appearances, is as great as ever: 'What is in Silvia's face but I may spy / More fresh in Julia's with a constant eye?' (v. iv. 114–15). This dependence, whatever we think of it, has finally to be accepted; in later plays the issue will get a fuller airing. In watching the two couples join hands, there is the technical satisfaction of seeing a dance pattern completed. In one's theatrical experience of the play, this satisfaction runs very deep, and its importance should not be underestimated. But one cannot help noticing that the final image of harmony includes the glib forgiveness of those comic-opera outlaws, banished for such 'petty crimes' as murder (IV. i. 52), but forgivable, it appears, because they have attempted to raise the tone of their profession (IV. i. 55–76; v. iv. 152–7). (H. B. Charlton's witty and accurate analysis of the outlaws, comparing them with the Pirates of Penzance, falls short only in denying that Shakespeare, like Gilbert, means to be funny.)[18] Even the final harmony of the comic ending is shown to have its laughable side, and is thus placed at a slight distance, recognized as a matter of literary artifice.

This is quite different from the ending of *The Comedy of Errors*, where the positive value of the family reunion is explored at length, and allowed to affect us quite seriously. The ending of *The Two Gentlemen* is, by comparison, rushed and somewhat apologetic, and the satisfactions it offers are more fragile.[19] When we come to the ending of the other play we realize that behind its comic dislocation of various experiences is a solid centre, one experience that is not mocked. *The Two Gentlemen of Verona* is a

[18] See H. B. Charlton, *Shakespearian Comedy* (London, 1966), pp. 38–9.
[19] Leech suggests that 'the appearance of condensation in the last scene . . . may be due, not to abridgement as Dover Wilson suggested, but to Shakespeare's purpose of reducing involvement by the very speed with which incident followed incident' (Arden introduction, p. lxix).

play without such a centre: the experience of love is distanced and exposed by techniques similar to those of the other play, but this time there is nothing to put in its place. Love, for all its frailties and limitations, is all that the central characters have. And that limited (though real) defence is the only defence it can put up. The comic strategy of the play is formidable, but one feels the play would give more satisfaction if this strategy were exercised against a more resilient object. That, however, is to ask for a different play. *The Two Gentlemen of Verona* is not so easy to like as the later comedies, but it has a quality of its own – cool, reticent and somewhat rueful, counselling us, if it counsels anything, not to expect too much. On the occasions – still comparatively rare – when the play is defended, it is usually defended as a testing ground for ideas that Shakespeare will develop more fully in later work. Such a defence is valid as far as it goes, but takes too little account of the play's own unique qualities – though ironically, in counselling the acceptance of small satisfactions, it shares in the play's essential spirit.

3 The Taming of the Shrew

In the plays we have just looked at, much of the comic tension sprang from confrontations between characters inhabiting different orders of experience, reflected often by collisions of style. *The Taming of the Shrew* opens with a similar effect, but takes it one stage further. The wonder felt by Antipholus of Syracuse at confronting a new world is now accompanied by an actual transformation of character. There is at first an obvious contrast in style between the racy prose of Christopher Sly and the more formal verse of the Lord and his servants. But as they practise on his imagination, telling him of the rich life that is rightfully his, he slips into verse, with some attempt at dignity;[1] he crosses the border between one experience and another. In our eyes, of course, he never ceases to be Christopher Sly, and this gives his new role a comic piquancy (with a touch of pathos, if the actor wants to exploit it); but he is Christopher Sly with his mind opened to new possibilities, and – like the lovers of *A Midsummer Night's Dream,* waking up after their night in the forest – unsure of what is dream and what is reality:

> Am I a lord and have I such a lady?
> Or do I dream? Or have I dream'd till now?
> I do not sleep: I see, I hear, I speak;
> I smell sweet savours, and I feel soft things.

[1] The change in Sly's speech is analysed in some detail by Brian Vickers, *The Artistry of Shakespeare's Prose* (London, 1968), pp. 13–14.

> Upon my life, I am a lord indeed,
> And not a tinker, nor Christophero Sly.
>
> (Induction, ii. 66–71)

That final decision takes him further than Antipholus ever goes. The waking of Sly, to find himself provided with fresh garments, attendance, a new wife and a whole new identity, also seems like a parody-in-advance of the waking of Lear. It is a dramatic moment of a kind that will continue to fascinate Shakespeare throughout his career, as a character poised on the brink of some unimaginable joy or horror, with his old sense of the normal crumbling, gropes to re-establish some kind of certainty.

In Sly's case, the new life is accepted as truth, and he moves into it with some difficulty, but with increasing confidence. Moreover, in the play as we have it we never see him disillusioned. His acceptance of his new role sets off a chain reaction that runs through the rest of the play, as new experiences are opened out for the characters and for the audience.[2] One might even say that the process had already begun when the audience settled as Sly and the Hostess appeared. To study a work of art is to move into a new experience; and the analogy between this and what happens to Sly is established in a variety of ways. He is the central character in a play of the Lord's making (which includes, as a normal play would, a boy playing a woman); his imagination is played upon by descriptions of 'wanton pictures' (Induction, i. 45); and finally, as he is entertaining the Lord, the Lord provides a play to entertain him. Within that play, new perspectives continue to open. Lucentio and Tranio begin the play, but their scene is interrupted by the arrival of the Baptista family. Tranio sees them as 'some show to welcome us to town' (i. i. 47); Lucentio is sent into a dreamlike state by the sight of Bianca. Most important, Katherina's mind is worked on by Petruchio as Sly's is by the Lord,[3]

---

[2] See G. K. Hunter, *John Lyly: the Humanist as Courtier* (London, 1962), p. 309; and G. R. Hibbard, introduction to his New Penguin edition of *The Taming of the Shrew* (Harmondsworth, 1968), p. 9. Hunter describes the process as opening a series of Chinese boxes, and Hibbard sees it as a number of cases of conditioning.
[3] This analogy has frequently been pointed out. See, for example, Maynard Mack, 'Engagement and detachment in Shakespeare's plays', in Richard Hosley (ed.), *Essays on Shakespeare and Elizabethan Drama in Honor of Hardin Craig* (Columbus, Missouri, 1962), p. 280.

producing a similar sense of dislocation:

> she, poor soul,
> Knows not which way to stand, to look, to speak,
> And sits as one new-risen from a dream.   (IV. i. 168–70)

Finally, she acquires a new identity: Baptista must provide 'Another dowry to another daughter, / For she is chang'd, as she had never been' (v. ii. 114–15).

But each of these changes is subtly different from the others; and it would certainly be too simple to say that each new perspective takes us one step closer to reality, or one step further away from it. Sly's new identity is false; Katherina's has, one feels, more validity. The move from the induction to the main play is a massive transformation; Tranio's comment on the Baptista family, a touch in passing. The audience remains detached from Sly's experience when he becomes a lord, but begins to share it when he watches the play. Nor is each new perspective *totally* new: often, the new experience will build upon something in the old one. Sly, in his first dispute with the Hostess, already has exalted ideas: 'Y' are a baggage; the Slys are no rogues. Look in the chronicles: we came in with Richard Conqueror' (Induction, i. 3–4). He has enough good sense to resist transformation for a while, but that speech may help to suggest why he finally succumbs. Also, the scene of his waking introduces some issues that are picked up and elaborated in the main play. Most obviously, he has some difficulty establishing his correct relation to his 'wife':

SLY: Are you my wife, and will not call me husband?
        My men should call me 'lord'; I am your goodman.
PAGE: My husband and my lord, my lord and husband;
        I am your wife in all obedience.

> (Induction, ii. 102–5)

The Page says briefly what Katherina will say at much greater length. Also worth noting is the way Sly's new life is presented by the Lord:

> Wilt thou have music? Hark! Apollo plays,   [*Music.*
> And twenty caged nightingales do sing.
> Or wilt thou sleep? We'll have thee to a couch

> Softer and sweeter than the lustful bed
> On purpose trimm'd up for Semiramis.
> Say thou wilt walk: we will bestrew the ground.
> Or wilt thou ride? Thy horses shall be trapp'd,
> Their harness studded all with gold and pearl.
> Dost thou love hawking? Thou hast hawks will soar
> Above the morning lark. Or wilt thou hunt?
> Thy hounds shall make the welkin answer them
> And fetch shrill echoes from the hollow earth.
>
> (Induction, ii. 33–44)

Music, sex, and particularly sport – these will all be important in the main play. That play may be a new world, but we see on reflection that it is built out of materials from the old one, expanded and elaborated. The barriers that separated different experiences of life in the earlier plays are now less tight, and there is more traffic across them.

In modern productions it is usual for Sly to remain on stage, constantly reminding us that the Shrew play is a theatrical illusion and keeping us at some distance from it. Directors have used this device in a lively and entertaining way,[4] but the text suggests a different relation between Sly and the play world. At first, we move into the play world with a jolt: after the surprisingly subtle comedy of the Induction, the opening of the main play seems stilted and mechanical. Character and situation are arbitrarily laid before us, as Lucentio bombards Tranio with information he must surely know already, information that is obviously designed for the audience:

> Tranio, since for the great desire I had
> To see fair Padua, nursery of arts,
> I am arrived for fruitful Lombardy
> The pleasant garden of great Italy,
> And by my father's love and leave am arm'd
> With his good will and thy good company,
> My trusty servant well approv'd in all,

---

[4] This was particularly true of Michael Langham's production at Stratford, Ontario in 1962 and Trevor Nunn's production for the Royal Shakespeare Company in 1967. In both productions the ending, with Sly waking from his dream, was borrowed from *The Taming of a Shrew*.

Here let us breathe, and haply institute
A course of learning and ingenious studies.
Pisa, renowned for grave citizens,
Gave me my being and my father first . . .

(I. i. 1–11)

– and so on. The constant references to Italian place names, and the (for Shakespeare) unusually frequent snatches of Italian in the dialogue, help to establish the special, separate quality of the play world – particularly since Sly has been so firmly placed in Warwickshire (Induction, ii. 16–23). In the anonymous *The Taming of a Shrew* we are distanced from the play by the players' bustling preparations, and their search for properties. Shakespeare achieves the same effect more subtly, by the style of the play itself.

But the distancing does not last: gradually the writing relaxes, and by the time Katherina meets Petruchio the stiffness is gone, and some of the earthiness of the Sly scenes is restored. In the process Sly himself disappears, perhaps because the audience has replaced him: the play world has acquired for us the same level of reality that the Induction had: we are watching, not a play within a play, but a play. And we remain in that state till the end, for, unlike the Sly of *The Taming of a Shrew*, Shakespeare's Sly does not return to us.[5] But at least he has made us aware of the play world as a special experience, in a more explicit way than in *The Comedy of Errors* or *The Two Gentlemen of Verona*. In establishing this sense of

[5] The ending of *The Taming of a Shrew* has obvious attractions, and remains popular in the theatre. See above, note 4, p. 44; and Arthur Colby Sprague and J. C. Trewin, *Shakespeare's Plays Today* (London, 1970), p. 54. One wonders if there was a similar ending, now lost, for Shakespeare's play. Richard Hosley has argued persuasively against this possibility, in 'Was there a "dramatic epilogue" to *The Taming of the Shrew*?', *Studies in English Literature 1500–1900*, I (spring 1961), pp. 17–34. Peter Alexander has pointed out that the stage direction '*They sit and mark*' at the end of I. i indicates that Shakespeare intended the 'presenters' to remain on stage. See 'The original ending of *The Taming of the Shrew*', *Shakespeare Quarterly*, XX (1969), pp. 114–15. But the fact remains that in the play as we have it Sly and his companions have no dialogue after I. i. They may be intended to watch for a while, but to leave the stage well before the ending – perhaps to play the new characters required in Act IV. It may be that, in an earlier version, Sly had the fuller role he enjoys in *The Taming of a Shrew*; but if so, Shakespeare may have made the change for artistic reasons, and not just to suit the resources of a smaller company (as Alexander argues, p. 116). For purposes of criticism, we must, I think, deal with the play as we have it, which is clear enough, and not with hypothetical earlier versions.

distance at the beginning, Shakespeare is following a method already familiar in such plays as Greene's *James IV* and Peele's *Old Wives' Tale*, and one that would become a favourite of Jonson's. This is Shakespeare's only use of it; elsewhere, he establishes the play world first, dislodging it only at the end. But this time he has a reason for starting us outside the play and then moving us into it: he is concerned, as G. R. Hibbard has pointed out, with processes of conditioning,[6] and he reminds us that we, as an audience, undergo such a process when we sit down to watch a play.

This device also reflects a concern with convention, since it calls our attention to the fact that the play is a special, limited experience; and in the play itself this concern persists. The contrast between the Bianca plot and the Petruchio plot presents a contrast in conventions, both social and dramatic. The Bianca plot is recognizably very conventional indeed: in manner and temper, it is much closer to Gascoigne's *Supposes* than, for example, *The Comedy of Errors* is to *Menaechmi*. The story of rival wooers is one of the most common motifs in Western comedy, Italian comedy in particular. Disguise is also part of the stock in trade of comedy, and it is used here more frequently and elaborately than anywhere else in Shakespeare. Equally conventional is Lucentio's dreamy, romantic posture as a lover. As in *The Two Gentlemen of Verona*, the master's lovesick trance is comically juxtaposed with the servant's awareness of practical reality:

LUCENTIO: O, yes, I saw sweet beauty in her face,
           Such as the daughter of Agenor had,
           That made great Jove to humble him to her hand,
           When with his knees he kiss'd the Cretan strand.
TRANIO: Saw you no more? Mark'd you not how her sister
           Began to scold and raise up such a storm
           That mortal ears might hardly endure the din?
LUCENTIO: Tranio, I saw her coral lips to move,
           And with her breath she did perfume the air;
           Sacred and sweet was all I saw in her.
TRANIO: Nay, then, 'tis time to stir him from his trance.

                                    (I. i. 162–72)

[6] See note 2, p. 42.

– and Tranio goes on to urge him, in practical terms, to win Bianca. But even when Lucentio wins her, there is still something literary and academic in his love, of which his disguise as a schoolmaster is a comic reflection:

BIANCA: What, master, read you? First resolve me that.
LUCENTIO: I read that I profess, 'The Art to Love.'
BIANCA: And may you prove, sir, master of your art!
LUCENTIO: While you, sweet dear, prove mistress of my heart.

(IV. ii. 7–10)

This interview, like Lucentio's earlier speeches, is comically distanced by an onstage audience: as the lovers court, Tranio and Hortensio comment on the fickleness of womankind (though it is characteristic of the play's ironies that neither of them has the right to complain of deceit, since both are at this point disguised).

The courting of Bianca follows literary convention: and this is played off against the social conventions followed by her father, the romanticism of the one contrasting with the realism of the other.[7] Bianca is literally put up for auction, and sold to the highest bidder. This is, by the social conventions of the time, the orthodox way to arrange a marriage. And Padua is, like Ephesus, a town where money matters. Commerce works its way into the characters' imagery, as when Baptista and Tranio comment on Katherina's match:

BAPTISTA: Faith, gentlemen, now I play a merchant's part,
            And venture madly on a desperate mart.
TRANIO: 'Twas a commodity lay fretting by you;
            'Twill bring you gain, or perish on the seas.
BAPTISTA: The gain I seek is quiet in the match.

(II. i. 318–22)

This passage introduces the auction of Bianca, in which the gain Baptista seeks is no longer metaphorical. The characters in the Bianca plot are also sticklers for social convention: Tranio in particular is always keeping the other characters on their dignity, advising the pedant, 'hold your own, in any case, / With such

---

[7] On the play's depiction of contemporary marriage customs, see Hibbard, Penguin introduction, pp. 29–35.

austerity as longeth to a father' (IV. iv. 6–7); and lecturing Vincentio: 'Sir, you seem a sober ancient gentleman by your habit,
but your words show you a madman' (V. i. 62–3). But the fact that
these speeches come from Tranio, the disguised servant, reminds
us that social convention, like literary convention, is being mocked
and dislocated. It is Tranio who puts in the winning bid for
Bianca, and produces a sober and generous father for Baptista's
benefit; the matchmaking, apparently conducted in the regula-
tion manner, is really a charade serving the purposes of romantic
love.

As in *The Comedy of Errors*, a world of romance and a world of
money collide. But the ultimate outcome is rather different. In the
end, the marriage of Bianca and Lucentio is shown as satisfying
both the conventions of romance and the conventions of society:
the young man is both a successful lover and a good catch. But
this satisfaction does not outlast the final scene. An extra factor is
introduced, which plays havoc with both conventions – the
character of Bianca herself. The heroine of *Supposes*, though tech-
nically the centre of the action, appeared only briefly; but Bianca
is given a character, and a will, of her own. Her sweet disposition
is part of a deeper strategy, as Katherina recognizes: 'Her silence
flouts me, and I'll be reveng'd' (II. i. 29). When we see her with
her rival tutors, her essential nature is revealed:

> I am no breeching scholar in the schools,
> I'll not be tied to hours nor 'pointed times,
> But learn my lessons as I please myself.

> (III. i. 18–20)

And throughout the scene she keeps a subtle but firm control over
the men. Her conduct at the end will be more surprising for
Lucentio than for the audience. Both socially and artistically, he
has won a conventional sweetheart in a conventional way; and
when the prize turns out to have been a baited trap, not merely
the character but the conventions he has operated under are
mocked.

The inadequacy of both conventions is that they take too little
account of personality. Bianca can play her role in a courtship,
and her role in a business transaction, without revealing her true

face. But the play, unlike so many romantic comedies, goes on for one scene after marriage, and Lucentio learns to his dismay what lay behind that romantic sweetness. On the other hand, Petruchio has been concerned with personality all along. The taming plot presents in a deeper, more psychological way ideas that are handled superficially and externally in the romantic plot. Education is one such idea: Bianca is surrounded by instructors, none of whose credentials would bear examination; they have really come to win her, not to teach her (the one real pedant in the play is disguised as someone else). But Petruchio, in his 'taming-school' (IV. ii. 54), really does teach Kate, and teaches her that inner order of which the music and the mathematics offered to Bianca are only a reflection. Disguise is also treated differently in the two plots: Petruchio disguises himself as a ruffian and a bully (I will argue later that this *is* only a disguise); and he achieves more with this psychological transformation than do the suitors of the other plot, no matter how many hats, robes and false noses they may don. This repeats a process I have mentioned before: one world builds on features of another world, but develops them in its own way. The Bianca plot is introduced first, and the taming plot may be said to be (in part) a reflection of it at a deeper level; but in the bulk of the play the two plots run along side by side, and we are led to compare them. The most striking effect, perhaps, is in v. i, when the false Vincentio confronts the real one. Here the external, farcical confusion of the Bianca plot reaches its climax; and this frantic scene is watched by Katherina and Petruchio, who are above the battle, having achieved their own peace already in a scene with the same Vincentio, playing a game of confusion with ideas rather than names and faces.

Petruchio, like Lucentio, has a literary tradition behind him; but it is the older, more elusive tradition of folk tale.[8] Lucentio is irrational, but in a familiar way; he lives in a daylight world, and we have no difficulty understanding anything he does. Petruchio's behaviour can in the end be rationalized, but it strikes us at first as strange and eccentric, a series of private jokes he does not

[8] Folktale analogies with the taming plot are discussed by Jan Harold Brunvald 'The folktale origin of *The Taming of the Shrew*', *Shakespeare Quarterly*, XVII (autumn 1966), pp. 345–59.

always share with us: motive and action are connected in an oblique, sometimes puzzling way. He has a tinge of the exotic, bringing with him suggestions of a world of adventure quite different from the closeted worlds of money and learning inhabited by the other characters:

> Have I not in my time heard lions roar?
> Have I not heard the sea, puff'd up with winds,
> Rage like an angry boar chafed with sweat?
> Have I not heard great ordnance in the field,
> And heaven's artillery thunder in the skies?
> Have I not in a pitched battle heard
> Loud 'larums, neighing steeds and trumpets' clang?
>
> (I. ii. 197–203)

He invades the ordered propriety of Padua like a natural force, and the feelings of the inhabitants are considerably ruffled in the process. (His behaviour at his wedding is much more piquant for being seen through the outraged eyes of Gremio than it would be if we saw it straight.) No small part of the disruption is that he professes the conventional social motives, but more blatantly than is socially acceptable:

> I come to wive it wealthily in Padua;
> If wealthily, then happily in Padua.
>
> (I. ii. 73–4)

> She is my goods, my chattels, she is my house,
> My household stuff, my field, my barn,
> My horse, my ox, my ass, my any thing,
> And here she stands; touch her whoever dare. . . .
>
> (III. ii. 226–9)

The citizens of Padua would probably agree with both attitudes; but it is part of their decorum not to insist on them so brazenly (though Baptista comes quite close). And Petruchio at times is simply rude: 'If she and I be pleas'd, what's that to you?' (II. i. 295). He woos roughly, dresses like a madman and brawls at his own wedding; and the native population responds with a mixture of chuckling appreciation and shock. But the occasional attempts by other characters to insist on proper behaviour are undermined by irony. Gremio says of his wooing, 'You are too blunt; go to it orderly' (II. i. 45), but since Petruchio's entrance has been accompanied by no fewer than three other characters in disguise (one of them introduced by Gremio himself) the old man's insistence on the proprieties seems comically out of place. Similarly, the character who rebukes him most roundly for his appearance at the wedding – 'See not your bride in these unreverent robes; / Go to my chamber, put on clothes of mine' (III. ii. 108–9) – is Tranio, who has much less right to the clothes he is wearing than Petruchio does.

Katherina is a match for him in that she too is unorthodox. Instead of playing, as Bianca does, the dutiful, submissive daughter, she asserts her own will quite overtly. She objects to being treated simply as part of Bianca's wedding arrangements: 'I pray you, sir, is it your will / To make a stale of me amongst these mates?' (I. i. 57–8). It should be noted that she has wrung one important concession from her father by her behaviour: he insists that whoever marries her must do so 'when the special thing is well obtain'd, / That is, her love, for that is all in all' (II. i. 127–8). There is obviously no point in trying to match her against her will. But he makes no such conditions with Bianca, whose will he assumes he can control, whose love he thinks he can give to the highest bidder:

> 'Tis deeds must win the prize, and he of both
> That can assure my daughter greatest dower
> Shall have my Bianca's love.

(II. i. 334–6)

The shrew's unorthodox behaviour has its value, forcing attention to her personality and her wishes, keeping her from being simply a counter in a social game.

It is in this sense, however, that Petruchio 'kills her in her own humour' (IV. i. 164), for he attacks her through a disruption of orthodox behaviour far more drastic than her own. It is more drastic, paradoxically, because it operates at a seemingly more trivial level: he disrupts the ordinary social amenities that she has taken for granted all her life – food, sleep, clothing. The devastating effect on Katherina demonstrates the truth of the Abbess's lecture to Adriana in *The Comedy of Errors*: 'In food, in sport, and

life-preserving rest, / To be disturb'd would mad or man or beast'
(v. i. 83–4). Our comfort and our sense of well-being depend on
the smooth operation of the normal domestic round. Yet in denying her this Petruchio claims, paradoxically, that he is acting the
loving husband:

> As with the meat, some undeserved fault
> I'll find about the making of the bed;
> And here I'll fling the pillow, there the bolster,
> This way the coverlet, another way the sheets;
> Ay, and amid this hurly I intend
> That all is done in reverend care of her.
>
> (IV. i. 183–8)

He concludes, 'this is a way to kill a wife with kindness' (IV. i. 192).
Throughout his behaviour runs this constant sense of paradox, of
a crazy inversion of motive and action: with a fine display of
choler, he throws the meat away – because it engenders choler
(IV. i. 141–61); in their bedchamber, on their wedding night, he
preaches 'a sermon of continency to her, / And rails, and swears,
and rates' (IV. i. 166–7). Simple bullying would, one feels, produce an equally simple reaction, enraged resistance or blind submission. But Petruchio's paradoxical behaviour teases Katherina's
mind into action. She picks up the incongruity in his 'kindness':

> And that which spites me more than all these wants –
> He does it under name of perfect love;
> As who should say, if I should sleep or eat,
> 'Twere deadly sickness or else present death.
>
> (IV. iii. 11–14)

She offers no explicit explanation; but clearly her mind is running
on the nature of 'perfect love', and her worries over food and sleep
are a stimulus to reflection on this deeper issue.

In place of the clear motives and two-dimensional action of the
Bianca plot, we have a more oblique dramatic method. There is
no explicit statement from Katherina or Petruchio as to why this
bizarre, inverted image of love should have the effect it does. We,
like Katherina, are teased into working it out for ourselves. In
rejecting clothing that is merely 'fashionable' (IV. iii. 69–70, 94–7),

or in overcoming Katherina's scruples about kissing in the street (v. i. 128–35), Petruchio appears at first glance to be insisting on the unimportance of the more superficial social conventions. As he puts it, ''tis the mind that makes the body rich' (IV. iii. 168). And he had flouted conventional taste at his wedding, with an equally solemn assurance that 'To me she's married, not unto my clothes' (III. ii. 113). The usual clichés about appearance and reality come to mind at once. But I wonder. In taking such elaborate care to dress absurdly at his wedding, and in criticizing the tailor's efforts so severely and in such detail, Petruchio actually demonstrates a concern for the importance of clothing, and a considerable fascination with it. And his behaviour over Katherina's dress is of a piece with his other attacks on her domestic comfort. He seems to be demonstrating to her the *importance* of small social amenities, by denying them to her and forcing her to realize how much she depends on them. Over and over again, her dismay and indignation – at having her groom show up late for the wedding, at not being allowed to attend her own marriage feast, at being denied food and sleep, at not being allowed to dress in the fashion, like other gentlewomen – push her, unwittingly, into being a spokesman for conventional decent behaviour. I say 'unwittingly', for her responses at this point do seem to be instinctive and automatic; one imagines that if she realized too clearly what Petruchio was doing, her stubborn nature would find some means of resisting; his attack has to be oblique and paradoxical if he is to penetrate her defences – as he does.

What Petruchio is doing, as G. R. Hibbard has pointed out, is forcing Katherina 'to see the value of that order and decency for which she previously had no use'.[9] And, expert teacher that he is, he does this not by telling her about it himself, but by manœuvring her into telling him. She also learns sympathy for the victims of bullying, as she finds herself begging forgiveness for Petruchio's servants (IV. i. 140).[10] Petruchio's ironic claim to be tormenting her out of love may also be a way of demonstrating how much love – love within marriage, as distinct from the romantic love

[9] Penguin introduction, p. 21.
[10] See Hibbard, Penguin introduction and Derek Traversi, *William Shakespeare: The Early Comedies* (London, 1964), p. 20.

of Lucentio – expresses itself through the provision of ordinary decent comfort. All these may seem like curious lessons for Petruchio to be teaching, since he impresses us at first as a breezy disrupter of convention; but here we touch on the essential paradox of the character. After all the brawling and shouting, the end and aim of his campaign is summed up:

> Marry, peace it bodes, and love, and quiet life,
> An awful rule, and right supremacy;
> And, to be short, what not that's sweet and happy.
>
> (v. ii. 108–10)

His programme is a comic exorcism of noise and violence, to achieve peace and order in the end. When we hear him assuring Vincentio that his son is well married – and this is *after* his own marriage is comfortably settled – he speaks in what, for him, is a new, surprising manner:

> Wonder not,
> Nor be not grieved – she is of good esteem,
> Her dowry wealthy, and of worthy birth;
> Beside, so qualified as may beseem
> The spouse of any noble gentleman.
>
> (IV. v. 62–6)

The madcap seems as much concerned with the respectable, non-romantic side of marriage as any citizen of Padua.

But while analysing Petruchio's methods, and abstracting a philosophical pattern from them, may be a necessary critical exercise, it is not finally an adequate account of the play. Something more intangible has to be reckoned with: the spirit in which Petruchio goes to work. It is here that the modern sensibility is on dangerous ground with *The Taming of the Shrew*. We feel a little uncomfortable with the harshness of Petruchio's method, with the very real suffering he inflicts; we try to reassure ourselves that he and Katherina are really in love all the time – romantically in love, in the manner we are used to in comedy – and toying affectionately with each other.[11] We think hopefully of Beatrice and

[11] Modern attempts to soften the play have been surveyed – and amusingly dissected – by Robert B. Heilman, 'The "Taming" untamed, or the return of the shrew', *Modern Language Quarterly*, XXVII (June 1966), pp. 147–51.

Benedick. In the theatre, performers are at great pains to assure us that since the couple love each other, no real harm is being done; and since the dialogue is uncooperative, they frequently resort to mime to make the point clear.[12] It is true enough that Petruchio is not just a sadist who beats his wife into dumb submission; but to react against this view by importing too much romantic softness into the play would be to falsify it in the other direction.

One cannot deny that the taming is a rough, brutal business, and for all its effect on Katherina's mind the initial impact is physical. She journeys, dirty, wet and starving, to an ice-cold house, where she is denied food and sleep. And yet the effect is different from the earlier, cruder shrew plays (such as *Tom Tyler and his Wife*) where if the shrew submits at all it is, in M. C. Bradbrook's words, 'either to high theological argument or to a taste of the stick'.[13] The taming of Katherina is more interesting, more fun to watch; otherwise the play would not be so consistently successful in the theatre. It is not just that we sense the philosophical purpose behind the knockabout; there is something attractive in the knockabout itself. A clue is provided, I think, in one of the key images Petruchio uses to describe his method:

My falcon now is sharp and passing empty,
And till she stoop she must not be full-gorg'd,
For then she never looks upon her lure.
Another way I have to man my haggard,
To teach her come, and know her keeper's call,
That is, to watch her, as we watch these kites
That bate and beat, and will not be obedient.

(IV. i. 174–80)

[12] In the Royal Shakespeare Company's 1962 production (redirected by Maurice Daniels from John Barton's 1960 production) Katherina was rewarded for her submission by being given back the hat Petruchio had refused her; in Trevor Nunn's 1967 production for the same company, their first meeting began with a long pantomime in which Petruchio pretended to have only one arm. Katherina approached him with an expression of sympathy; her reaction when the 'missing' arm suddenly appeared combined indignation with wry amusement. She and Petruchio were thus established as characters who enjoyed playing games with each other. In both cases the effect was to soften the characters' relationship, to assure us that no real wounds were being inflicted.
[13] 'Dramatic rôle as social image: a study of *The Taming of the Shrew*', *Shakespeare Jahrbuch*, XCIV (1958), p. 134.

The style of the speech reflects the tough, alert mind of the seasoned sportsman. Katherina is trained, quite literally, as one would train a hawk. (In contrast, Bianca is described in the following scene as a 'proud disdainful haggard' (IV. ii. 39) who will not be tamed.) Petruchio greets her submission with another image drawn from sport: 'thus the bowl should run, / And not unluckily against the bias' (IV. v. 24–5). The taming of Katherina is not just a lesson but a game – a test of skill and a source of pleasure. The roughness is, at bottom, part of the fun: such is the peculiar psychology of sport that one is willing to endure aching muscles and risk the occasional broken limb for the sake of the challenge and the pleasure it provides. And the sports most often recalled throughout the play are blood sports, hunting and hawking – thus invoking in the audience the state of mind in which cruelty and violence are acceptable, even exciting, because their scope is limited by tacit agreement and they are made the occasion for a display of skill.

Similarly, the cruelty is made limited and acceptable by reminders that Petruchio is putting on an act. The memory of Sly may create some detachment in any case; but even in terms of the shrew play Petruchio is seen as a performer. In their first interview, Katherina says of his bombast, 'Where did you study all this goodly speech?' (II. i. 255). And a slight but visible gap opens between the character and his performance when, after his flamboyant abuse of the tailor, he asks Hortensio, aside, to assure his victim that he will be paid (IV. iii. 160). When, by the end of the play, we realize the value Petruchio places on settled domesticity, the suggestion that his brawling was a performance becomes a virtual certainty. (It might also be noted, by the way, that Petruchio uses the sense of detachment given by a performance as the basis of one of his most ingenious taming devices: he assures the other characters that Katherina's shrewishness is only a pretence, since ''Tis bargained 'twixt us twain, being alone, / That she shall still be curst in company' (II. i. 296–7). This robs Katherina of the chief means of exerting her will, since the others can no longer be sure if her displays of temper are serious. This device, however, is not developed, since, from this point on, the real issue is not her relation to the other characters but her relation to Petruchio.)

We can enjoy Petruchio's brutality, then, because it is limited and conventionalized; and this, rather than any notion of romantic love, is the real source of our pleasure in the taming. This is, when viewed dispassionately, a peculiar frame of mind, but it is common enough in spectators of sport and drama. However, it is not automatically created by drama (as it is by some sports) and one of the functions of the Induction is to invoke this state of mind in preparation for Petruchio. The Lord is in many ways analogous to Petruchio. When he first appears we hear him speaking of his hounds, with appreciation, enjoyment and concern:

> Huntsman, I charge thee, tender well my hounds;
> Brach Merriman, the poor cur, is emboss'd;
> And couple Clowder with the deep-mouth'd brach.
> Saw'st thou not, boy, how Silver made it good
> At the hedge corner, in the coldest fault?
> I would not lose the dog for twenty pound.
>
> (Induction, i. 14–19)

(We may recall this passage later when Petruchio, returning home, demands 'where's my spaniel Troilus?' – IV. i. 134.) The Lord is also a connoisseur of acting:

>   This fellow I remember
> Since once he play'd a farmer's eldest son.
> 'Twas where you woo'd the gentlewoman so well.
> I have forgot your name; but, sure, that part
> Was aptly fitted and naturally perform'd.
>
> (Induction, i. 81–5)

He later tries a hand at acting himself, impersonating one of his own servants. Quickly but firmly, Shakespeare establishes the Lord as a cultivated lover of pleasure. And, like Petruchio, he has a sense of propriety beneath his sense of fun. The first sight of Sly offends him: 'O monstrous beast, how like a swine he lies! / Grim death, how foul and loathsome is thine image!' (Induction, i. 32–3). His joke on Sly is one more sport, a pleasant relaxation after the day's hunting; but he sees that if it is to remain sport, it must remain under control: 'It will be pastime passing excellent, / If it be husbanded with modesty' (Induction, i. 65–6). He looks forward to the page's performance, and the servants' reactions, but adds,

> I'll in to counsel them; haply my presence
> May well abate the over-merry spleen,
> Which otherwise would grow into extremes.
>
> (Induction, i. 134–6)

To a compassionate eye, the Lord's treatment of Sly, like Petruchio's of Katherina, is cruel fun; but we are not allowed to be so compassionate. Sport and acting are both invoked to give us the detachment necessary to take pleasure in the trick, and the Lord's essential restraint ensures that the balance is maintained.

The appeal to our sense of sport also has important implications for the development of Katherina herself: we watch her progress, not just as a wife, but as a player in Petruchio's game. Their first interview is revealing. He begins by laying out his plan of attack quite simply: he will turn everything she does upside down, and throw her into a state of confusion (II. i. 169–80). But when she appears, his early attempt to dominate the conversation breaks down as she engages him in tight, fast repartee, demonstrating that she is a keen fighter, worthy of his best efforts; and the result, as we have seen, is that his simple device of contradiction is replaced by a more subtle and intricate strategy. This increases the pleasure of the game, since there is no sport in playing too weak an opponent. And in her final transformation her sporting nature is not crushed but redirected. The location of the scene is unusual: often enough, in Shakespeare's comedies, we see the beginning or end of a journey; but here, as the dialogue emphasizes, we are on the open road, in transit between Petruchio's house and Baptista's – as it were, on neutral ground, in a free area where anything can happen. And here Katherina finally displays the fruits of Petruchio's teaching. Her obedience is signalled by submission to her husband on the most basic of matters – perception itself. She sees literally with his eyes, her mind becomes a reflection of his:

> Then, God be bless'd, it is the blessed sun;
> But sun it is not, when you say it is not;
> And the moon changes even as your mind.
>
> (IV. iv. 18–20)

But there is a sly rebuke in that last line, and with it an awareness
that they are really playing a game. Through this awareness
something like the initial balance between them is restored. Attacking her on the physical and social levels, he could break her
down; but in a battle of pure wit they are well matched, and it is
to this level that their relationship now returns. We see this more
clearly – and we see how it squares with her new obedience –
when she not only accepts her husband's description of Vincentio
as a young maid, but matches the relish with which he pursues the
jest, and adds a few touches of her own:

> Young budding virgin, fair and fresh and sweet,
> Whither away, or where is thy abode?
> Happy the parents of so fair a child;
> Happier the man whom favourable stars
> Allots thee for his lovely bed-fellow.   (IV. v. 36–40)

As a wife she submits, but as a player in the game she is now a full
and skilful partner. Most important, she is helping to create her
own role as an obedient spouse, and the process of creation gives
her pleasure. Her obedience is not meekly accepted, but embraced and enjoyed.[14]

It is this sense of pleasure that one misses most in the other
shrew play, *The Taming of a Shrew*. In external action the taming
scenes are much the same, but their development is too bare and
economical; the fullness of detail is missing, and with it the zest
displayed by Katherina at the beginning and end, and by Petruchio throughout. But this sense of the importance of pleasure is not
just a palliative to make the taming acceptable: it is close to the
heart – arguably it *is* the heart – of the play's vision of social life.
It is presented as the *raison d'être* of the play performed for Sly, and
for us:

[14] I have drawn the analogy between the Lord and Petruchio: at this point,
John Russell Brown draws the analogy between Katherina and Sly, both of
whom 'show the gusto of actors who have been given congenial roles'. See
Shakespeare and his Comedies (2nd edition, revised: London, 1968), p. 98. Nevill
Coghill also points to the 'sense of fun' Katherina displays in this scene, though
he comes to a conclusion about their relationship rather different from mine:
'like most of those wives that are the natural superiors of their husbands, she
allows Petruchio the mastery in public'. See 'The basis of Shakespearian
comedy', *Essays and Studies*, III (1950), p. 12.

Your honour's players, hearing your amendment,
Are come to play a pleasant comedy;
For so your doctors hold it very meet,
Seeing too much sadness hath congeal'd your blood,
And melancholy is the nurse of frenzy.
Therefore they thought it good you hear a play
And frame your mind to mirth and merriment,
Which bars a thousand harms and lengthens life.

(Induction, ii. 126–33)

This genial theory of the function of art is matched shortly afterwards by Tranio's view of education: while acknowledging the importance of 'This virtue and this moral discipline' he insists, 'No profit grows where is no pleasure ta'en' (I. i. 30, 39). The same may be said of Petruchio's education of his wife. The final image of social pleasure is the wedding feast – which, for the only time in Shakespeare, is held on stage. Throughout we have been reminded of the civilizing influence of food and drink. It softens the rivalry of Bianca's suitors: Tranio proposes they should 'do as adversaries do in law – / Strive mightily, but eat and drink as friends' (I. ii. 274–5). It consoles Gremio in his defeat: 'My cake is dough, but I'll in among the rest; / Out of hope of all but my share of the feast' (v. i. 125–6). And it provides the setting for Katherina's display of obedience, placing it in a context of social pleasure and pastime.

In the wager the men lay on their wives, the analogy with sport is invoked once more, and more explicitly than ever. When Katherina spars with the Widow, their husbands cheer them on:

PETRUCHIO: To her, Kate!
HORTENSIO: To her, Widow!
PETRUCHIO: A hundred marks, my Kate does put her down.

(v. ii. 33–5)

And when Petruchio objects to the stake –

Twenty crowns!
I'll venture so much of my hawk or hound,
But twenty times so much upon my wife.

(v. ii. 71–3)

– the difference in the wagers seems to be one of degree, not kind. He displays a confident player's zest for the game; and he displays also a complete trust in his partner, a confidence in her ability to play her own hand. If he enjoys making the wager, Katherina enjoys winning it: the sheer length of her speech, the care she lavishes on its rhetoric, tell us that. Here, as with the taming itself, we must not be too quick to adjust the play to our own assumptions about love and marriage. The fact that Katherina relishes her speech as a performance does not necessarily mean she is ironic or insincere.[15] She is simply enjoying herself. Her submission to her husband is not something to be admitted with shame, or rationalized, but celebrated – particularly in the presence of women who have just failed the test she has so triumphantly passed.

Sport, playacting, education – the taming of Katherina is not finally any of these things, but something *sui generis*, the working out of a personal relationship. But these other activities are analogous, and are placed in the play as points of reference. The achievement of 'peace . . ., and love, and quiet life' (v. i. 108) in Petruchio's marriage is seen as part of a whole range of activities whereby men try to bring order and pleasure into their lives. In showing this, the play also shows us as creatures of convention: our most pleasurable activities are organized, limited, bounded by rules; and Petruchio's ultimate lesson may be that order and pleasure are inseparable. We also load ourselves with superficial conventions: the play identifies romantic love and a stuffy sense of propriety as two of these, and comically explodes them. But sport and playacting – both highly conventionalized activities – are seen as genuine sources of strength and enjoyment, and Petruchio's application of these activities to his marriage, while it may seem bizarre to the citizens of Padua, is triumphantly justified.

The characters of *The Comedy of Errors* and *The Two Gentlemen of*

---

[15] Critics have varied widely in their reactions to the speech. Coghill, ibid., clearly sees it as ironic. For George Ian Duthie, in *Shakespeare* (London, 1951), Katherina speaks 'with fervent conviction' (p. 58). Charles Brooks concludes 'she plays her part so well that only she and Petruchio know how much is serious and how much put on'. See 'Shakespeare's romantic shrews', *Shakespeare Quarterly*, XI (summer 1970), p. 354.

Verona are comically trapped by limited orders of understanding; they find it difficult, if not impossible, to rise out of their private worlds and see them in relation to other worlds (though Julia is to some degree an exception). But in *The Taming of the Shrew* Petruchio, Katherina and the Lord have a special vision, an awareness of life as a play or a game, that gives them a power to control not only their own lives but other people's. They have a sense of convention, and therefore a power to manipulate convention, to create experiences rather than have experiences forced upon them. The Lord in creating a new identity for Sly, Petruchio in creating a new life for Katherina, and she herself when she finally joins in this act of creation – all of them convey some of what we imagine to be their own creator's zest in the act of making a new world come to life.

4 Love's Labour's Lost

With its dance movements, its wit combats and its symmetrical teams of wooers, *Love's Labour's Lost* may claim to be Shakespeare's most formal play. The awareness of convention that characterized *The Taming of the Shrew* is here extended in a variety of ways. In that play, we saw the main action, initially at least, as a show put on for a drunken tinker. But that was a play put on by professional actors; *Love's Labour's Lost* is full of enthusiastic amateurs. The performing instinct affects the characters' normal behaviour: not only do they recite poems, adopt disguises and stage shows, but even in what purports to be normal conversation the style may be suddenly heightened and patterned, turned from casual talk into a self-conscious dance of language. When Navarre and his book-men first meet the Princess and her ladies, they inquire their names of Boyet, one after another, in a passage of jingling rhymes and puns which begins calmly enough but rapidly accelerates, with shorter lines and faster repartee (II. i. 193–213). The same stylized, lilting, punning dialogue characterizes the encounter between the masked ladies and the men disguised as Russians (v. ii. 195–264). The two parties seem incapable of approaching each other informally; some convention of behaviour appears to dictate that relations between the sexes should be conducted in a stylized way. But this manner is not confined to the big ensemble scenes of courtship: over and over, individual characters will, at a moment's notice, stage their own little performances, set off by rhyme, and often by a special metre – as when Boyet describes the effect of love on the King, and makes quite a substantial set piece of it (II. i. 233–48). This capacity is not confined to the courtiers: the comic routines of the clowns, such as the play on the idea of 'l'envoy' (III. i. 75–111) may be coarser in texture, but they are equally stylized. Costard joins with the ladies and Boyet in their bawdy playing with hunting terms, and for the moment they all share the same style (IV. i. 101–32). The wit game, like village cricket, is a great social leveller.

We may wonder at times if the characters are simply creatures of literary artifice, or creatures of a more 'real' or 'normal' world who consciously *adopt* literary artifice. Even if we leave aside the consideration that a 'real' world on the stage is still a literary construction, there is no simple answer to this question. When in IV. iii the bookmen enter one by one, confess their love, then hide to spy on the next victim, only Berowne seems conscious of the artificiality of the action they are engaged in – ' "All hid, all hid" – an old infant play' (IV. iii. 74). The others simply fall unconsciously into the formal pattern. Berowne's remark, however, is typical of many deflating comments throughout the play: characters may not admit the artifice of their own behaviour, but they are quite willing to point out the artifice of other people's. Denounced by Berowne, Boyet passes off the attack as a performance (which to some extent it is) and thus draws some of its sting: 'Full merrily / Hath this brave manage, this career, been run' (v. ii. 481–2). After a stylized, punning exchange between Katharine and Rosaline, the Princess congratulates them – and perhaps restrains them, for their joking has become sharp and personal: 'Well bandied both, a set of wit well play'd' (v. ii. 29). In both instances, we notice that the image is drawn from sport – tilting in one case, tennis in the other. Sometimes the performer himself will be self-conscious. Berowne is aware that he is a word-spinner: 'I'll prove her fair, or talk till doomsday here' (IV. iii. 270). And Moth's set piece on white and red is introduced by the following exchange:

ARMADO: Define, define, well-educated infant.
  MOTH: My father's wit, and my mother's tongue assist me!

ARMADO: Sweet invocation of a child, most pretty and
                   pathetical!

(I. ii. 90–4)

Both are aware of Moth as a performer, and beneath the page's
cheeky manner is some of a young performer's nervousness; this
suggestion is later confirmed when he 'dries' before the ladies. A
welcome touch of humanity is added to a character who might
otherwise seem a coldly efficient joke machine.

   The characters' sporadic awareness that they are putting on
performances recalls the special awareness of Petruchio, Katherina and the Lord in *The Taming of the Shrew*. The characters are
not simply creatures of convention: they are also *aware* of conventions, and manipulate them, using them to describe or evoke
special states of mind. Again, as in *The Taming of the Shrew*, the
special state most frequently evoked is that of the game-player,
homo ludens. But while the other play suggested a rough outdoor
fun, the interest here – even when the same sports are referred to –
is more in elegance and precision: 'finely put on' (IV. i. 106). Just
as, in the bawdy set piece in which Boyet, Costard and the ladies
play with hunting, archery and bowling, sex becomes a matter of
arrows hitting targets (IV. i. 101–32), so throughout the wit exchanges the primary value is not feeling but accuracy. However
coarse or brutal the joking may be (and the characters are at no
pains to spare each other's feelings) what matters is that the shaft
should hit its mark. Even the pedants are not as cloistered as we
might think, but show some sporting instincts. We first see them
as spectators of the Princess's hunt, and conversation about it
dominates their first scene (IV. ii). Their own sport is playing with
language – again, accuracy is the primary aim, though Holofernes's idea of accuracy may appear stuffy and old-fashioned –
and they get their own kind of pleasure from it. Their first scene
ends with Holofernes's words, 'Away; the gentles are at their
game, and we will to our recreation' (IV. ii. 155–6): their recreation being a literary conversation over dinner, in which
Holofernes will do most of the talking. Their second scene, in
which they plan the show of the Nine Worthies, ends with a
similar cry from Holofernes: 'To our sport, away' (V. i. 135). Dull,

too, sees the show of the Nine Worthies as a chance for some fun, though his idea of what is appropriate to the figures of classical antiquity is cheerfully incongruous: 'I'll make one in a dance, or so; or I will play / On the tabor to the Worthies, and let them dance the hay' (v. i. 133-4). The play evokes a world of social pastime and recreation, in which courtship and even learning are woven into the figures of a dance; and the play's fascination with the actions of groups, rather than those of individuals, reflects this interest in recreation: the individual surrenders some of his individuality, to become part of a team, a figure in a larger pattern.[1]

In *The Taming of the Shrew* dependence on convention was simply accepted, and the play conveyed a feeling of pleasure and satisfaction in seeing how well the conventions worked, how much could be achieved in human terms by sport and playacting. But in *Love's Labour's Lost* there is a new spirit of edgy suspicion. The Lord and Petruchio were firmly in control, using conventions to manipulate the minds of Sly and Katherina, who responded with increasing eagerness. But here the characters are more sharply in competition with each other: the difference is between teaching someone to use a weapon and seeing if you yourself can use the weapon better. The result is that the conventions which appeared so powerful are now being explored for weaknesses. The show put on for Sly took over the stage and became the play's main reality; the shows put on for the Princess and her ladies are torn to pieces. The men come masked and disguised, only to find that the ladies too are masked and (having changed identities) even more deeply disguised, determined to beat them at their own game. The characters' awareness of convention, which led simply to pleasure in the other play, now produces a more complex and sceptical response.

In discussing earlier plays, I have suggested some of the comic devices by which Shakespeare can dislocate an experience and show its limits; here these devices are skilfully and elaborately deployed in order to dislocate the various conventions on which the characters depend. The most frequently used device is that of

---

[1] See C. L. Barber, *Shakespeare's Festive Comedy* (Cleveland, 1967), p. 89. On the play's interest in games, see also Ralph Berry, 'The words of Mercury', *Shakespeare Survey*, XXII (1969), p. 72.

addressing a speech to an unsympathetic or uncomprehending audience, as in *The Comedy of Errors*; though in *Love's Labour's Lost* the listener's lack of sympathy usually results not from misunderstanding but from a deliberate refusal to co-operate. Moth meets the problem in its most basic form: 'They do not mark me, and that brings me out' (v. ii. 172). Attempts at wooing are constantly bedevilled in this way: love letters are read by the wrong people, who comment disapprovingly on the style: protestations of love are either misdirected (as in the Masque of Russians), or rebuffed, or both. The ladies' characteristic tactic is to take the conventional utterances of love at their face value, thereby reducing them to nonsense:

BEROWNE: White-handed mistress, one sweet word with thee.
PRINCESS: Honey, and milk, and sugar; there is three.

(v. ii. 230–1)

You can reduce any convention to nonsense by taking it too literally – as Shakespeare himself does in Sonnet CXXX, 'My mistress' eyes are nothing like the sun.' There is a more subtle effect earlier in the same scene:

KING: Say to her we have measur'd many miles
       To tread a measure with her on this grass.
BOYET: They say that they have measur'd many a mile
       To tread a measure with you on this grass.
ROSALINE: It is not so. Ask them how many inches
       Is in one mile? If they have measured many,
       The measure, then, of one is eas'ly told.

(v. ii. 184–90)

The use of Boyet as a go-between is even more damaging than the obvious trick of taking the image literally. He dislodges the words from their original speaker and robs them of the conviction with which they were first uttered: '*They say* that they have measur'd many a mile.' The poor phrase is already helpless before Rosaline goes to work on it.

Berowne, as a one-man audience for his fellows' confessions of love, also has a dislocating effect. They are mostly aware of their own private feelings, which seem very important and serious to them. But, from his special vantage point – 'Like a demigod here sit I in the sky' (IV. iii. 75) (and whatever that means in stage terms, there is no doubt what it means in psychological ones) – he sees them as we do, losing their individuality, and their seriousness, to a pattern of comic repetition that reduces the importance of individual feeling:

> KING: In love, I hope; sweet fellowship in shame!
> BEROWNE: One drunkard loves another of the name.
> LONGAVILLE: Am I the first that have been perjur'd so?
> BEROWNE: I would put thee in comfort: not by two that I
> know.
>
> (IV. iii. 45–8)

> DUMAIN: Once more I'll read the ode that I have writ.
> BEROWNE: Once more I'll mark how love can vary wit.
>
> (IV. iii. 95–6)

But of course Berowne himself is one of the 'four woodcocks in a dish' (IV. iii. 78); and he himself realizes how much he is included in his sardonic view of the others. They get their revenge later in the scene, when his praise of Rosaline is greeted with the same scorn that he had heaped on their efforts. He is not allowed a sympathetic hearing for his declarations, any more than they are (IV. iii. 228–77).

The self-satisfaction with which Armado and the pedants display their facility with words is likewise dislocated by the reactions of an onstage audience, though here the attacks are less direct. Armado's delicate loftiness is played off against the teasing of Moth; and when Armado and Holofernes join together for a display of what they conceive to be grand language, their encounter is introduced by Moth's remark, 'They have been at a great feast of languages and stol'n the scraps' (V. i. 33–4) and concludes with the following exchange between Holofernes and Dull:

> HOLOFERNES: Via, goodman Dull! Thou hast spoken no word
> all this while.
> DULL: Nor understood none neither, sir.
>
> (V. i. 129–31)

What is high talk to the speakers is, to the listeners, just so much noise. For the most part, this device of playing the speaker off against his listener is used for its obvious comic value; but, as in *The Comedy of Errors*, our failure to reach each other's minds is not always funny. In the last scene the King speaks, as before, in the language of love, but it is embarrassingly out of place, and the Princess replies 'I understand you not; my griefs are double' (v. ii. 740). To the grief of her father's death is added the pain of watching her suitor behave so tactlessly in a serious situation. Once again the conventional utterance of love is dislocated; but here it is seen, not as laughable, but as painfully inappropriate.

Broken or interrupted ceremonies are another device by which conventions are challenged: one thinks of the ceremony of oath-taking, which Berowne disrupts, and the masque in which the ladies refuse to dance (were this to happen in a real masque, the result would likely be an international scandal). The show of the Nine Worthies is destroyed at the most basic level, as the audience simply refuses to accept the convention of theatrical illusion:

COSTARD: *I Pompey am* –
BEROWNE: You lie, you are not he.

> (v. ii. 543)[2]

The players are forced out of their disguises, with particularly humiliating results for Armado's portrayal of Hector. We learn much more about the performers in this scene than about the characters they portray: Sir Nathaniel, in particular, becomes a clearer character than ever before:

> There, an't shall please you, a foolish mild man; an honest man, look you, and soon dash'd. He is a marvellous good neighbour, faith, and a very good bowler; but for Alisander – alas! you see how 'tis – a little o'er parted.

> (v. ii. 574–8)

The result is to emphasize how fragile their impersonations are, how far they are from being the great figures of legend they are pretending to be.

[2] See Anne Righter (Barton), *Shakespeare and the Idea of the Play* (Harmondsworth, 1967), p. 99.

Contrasts of style also have their function in this process: we see this in the difference between the formality of the lords and the sharp responses of the ladies; and between Armado's elaborate meditations on love when he is alone, and the blunt utterance he slips into when faced with Jaquenetta, whose mind is incapable of grasping words of more than one syllable:

ARMADO:	I do betray myself with blushing. Maid!
JAQUENETTA:	Man!
ARMADO:	I will visit thee at the lodge.
JAQUENETTA:	That's hereby.
ARMADO:	I know where it is situate.
JAQUENETTA:	Lord, how wise you are!
ARMADO:	I will tell thee wonders.
JAQUENETTA:	With that face?
ARMADO:	I love thee.
JAQUENETTA:	So I heard you say.

(I. ii. 126–35)

One of the most elaborate and telling effects, however, is in the opening scene. The oath-taking ceremony, and Berowne's rebellion, are written in a more or less uniform style: smooth, formal, self-consciously clever. Berowne is, for all his objections, one of them, and it is no surprise when he finally subscribes. The real challenge to the credibility of the King's legislation comes with the entrance of Dull and Costard, and the reading of Armado's letter. We hear a different range of voices now: Dull's comic, futile self-importance; Costard's cheeky earthiness, which includes a few parodies of the high style – 'Such is the simplicity of man to hearken after the flesh' (I. i. 212–13); and, best of all, Armado's delicate hovering several miles above reality:

KING:	'sorted and consorted, contrary to thy established proclaimed edict and continent canon, which, with, O, with – but with this I passion to say wherewith –'
COSTARD:	With a wench.
KING:	'with a child of our grandmother Eve, a female; or, for thy more sweet understanding, a woman. . . .'

(I. i. 245–50)

The courtiers poke fun at Armado, but the irony is that he is up-
holding their standards, and the joke is therefore partly on them.
When at the end of the scene Berowne predicts 'These oaths and
laws will prove an idle scorn' (i. i. 288), we may reflect that, with
authority represented by Armado and Dull, and with the prisoner
Costard scoring most of the points, the prediction has already been
fulfilled: the vow and its attendant legislation have been presented from a new and comically unflattering perspective.[3]

So radically does the play question conventions that even words
themselves, the most basic of conventions, come under suspicion.[4]
Language is based on a tacit agreement that certain combinations
of sound carry certain meanings. But in the very first encounter of
the King and the Princess, his apparently innocuous speech of
greeting is seized upon, and his use of words mercilessly dissected:

> KING: Fair Princess, welcome to the court of Navarre.
> PRINCESS: 'Fair' I give you back again; and 'welcome' I have
> not yet. The roof of this court is too high to be yours,
> and welcome to the wide fields too base to be mine.
>
> (ii. i. 90–3)

Costard, like Dogberry after him, uses words with a fine un-
concern for their agreed meanings: 'and therefore welcome the
sour cup of prosperity! Affliction may one day smile again; and
till then, sit thee down, sorrow' (i. i. 292–4). In another play, this
might be an incidental comic effect; but here, a sense that language is unreliable is basic to the play's vision. The mistaking of
words is still a comic effect, but it is far from incidental.

The play, in short, shows conventions – even words themselves –
as comically vulnerable. And here is where the lovers' problem
lies. As we saw in *The Two Gentlemen of Verona*, love depends for its

---

[3] See Bobbyann Roesen (Anne Barton), '*Love's Labour's Lost*', *Shakespeare Quarterly*, IV (October 1953), p. 414; here the scene is compared to the scene in *Measure for Measure* where Elbow brings Pompey for trial, and demonstrates the futility of Angelo's kind of justice.

[4] On the treatment of language in the play, see Berry, 'The words of Mercury', pp. 69–76; William Matthews, 'Language in *Love's Labour's Lost*', *Essays and Studies*, XVII (1964), pp. 1–11; and James L. Calderwood, '*Love's Labour's Lost*: a wantoning with words', *Studies in English Literature 1500–1900*, V (spring 1965), pp. 317–32.

fulfilment on expression, but the means of expression available to it are largely conventional and therefore open to mockery. Standard metaphors are used to describe love and courtship – metaphors drawn from war:

KING: Saint Cupid, then! and, soldiers, to the field!
BEROWNE: Advance your standards, and upon them, lords;
           Pell-mell, down with them! But be first advis'd,
           In conflict, that you get the sun of them.

                                             (IV. iii. 362–5)

from hunting:

BOYET: Who is the shooter? Who is the shooter?
ROSALINE: Shall I teach you to know?
BOYET: Ay, my continent of beauty.
ROSALINE: Why, she that bears the bow.
            Finely put off!
BOYET: My lady goes to kill horns; but, if thou marry,
            Hang me by the neck, if horns that year miscarry.
            Finely put on!
ROSALINE: Well, then, I am the shooter.
BOYET: And who is your deer?
ROSALINE: If we choose by the horns, yourself come not near.

                                             (IV. i. 101–8)

and from law:

BEROWNE: Our states are forfeit; seek not to undo us.
ROSALINE: It is not so; for how can this be true,
            That you stand forfeit, being those that sue?

                                             (V. ii. 425–7)

These are all commonplaces of Elizabethan love poetry; and they all have the effect of reducing love to generalizations – conflict, desire, bargaining. They compare love to something which is not love, and they find the common ground in some general experience. The bawdry in the references to war and hunting also reduces love to its physical expression, seen as a subject of mechanical jokes. Moth, in prescribing to Armado the correct behaviour for a lover, recites a series of formulae (III. i. 10–22). Berowne is aware of how painfully unoriginal love has made him, and expresses this in a cliché rhyme: 'Well, I will love, write, sigh, pray, sue, and groan; / Some men must love my lady, and some Joan' (III. i. 194–5). The trouble with these conventional expressions of love is that they offer no guarantee that the feelings the lover expresses are his own. The love poems the men produce could be written by anybody, for anybody. The Princess, I think, makes this point when she has her ladies exchange favours, tricking the men into courting the wrong women:

> The effect of my intent is to cross theirs.
> They do it but in mockery merriment,
> And mock for mock is only my intent.
>
> (v. ii. 138–40)

If courtship is simply a game or dance, it does not matter who your partner is, so long as the forms are observed. And indeed one feels that in this scene the speakers could be interchanged in a variety of ways, and it would make no difference: the lines they speak, like the masks they wear, could belong to anyone.

There is another danger in the conventions by which love expresses itself, a danger that the speaker will begin to revel in his own skill with words, not communicating but simply preening himself. The general danger of pride is suggested by the Princess:

> And, out of question, so it is sometimes:
> Glory grows guilty of detested crimes,
> When, for fame's sake, for praise, an outward part,
> We bend to that the working of the heart;
> As I for praise alone now seek to spill
> The poor deer's blood that my heart means no ill.
>
> (IV. i. 30–5)

Any activity can be corrupted if we do it, not for its own sake, but for the credit it gives us. The point is applied to language most directly through the figures of Holofernes, Nathaniel and Armado. The pedants are smug about their cleverness with words (IV. ii. 22–7, 63–9); and when Holofernes speaks it is not to communicate ideas so much as to display his best classroom manner:

> Most barbarous intimation! yet a kind of insinuation, as it were, in via, in way, of explication; facere, as it were,

replication, or rather ostentare, to show, as it were, his inclination, after his undressed, unpolished, uneducated, unpruned, untrimmed, or rather unlettered, or ratherest unconfirmed fashion to insert again my haud credo for a deer.

(IV. ii. 12–17)

Armado at least has some flair: 'the posteriors of this day; which the rude multitude call the afternoon' (V. i. 75–7). Like Holofernes he is showing off, but unlike Holofernes he is capable of something that might pass, in a dim light, for elegance. Even Costard is subject to linguistic display, preferring 'remuneration' to a plain three farthings (III. i. 129–34).

With this in mind, we can see why the Princess suspects the praise Boyet offers her:

> I am less proud to hear you tell my worth
> Than you much willing to be counted wise
> In spending your wit in the praise of mine.

(II. i. 17–19)

For all she knows, the King and his bookmen, too, may simply be showing off.[5] The women, in trying to assess the men's love, have to rely on the formal expressions the men offer; and these may be simply standard conventions with no application to individual reality, or displays of social elegance indulged in for their own sake. The Princess concludes:

> We have received your letters, full of love;
> Your favours, the ambassadors of love;
> And in our maiden council, rated them
> At courtship, pleasant jest, and courtesy,
> As bombast and as lining to the time;
> But more devout than this in our respects
> Have we not been; and therefore met your loves
> In their own fashion, like a merriment.

DUMAIN: Our letters, madam, show'd much more than
jest.

[5] According to Gates K. Agnew, 'Berowne and the progress of *Love's Labour's Lost*', *Shakespeare Studies*, IV (1968), 'through Berowne the fame-seeker's mentality comes to pervade the wooing game' (p. 44).

LONGAVILLE: So did our looks.

ROSALINE: We did not quote them so.

(v. ii. 765–74)

The men's love may have been sincere, but nothing in its expression allowed this sincerity to communicate. The Princess, describing it as 'bombast and as lining to the time', picks up the image of clothing used by Berowne in renouncing 'Taffeta phrases, silken terms precise, / Three-pil'd hyperboles' (v. ii. 406–7). The expression of love has been purely a matter of social display, of outward show. In *The Two Gentlemen of Verona*, the lady was 'deform'd' by the lover's peculiar vision of her (II. i. 56–8). Here, according to Berowne, the lovers themselves are deformed, betrayed by the means they have used to express themselves:

> Your beauty, ladies,
> Hath much deformed us, fashioning our humours
> Even to the opposed end of our intents.

(v. ii. 744–6)

We touch here on one of the crucial paradoxes of convention. The forms of expression the men have used have been, to take them at the most basic level, attempts to break out of the privateness of the individual mind and communicate with someone else. Yet the means of communication are, and have to be, agreed conventions of speech and behaviour, with a general applicability that makes them instantly recognizable. And their very generality detracts from the personal nature of the feeling the speaker wishes to communicate. The listener is aware only of words that have been used a thousand times before, and the experience of the speaker remains locked inside him after all.

This leads to a feeling of helplessness on both sides: 'I understand you not; my griefs are double.' This feeling is centred on the character of Berowne. Even his major attempt to identify and solve the problem of communication fails to get the response he would have hoped for:

> O, never will I trust to speeches penn'd,
> Nor to the motion of a school-boy's tongue,
> Nor never come in vizard to my friend,

> Nor woo in rhyme, like a blind harper's song.
> Taffeta phrases, silken terms precise,
> Three-pil'd hyperboles, spruce affectation,
> Figures pedantical – these summer-flies
> Have blown me full of maggot ostentation.
> I do forswear them; and I here protest,
> By this white glove – how white the hand, God
> knows! –
> Henceforth my wooing mind shall be express'd
> In russet yeas, and honest kersey noes.
> And, to begin, wench – so God help me, law! –
> My love to thee is sound, sans crack or flaw.

ROSALINE: Sans 'sans,' I pray you.

BEROWNE: Yet I have a trick
> Of the old rage; bear with me, I am sick.

>   (v. ii. 402–17)

He identifies the problem most sharply, perhaps, in the words 'Nor never come in vizard to my friend'. He has turned what should be a personal affair into a matter of external form, disguising rather than revealing himself. And the speech throughout has a surprising undercurrent of genuine feeling: the images of corruption and disease convey remorse and disgust. Yet Rosaline picks one word – one very small word – to show how far Berowne still is from achieving his objective; and the fact is that the renunciation of ornate expressions of love is in itself a poetic commonplace, a convention like all the others.[6] The way the speech drifts into rhyme towards the end shows that, like the speeches it is designed to replace, it is really a neat rhetorical package. Far from being impressed by Berowne's declaration, the women go on to tease the men further by revealing that when they came in vizards they were addressing the wrong friends. Berowne's speech is anything but the final point of rest that it may at first appear to be.

Berowne's characteristic posture throughout the play is to be trapped in a situation which he sees as ridiculous, but from which

[6] See M. C. Bradbrook, *Shakespeare and Elizabethan Poetry* (Harmondsworth, 1964), p. 29.

he is unable to extricate himself. This is true of the opening scene
of the oath-taking: he protests, but he signs.[7] It is true most particularly of his experience of love. Berowne has the range of vision
and feeling found so often in the major characters of the comedies;
but this does not give him the self-control or the power of action
enjoyed by Petruchio (and, to some extent, Julia). The clarity
with which he sees both sides of his dilemma leaves him, paralysed,
in the middle. He sees love from the outsider's perspective, as a
comic humiliation:

> O me, with what strict patience have I sat,
> To see a king transformed to a gnat!
> To see great Hercules whipping a gig,
> And profound Solomon to tune a jig,
> And Nestor play at push-pin with the boys,
> And critic Timon laugh at idle toys!
>
> (IV. iii. 161–6)

But he also sees love from inside, as a special, heightened awareness that transforms the world by transforming our perception of
it:

> It adds a precious seeing to the eye:
> A lover's eyes will gaze an eagle blind.
> A lover's ear will hear the lowest sound,
> When the suspicious head of theft is stopp'd.
> Love's feeling is more soft and sensible
> Than are the tender horns of cockled snails;
> Love's tongue proves dainty Bacchus gross in taste.
> For valour, is not Love a Hercules,
> Still climbing trees in the Hesperides?
>
> (IV. iii. 329–37)

What love is depends entirely on your point of view, and unlike
his fellows, who move from scorn to acceptance, Berowne holds
both perspectives in his mind at once. This double perspective also
affects his view of Rosaline:

[7] Agnew, 'Berowne and the progress of *Love's Labour's Lost*', pp. 40–1, discusses
the importance of Berowne's loyalty to his comrades.

And, among three, to love the worst of all,
A whitely wanton with a velvet brow,
With two pitch balls stuck in her face for eyes;
Ay, and by heaven, one that will do the deed,
Though Argus were her eunuch and her guard.

(III. i. 185–9)

O, but for my love, day would turn to night!
Of all complexions the cull'd sovereignty
Do meet, as at a fair, in her fair cheek,
Where several worthies make one dignity,
Where nothing wants that want itself doth seek.

(IV. iii. 229–33)

His dilemma, comic enough in itself, is made doubly so by its close similarity to the musings of Armado, who has just the same problem reconciling himself to his love for Jaquenetta.

Berowne's extravagant defences of Rosaline, and of love itself, are made in public. It is mostly in private that we hear his witty dissection of the feelings that have trapped him, and his wry acceptance of them. We cannot help feeling that he is putting a good face on things for his fellows, preserving his own credit by concealing the complexity of his real feelings. But his denunciations, like his defences, are extravagant, rhetorical and overheated. In both cases he is protesting too much. When he is most honest about his own position, his tone is quieter, more philosophical:

Well, I do nothing in the world but lie, and lie in my throat. By heaven, I do love; and it hath taught me to rhyme, and to be melancholy; and here is part of my rhyme, and here my melancholy.

(IV. iii. 9–13)

For Berowne, then, the problem of self-expression goes deeper than a simple failure to communicate with the lady. His dual awareness of love leads him, not to a steady and comprehensive assessment of it, but to the expression of extravagant half-truths, first on one side, then on the other. Over and over, he seems distressed at the sound of his own voice, embarrassed at what he has just said. After a long passage of rhetorical praise of Rosaline, he concludes 'Fie, painted rhetoric! O, she needs it not' (IV. iii. 235). After whipping himself and his companions into a frenzy of enthusiasm for love, he concludes:

> Allons! allons! Sow'd cockle reap'd no corn,
> And justice always whirls in equal measure.
> Light wenches may prove plagues to men forsworn;
> If so, our copper buys no better treasure.
>
> (IV. iii. 379–82)

If Berowne seems the most fully realized figure of the play, this may be because, like Petruchio, he embodies many of the play's processes in his own nature. Just as Petruchio was a creator, a teacher and an entertainer, doing for Katherina what the play did for the audience, so Berowne displays in his own mind the critical, comic testing of love and language that seems for much of the action to be the chief purpose of *Love's Labour's Lost*.

But the qualifications in that last statement are important. Love and language are not the only targets, nor is the debate that takes place in Berowne's nature the ultimate debate of the play. It is merely, for a while, the most prominent one. Love and language are dislocated by mockery; yet mockery itself is also examined from a detached and critical point of view. Mockery, like love, turns people into objects: just as a lady who is simply an object of adoration may feel she is being denied her full individuality, so the victim of a joke is denied whatever claim he may have to a sympathetic understanding. There is something a little unpleasant in the way the King treats Armado as a household pet (I. i. 172–4), while the man himself thinks he enjoys the King's friendship and favour (v. i. 82–101). More prominent, of course, is the mockery of the men by the women; and there are several passages where we find them gloating over the helplessness of their victims (v. ii. 266–81, for example). In particular, there is something sadistic in Rosaline's attitude to Berowne:

> That same Berowne I'll torture ere I go.
> O that I knew he were but in by th' week!
> How I would make him fawn, and beg, and seek,

And wait the season, and observe the times,
And spend his prodigal wits in bootless rhymes,
And shape his service wholly to my hests,
And make him proud to make me proud that jests!
So pertaunt-like would I o'ersway his state
That he should be my fool, and I his fate.

(v. iii. 60–8)

The emphasis on the mocker's own pride is important here, for it shows mockery as subject to the same peril as courtship: the danger that it could be just a vehicle for display, conveying only the self-esteem of the speaker. With this in mind, we may wonder if Berowne's ridicule of Boyet (v. ii. 315–34, 463–81), which seems to be developed out of all proportion, springs in fact from wounded self-esteem: Berowne and his fellows have had their egos sadly bruised by the women's mockery, and Berowne takes out his resentment on the nearest available object. He cannot regain his pride by flouting the ladies (his position with them is insecure enough as it is) and he therefore identifies Boyet as the real culprit, and flouts him. A similar motive may lie behind the men's savage mockery of the Nine Worthies (in which, we should note, the women do not join): Berowne suggests that "tis some policy / To have one show worse than the King's and his company' (v. ii. 510–11), and they make sure that it does indeed appear worse.[8]

It would be pleasant to believe that the women ridicule the men out of love, in order to point out their follies and educate them into being better lovers. But they never say so. The interest they display in the men when they first discuss them (II. i. 37–79) springs from past memory, and when the men actually appear the reaction they trigger is pure mockery. The Princess's explanation of this, which I have already quoted, is that they could not take the men's love seriously; nothing is said about using ridicule to draw them to a more valid expression of love. The ridicule

---

[8] It may also be suggested, though more tentatively, that Boyet joins in ridiculing the Worthies to regain his own credit, somewhat bruised by Berowne's attacks. Certainly the effect is to unite the two men against a common victim, for Berowne's reaction is 'Well said, old mocker; I must needs be friends with thee' (v. ii. 545).

appears, on the contrary, to be exercised for its own sake. And the
Princess herself, who is most articulate about the reasons for
mockery, is also the first to recognize its limits, and to temper its
effect. She is at some pains to counter the ridicule of the Nine
Worthies, giving a sympathetic hearing in particular to Armado
(whose touching defence of the dead Hector also rebukes the
mockery of his audience). While the others try to force the players
out of their disguises, she addresses them by the names of the
characters they portray.[9] Almost her first statement after the
sobering news of her father's death is an apology to the men for
the way they have been mocked:

> I thank you, gracious lords,
> For all your fair endeavours, and entreat,
> Out of a new-sad soul, that you vouchsafe
> In your rich wisdom to excuse or hide
> The liberal opposition of our spirits,
> If over-boldly we have borne ourselves
> In the converse of breath – your gentleness
> Was guilty of it.

(v. ii. 717–24)

Rosaline presents a more difficult case. Her instruction to
Berowne to 'jest a twelvemonth in an hospital' (v. ii. 859) is
intended

> to choke a gibing spirit,
> Whose influence is begot of that loose grace
> Which shallow laughing hearers give to fools.
> A jest's prosperity lies in the ear
> Of him that hears it, never in the tongue
> Of him that makes it.

(v. ii. 846–51)

As with love poetry, the problem is to communicate – in this case,
to give delight – not simply to display one's superiority. But this
criticism, as we have seen, applies with equal force to Rosaline
herself, and she gives no indication of realizing this. On one point
at least, her mind has already shown a dramatic change: she once
praised Berowne for the very quality she now finds objectionable,

[9] See Roesen, *'Love's Labour's Lost'*, p. 422.

and praised him in particular for his ability so to charm his hearers 'That aged ears play truant at his tales, / And younger hearings are quite ravished' (II. i. 74–5). She now feels less enthusiastic about Berowne's mockery than before. But does she also feel less enthusiastic about her own? If so, the next logical step would be the kind of apology for her own behaviour the Princess has made. That no such apology is given may be due to incomplete revision (of which there are other signs in the text); or it may be Shakespeare's intention to show that the character's self-esteem and her desire to control her lover are not broken down but simply applied in a new way; finally, it is possible for the actress, if she wishes, to deliver the speech as though Rosaline realized its application to herself: the general terms in which it is couched could aid, though they do not require, such an interpretation. However we take Rosaline's behaviour, one thing seems clear: far from using wit as an instrument of love, the women find it necessary to put wit to one side if love is to be established on a serious basis.

What we have seen up till now is a closed circle of worship and mockery, a sterile situation in which love cannot thrive. If the circle is to be broken, a different set of realities altogether must be introduced; and this is what happens in the last scene. As in *The Two Gentlemen of Verona* love is seen in relation to a broader range of experience; but the effect here is not simply a comic juxtaposition but an attempt to use the larger realities as a means of testing and strengthening love. First, Armado's attempt at dignified, heroic love is amusingly compromised – and his portrayal of Hector exploded – by the intrusion of animal reality:

ARMADO: I do adore thy sweet Grace's slipper.
BOYET: (*Aside to Dumain*) Loves her by the foot.
DUMAIN: (*Aside to Boyet*) He may not by the yard.
ARMADO: *This Hector far surmounted Hannibal* –
COSTARD: The party is gone, fellow Hector, she is gone; she is two months on her way.

(v. ii. 657–62)

This is what love leads to, and the discovery is presented in a spirit of coarse ribaldry (introduced by the sexual joke on 'yard').

Then, in a few moments, we are presented with another animal reality – death. The enclosed world of courtship is attacked from two sides at once. A new life begins in Jaquenetta's belly, and an old life ends somewhere in France: courtship is only a moment in a larger cycle. But Marcade's entrance, striking though it is, is not an intrusion of something totally new: throughout the play there have been suggestions of the larger sweep of time, and the presence of death.[10] In the opening lines, the three years' vow of study was seen as an attempt to win fame and so defy time and death (I. i. 1–7). We were reminded, too, of the death of Katherina's sister, grown melancholy through love (v. ii. 13–18); and of the decay to which time subjects the graces of youth: 'Such short-liv'd wits do wither as they grow' (II. i. 54). In the first meeting of the lovers we are reminded that the Princess has actually come on other business. Between the stylized skirmishes of wit there is a long passage on the surrender of Aquitaine – written in a fluid, natural style, full of political detail, utterly unlike the surrounding dialogue (II. i. 128–70). It is as though a passage from one of the history plays had been inserted, and the effect is to remind us that the games of courtship are only a small part of the general business of living – a reminder that is renewed in the last scene, when the Princess thanks the King 'For my great suit so easily obtain'd' (v. ii. 727).

Here is where the oath taken by Navarre and his bookmen, and so easily broken, becomes of special importance. The dedication to plain living and high thinking is easily ridiculed, and there is a natural comic satisfaction in seeing it crumble. Berowne's attacks on pedantry, the chief danger of learning, are witty and satisfying (I. i. 71–93); and when Armado cannot fall in love without assuring himself that he has classical precedent behind him we see the ridiculous side of the men's idealism (I. ii. 62–7). But at least the oath showed some attempt, however mistaken, to deal with the realities of time and death. And a foolish vow is still a vow: in the words of the Princess, ''Tis deadly sin to keep that oath, my lord, / And sin to break it' (II. i. 104–5). Throughout their courtship, the men are haunted by the betrayal of their vow, and

[10] For a contrary view, see Peter G. Phialas, *Shakespeare's Romantic Comedies* (Chapel Hill, 1966), p. 99.

Berowne even connects this with the drubbing the women give them: 'Thus pour the stars down plagues for perjury' (v. ii. 394). Berowne's attacks on the oath in the first scene, and his later excuses for breaking it, include blatant sophistry as well as refreshing common sense (I. i. 59–66; IV. iii. 359–61). Here again Berowne knows he and the others are doing wrong – 'God amend us, God amend! We are much out o' th' way' (IV. iii. 72) – but is unable to resolve the dilemma.

The Princess constantly reminds the King of his perjury (v. ii. 345–90, 440–2) and she returns to this point in the final scene:

> No, no, my lord, your Grace is perjur'd much,
> Full of dear guiltiness; and therefore this,
> If for my love, as there is no such cause,
> You will do aught – this shall you do for me:
> Your oath I will not trust; but go with speed
> To some forlorn and naked hermitage,
> Remote from all the pleasures of the world;
> There stay until the twelve celestial signs
> Have brought about the annual reckoning.
> If this austere insociable life
> Change not your offer made in heat of blood,
> If frosts and fasts, hard lodging and thin weeds,
> Nip not the gaudy blossoms of your love,
> But that it bear this trial, and last love,
> Then, at the expiration of the year,
> Come, challenge me, challenge me by these deserts;
> And, by this virgin palm now kissing thine,
> I will be thine . . .
>
> (v. ii. 778–95)

The other women follow this lead. The new vow – for that is what it is – repeats the old one's emphasis on penance and self-denial. The King must prove he is a worthy lover by proving he can be more than a lover: in particular, his lost integrity must be restored. The device of seeing romantic love in relation to other experiences, from being a comic technique exercised by the playwright, is now used by the characters themselves. As in *The Taming of the Shrew*, the characters are allowed to handle some of the instruments used only by the author in *The Comedy of Errors* and *The Two Gentlemen of Verona*. The new vow will not be a denial of love, but a means towards its fulfilment; and it will not deny the natural cycles of life (as Berowne argued the old one did – i. i. 102–7), but use them to test love: in particular, it will see if time, so obviously the medium of decay, can also be the medium of fulfilment.

It would, however, be misleading to suggest that the tasks imposed on the men involve the intrusion of raw, brutal reality on an artificial world. The vows themselves, to expire in 'a twelvemonth and a day' (v. ii. 815), are just as much a matter of literary convention as the courtship games they replace.[11] The play comes full circle, ending as it began, with the taking of a vow. And while this convention or that may be ridiculed, the necessity – the inevitability, even – of living by convention is never questioned. When Berowne renounces literary artifice, the sheer orthodoxy of his position reminds us that the breaking of conventions is itself conventional. Throughout the play a favourite device is to set up a pattern and break it, only to create a larger pattern. We see this in the masque:

ROSALINE: Since you are strangers and come here by chance,
We'll not be nice; take hands. We will not dance.
KING: Why take we hands then?
ROSALINE: Only to part friends.
Curtsy, sweet hearts; and so the measure ends.
(v. ii. 218–21)

The refusal to dance is in itself a small verbal dance movement.[12] When Berowne interrupts the ceremony of the oath, the effect is to create a small debate, as formal as the ceremony itself. I have argued that the real disruption comes with the entrance of Dull and Costard, and even that suggests a larger ceremonial pattern – masque and antimasque. The pattern of the opening scene is comically inverted in iv. iii, with the King, Longaville and Dumain expressing love by turns, Berowne pretending to hold out

[11] See Karl F. Thompson, 'Shakespeare's romantic comedies', *Publications of the Modern Language Association of America*, LXVII (December 1952), pp. 1084–5.
[12] See Barber, *Shakespeare's Festive Comedy*, p. 94.

and finally succumbing, and Costard appearing this time not as
the transgressor but as the one righteous man: 'Walk aside the
true folk, and let the traitors stay' (IV. iii. 209). As the one scene
parodies the other, so between them they create something larger
than either, an elegantly ironic design.

The play itself, in which so many conventions are tested and
broken, is one more convention. Our awareness of this is conveyed
by a variety of extra-dramatic references. Berowne, like Speed,
steps partly outside the dramatic illusion by his awareness that he
and his fellows are speaking in rhyme, and his readiness to poke
fun at this particular convention:

KING:	How well he's read, to reason against reading!
DUMAIN:	Proceeded well, to stop all good proceeding!
LONGAVILLE:	He weeds the corn, and still lets grow the weeding.
BEROWNE:	The spring is near, when green geese are a-breeding.
DUMAIN:	How follows that?
BEROWNE:	Fit in his place and time.
DUMAIN:	In reason nothing.
BEROWNE:	Something then in rhyme.

(I. i. 94–9)

In IV. iii, eavesdropping on the others, he has some of the function
of a 'presenter': 'Now, in thy likeness, one more fool appear!'
(IV. iii. 41). Then, in the final scene:

BEROWNE:	Our wooing doth not end like an old play: Jack hath not Jill. These ladies' courtesy Might well have made our sport a comedy.
KING:	Come, sir, it wants a twelvemonth and a day, And then 'twill end.
BEROWNE:	That's too long for a play.

(V. ii. 862–6)[13]

---

[13] In John Barton's production for the Royal Shakespeare Company in 1965,
Berowne's words were spoken directly to the audience; the effect was to make
them an apology from the stage, not unlike the conventional epilogue. The last
words of the play – 'You that way: we this way' – have a dubious textual history,
but if they are authentic they too might well be addressed to the audience. This
was done in Laurence Olivier's production for the National Theatre in 1968:
see Arthur Colby Sprague and J. C. Trewin, *Shakespeare's Plays Today* (London,
1970), p. 74.

We are made aware of the limits of the theatrical convention, as of the others, by seeing its fragility in a larger context. Like the show of the Nine Worthies, it rests on a basis of illusion that is perilous and easily broken; and, in the end, it can no more embody the 'world-without-end bargain' of love in a two-hours comedy than Alexander the Great can be embodied in the village curate.[14]

What it *can* show, however, is the problem of expressing love, and it does this with liveliness and grace, and with the joking acceptance of a hopeless dilemma that is shown most clearly in the figure of Berowne. For all its scepticism it is not an austere or bitter play, for it sees the attractions of everything it attacks. The love poems, at their best, have genuine charm; the Masque of Russians can be staged – and there is no reason why not – as a lively and colourful show. There is pleasure to be had even from inadequate conventions; there is fun to be had from demolishing them; and there is pleasure of a deeper kind in pressing beyond them to more satisfying conventions. The solemn anxiety expressed in some individual passages is only part of the play's ultimate effect. The final songs of Spring and Winter lie closer to its heart: they could be called a celebration of mutability. The cuckoo's 'word of fear' sounding through the spring meadows and the 'merry note' of the owl in the cold of winter suggest a comment on the men's final vows: the pleasures of spring, the season of courtship, are fragile; the testing and patience of winter may bring joy.[15] Other comedies may end with an image of security, but this play by its constant questioning of convention – up to and including the convention that at the end of a comedy Jack shall have Jill – has denied itself that. Instead, through the songs, it presents the instability of life as a general experience (everyone can talk about the weather) and a familiar one, all the more familiar for being so precisely described. Just as, in writing conventionalized love poetry, the private feelings of the lover are turned into something public and familiar and cease to be his

[14] See Philip Edwards, *Shakespeare and the Confines of Art* (London, 1968), pp. 44–8; and Righter, *Shakespeare and the Idea of the Play*, p. 101.
[15] In Michael Langham's production at Stratford, Ontario in 1961, the Spring song accompanied a final dance for the lovers; the Winter song was sung as they left the stage in opposite directions.

own, so in the songs the characters' experience of the insecurity of life is embodied in images which seem far away from that experience – images which are, in a sense, public property; and in that way some of the personal pain of the last scene is dissipated.[16] But if this creates a distance between the characters and the audience, by moving us away from them as individuals, it also creates a link. Seen directly, the problems of Berowne, Rosaline and the others were theirs, not ours; but the images of spring and winter provide a meeting point for the characters and the audience, a shared experience of the mutability of life. We should not forget, too, that these vivid and delightful songs were written by the two pedants (now 'the two learned men' – v. ii. 873), whose literary efforts have earned so much ridicule throughout the play. It is not so much that they are talented enough to write the songs (which one can hardly believe); rather, Shakespeare is kind enough to say they did, even at some cost to the consistency of the characterizations. This is typical of Shakespeare's generosity to characters who, like himself, labour in the mysteries of art and language: the problems they face are formidable; the chances for folly and misdirected zeal are legion; but in the last analysis, none of them, even the lowest, is to be despised. But the play's ultimate effect is to provide an image of insecurity, and the songs, by conveying a delight in the changes and surprises of life (how many writers would describe an owl as merry?) help to ensure that the image is a pleasurable one, that the play can break the rules of comedy only to extend them.

[16] See Cyrus Hoy, *The Hyacinth Room* (London, 1964), pp. 36–8.

5 · A Midsummer Night's Dream

When Titania meets Bottom in the wood near Athens, we see a fairy confronting a mortal, and finding him more wonderful than he finds her. For Titania, Bottom – ass's head and all – is an object of rare grace and beauty; for Bottom, the queen of the fairies is a lady he has just met, who is behaving a bit strangely, but who can be engaged in ordinary, natural conversation:

TITANIA: I pray thee, gentle mortal, sing again.
           Mine ear is much enamoured of thy note;
           So is mine eye enthralled to thy shape;
           And thy fair virtue's force perforce doth move me,
           On the first view, to say, to swear, I love thee.
BOTTOM: Methinks, mistress, you should have little reason for
           that. And yet, to say the truth, reason and love keep
           little company together now-a-days. The more the
           pity that some honest neighbours will not make them
           friends. Nay, I can gleek upon occasion.
TITANIA: Thou art as wise as thou art beautiful.

(III. i. 125–35)

This is, by now, a familiar effect. Behind the sharply contrasted voices are two utterly different kinds of understanding, and each one comically dislocates the other. Titania's love is addressed to a hearer who uses it simply as the occasion for a bit of cheerful philosophizing. And the philosophy, in turn, is wasted on the listener. It is all very well for Bottom to chatter away about reason and love; he has the detachment of the totally immune. But Titania is caught up in the experience of which Bottom is only a detached observer, and, ironically, his cool philosophy only gives her one more reason for adoring him.

But while the essential technique is familiar, there is an important difference in the way it is used. When Speed and Launce commented on the loves of their masters, or when the ladies of France mocked the men who were courting them, we felt that the mockers had (temporarily, at least) a special authority, that they were sharing with the audience a more sophisticated awareness than that of their victims. In the confrontation of different understandings, we felt able to take sides. But in the confrontation of Bottom and Titania, the audience's judgement is delicately suspended between both parties. Each one's assessment of the other is amusingly wrong: Bottom is hardly an object of beauty and grace, nor is plain 'mistress' an adequate form of address for Titania. On reflection, there is something to be said for each of these mistaken views: for all his mortal grossness, Bottom *has* been touched by magic; and the fairy queen is in the grip of a passion we have already seen affecting mortals, and affecting them in a similar way. Yet this only compounds the joke, for while both have been transformed, shifted from their true natures, both are unaware of being anything but their normal selves. The special, sophisticated awareness of the ladies in *Love's Labour's Lost* made the dislocations of that play critical and satiric. But in *A Midsummer Night's Dream* no character has that kind of awareness: each is locked in his own private understanding, confident, self-enclosed and essentially innocent. The closest analogy, perhaps, is with *The Comedy of Errors*, where one brother thought he was subjected to enchantment, the other appeared to be going mad and only the audience knew the true state of affairs. But there at least the characters knew that something very strange was happening: Bottom and Titania, in a situation more genuinely fantastic than anything in *The Comedy of Errors*, accept it without bewilderment, Titania moving to gratify her love at once, and Bottom accepting his new role with cheerful equanimity. The keynote, again, is innocence.

Bottom and Titania present the play's most striking image, a pairing of disparate beings whose contact only emphasizes the difference between them. It looks for a moment as though the barrier between the mortal and immortal worlds has fallen; but on inspection, the barrier proves as secure as ever. Instead of a fusion of worlds we are given a series of neat comic contrasts. And throughout the play, we see four different groups of characters – the lovers, the clowns, the older Athenians and the fairies – each group preoccupied with its own limited problems, and largely unaware of the others. When they make contact, it is usually to emphasize the difference between them. All are to some degree innocent, though (as we shall see) the degree of innocence varies. But the play weaves them all together. Each group, so self-absorbed, is seen in a larger context, which provides comic perspective. Each in turn provides a similar context for the others, and if here and there we feel tempted to take sides, we can never do so for very long; for while each group has its own folly, it has its own integrity as well, and its own special, coherent view of life.

We are reminded throughout of the workings of perception, and in particular of the way we depend on perception – special and limited though it may be – for our awareness of the world. When Hermia finds Lysander, who has run away from her, her first words appear to be a digression:

> Dark night, that from the eye his function takes,
> The ear more quick of apprehension makes;
> Wherein it doth impair the seeing sense,
> It pays the hearing double recompense.
> Thou art not by mine eye, Lysander, found;
> Mine ear, I thank it, brought me to thy sound.

(III. ii. 177–82)

The natural question – 'But why unkindly didst thou leave me so?' – is asked only after she has discoursed in general terms on how the senses work. In the clown scenes, there is a recurring joke by which the senses are comically transposed (III. i. 81–2; IV. i. 206–9; V. i. 190–1).[1] For the most part, however, the general point

---

[1] This appears to have been a standard comic routine. In *Mucedorus* the clown Mouse declares, 'I can keepe my tongue from picking and stealing, and my

is absorbed into the particular dramatic situations of the play. The conflict between Hermia and her father, for example, is seen as a difference of perception:

HERMIA: I would my father look'd but with my eyes.
THESEUS: Rather your eyes must with his judgment look.

(I. i. 56–7)

✔ When Hermia and Egeus look at Lysander, they see two different people, for she sees with the eyes of love, he with the eyes of cantankerous old age, obsessed with its own authority.

✔ In the opening scene, the lovers are on the defensive, set against the hostility of Egeus and the more restrained, regretful opposition of Theseus. Egeus's lecture to Lysander presents love from an outsider's point of view, as trivial, deceitful and disruptive of good order:

> Thou hast by moonlight at her window sung,
> With feigning voice, verses of feigning love,
> And stol'n the impression of her fantasy
> With bracelets of thy hair, rings, gawds, conceits,
> Knacks, trifles, nosegays, sweetmeats, messengers
> Of strong prevailment in unhardened youth;
> With cunning hast thou filch'd my daughter's heart;
> Turn'd her obedience, which is due to me,
> To stubborn harshness.

(I. i. 30–8)

Against this crabbed but concrete and detailed attack, Hermia's defence, though deeply felt, is inarticulate: 'I know not by what power I am made bold . . .' (I. i. 59). But it suggests that love is a force bearing down all normal authority, and arming the lover with strength to meet the hostility of the outside world. It gives Hermia the courage to defy her father and the Duke in open court, and to accept the pains and trials love must always bear:

---

handes from lying and slaundring, I warrant you, as wel as euer you had man in all your life' (I. iv. 128–31) – *The Shakespeare Apocrypha*, ed. C. F. Tucker Brooke (Oxford, 1967). But in *A Midsummer Night's Dream* – as in Costard's 'mistaking words' in *Love's Labour's Lost* (I. i. 292–4) – the stock device is used to serve the play's special comic vision.

> If then true lovers have been ever cross'd,
> It stands as an edict in destiny.
> Then let us teach our trial patience,
> Because it is a customary cross . . .   (I. i. 150–3)

✔ Love, to the outsider, appears foolish; but in accepting its demands the lovers acquire their own kind of integrity.

Their vision of the world is transformed. In Hermia's words,

> Before the time I did Lysander see,
> Seem'd Athens as a paradise to me.
> O, then, what graces in my love do dwell,
> That he hath turn'd a heaven into a hell!   (I. i. 204–7)

And for Helena the forest is similarly transformed by the presence
of Demetrius:

> It is not night when I do see your face,
> Therefore I think I am not in the night,
> Nor doth this wood lack worlds of company,
> For you, in my respect, are all the world.
>
> (II. i. 221–4)

But there is also something comically irrational in these transformations. In particular, the lover's perception of his beloved,
and his judgement of her, are peculiar and inexplicable, so much
so that even to the lovers themselves love seems blind. As ~~Hermia~~ HELENA
says of Demetrius,

> And as he errs, doting on Hermia's eyes,
> So I, admiring of his qualities.
> Things base and vile, holding no quantity,
> Love can transpose to form and dignity.
> Love looks not with the eyes, but with the mind;
> And therefore is wing'd Cupid painted blind.
> Nor hath Love's mind of any judgment taste;
> Wings and no eyes figure unheedy haste;
> And therefore is Love said to be a child,
> Because in choice he is so oft beguil'd.
>
> (I. i. 230–9)

It is not Hermia's beauty that inspires Demetrius's love: 'Through

Athens I am thought as fair as she' (I. i. 227). It is rather that love imposes its own peculiar kind of vision, which renders any other opinion – including that of common sense – irrelevant. How far Helena's own senses have been taken over by this vision may be judged by her decision to betray her friend to Demetrius:

> for this intelligence
> If I have thanks, it is a dear expense.
> But herein mean I to enrich my pain,
> To have his sight thither and back again.   (I. i. 248–51)

In love, the mere sight of the beloved acquires an importance that by any normal standards would be absurd.

The lovers may find each other's choices inexplicable, but at least they share the same kind of experience: they are in the grip of a power that renders choice and will meaningless. One sign of this is that the lovers lack the conscious awareness of convention that distinguishes Berowne and the ladies in *Love's Labour's Lost*. They slip naturally into a stylized manner of speech:

LYSANDER: Ay me! For aught that I could ever read,
            Could ever learn by tale or history,
            The course of true love never did run smooth;
            But either it was different in blood –
HERMIA: O cross! too high to be enthrall'd to low.
LYSANDER: Or else ingraffed in respect of years –
HERMIA: O spite! too old to be engag'd to young.
LYSANDER: Or else it stood upon the choice of friends –
HERMIA: O hell! to choose love by another's eyes.

                           (I. i. 132–40)

There is something ceremonial about this passage, with its liturgical responses, and like all ceremonies it presents the individual experience as part of a larger and more general pattern. The individual can assert his independence of this process only by showing his awareness of it and standing partly outside it, as Berowne attempts to do. But Lysander and Hermia surrender to the ceremony, taking its patterned language as a normal mode of speech. Later in the same scene, Hermia falls into a playful, teasing style as she swears to meet Lysander:

I swear to thee by Cupid's strongest bow,
By his best arrow with the golden head,
By the simplicity of Venus' doves,
By that which knitteth souls and prospers loves,
And by that fire which burn'd the Carthage Queen,
When the false Troyan under sail was seen,
By all the vows that ever men have broke,
In number more than ever women spoke,
In that same place thou hast appointed me,
Tomorrow truly will I meet with thee.

(I. i. 169–78)

There is, this time, a deliberate playfulness in the way the literary allusions pile up, as she teases her lover by comparing male infidelity and female faith. But the speech flows swiftly and easily, and the joking does no damage; she can afford to toy with her love because she is so sure of it. (There is a similar quality in their affectionate banter about sleeping arrangements in the forest – II. ii. 39–61.) The joking with love is not that of an outsider exposing its weakness, but that of an insider confident of its strength, and feeling that strength by subjecting it to a little harmless teasing. And once again, the character herself gives no indication that this manner of speech is anything other than perfectly natural.

The exchange on the course of true love is slow and brooding; Hermia's speech, swift and gay. The common factor is an air of literary artifice that sets the lovers' experience apart as something special; and throughout the play the range of expression achieved within this framework of artifice is remarkable. We see this, for example, when Lysander awakes to find himself in love with Helena:

The will of man is by his reason sway'd,
And reason says you are the worthier maid.
Things growing are not ripe until their season;
So I, being young, till now ripe not to reason;
And touching now the point of human skill,
Reason becomes the marshal to my will,
And leads me to your eyes, where I o'erlook
Love's stories, written in Love's richest book.

HELENA: Wherefore was I to this keen mockery born?
When at your hands did I deserve this scorn?
Is't not enough, is't not enough, young man,
That I did never, no, nor never can,
Deserve a sweet look from Demetrius' eye,
But you must flout my insufficiency?
Good troth, you do me wrong, good sooth, you do,
In such disdainful manner me to woo.

(II. ii. 115–30)

Lysander's speech is formal, solemn, sententious – and thoroughly dislocated by its context. He describes his love as natural and reasonable, but we know it is purely arbitrary. Here the character's unawareness of his own dependence on convention becomes sharply comic. Helena's irritable retort gives us, by contrast, the sound of a natural speaking voice; there is a striking difference in tone and pace. And yet it too is in rhyming couplets: her seemingly natural utterance is still contained within the framework of a convention; her anger, no less than his infatuation, is part of the larger, dance-like pattern in which all four lovers are unconsciously moving.

The lovers see their experiences in the forest as chaotic; but for the audience the disorder, like the disorder of a Feydeau farce, is neatly organized, giving us pleasure where it gives them pain.[2] When Hermia accuses Demetrius of killing Lysander, the patterned language and the rhymed couplets cool the emotional impact the scene might have had (III. ii. 43–81). Over and over, the violence of the ideas is lightened by jingling rhythm and rhyme: 'I'll follow thee, and make a heaven of hell, / To die upon the hand I love so well' (II. i. 243–4). It is not so much that, as Enid Welsford suggests, 'the harmony and grace of the action would have been spoilt by convincing passion';[3] it is more that the manner of the action in itself ensures that the passion is convincing only to the characters. They lash out frantically at each other, but

[2] There are similar effects in *The Comedy of Errors* and *Love's Labour's Lost*, in which the scenes of most intense confusion – such as Antipholus of Ephesus's vain attempt to break into his own house, and the Russian masque in which the men court the wrong ladies – contain some of the most patterned writing in their respective plays.

[3] *The Court Masque* (New York, 1962), p. 332.

the audience is too far away to share in their feelings. Our detachment is aided by the presence of Puck and Oberon, acting as an
onstage audience and providing a comic perspective. What is
serious and painful to the lovers is simply a 'fond pageant' of
mortal foolishness to the watchers (III. ii. 144). Puck in particular
regards the whole affair as a show put on for his amusement (and
incidentally if we can remember this in the final scene it adds a
level of irony to the lovers' laughter as they watch Pyramus and
Thisbe: they too, not so long ago, amused an audience with antics
that they thought were serious).[4] The irony is compounded when
the lovers indignantly accuse each other of playing games with
serious feelings: 'Wink at each other; hold the sweet jest up; / This
sport, well carried, shall be chronicled' (III. ii. 239–40). Helena's
accusation is very close to the truth – except that it should be
directed at the audience.

But our feelings are subtly managed here: there are two
watchers – Puck, with his delight in chaos, and Oberon, who
wishes to bring chaos to an end. We share in both these attitudes.
When Helena recalls her childhood friendship with Hermia, the
rhyme slips away and it becomes a little easier to take the characters' feelings seriously (III. ii. 195–219). From this point on, the
formality breaks down into undignified, farcical squabbling, with
physical knockabout and coarse insults – relieved, on one occasion,
by a surprisingly quiet and dignified speech from Helena:

> Good Hermia, do not be so bitter with me.
> I evermore did love you, Hermia,
> Did ever keep your counsel, never wrong'd you;
> Save that, in love unto Demetrius,
> I told him of your stealth unto this wood. . . .
> And now, so you will let me quiet go,
> To Athens I will bear my folly back,
> And follow you no further. (III. ii. 306–16)

While still enjoying the confusion, we are beginning to feel that it
had better stop soon. And Oberon and Puck see that it does.

But we are kept at a distance from the lovers' final union, no

---

[4] See G. K. Hunter, *William Shakespeare: The Late Comedies* (London, 1962),
p. 14; and Bertrand Evans, *Shakespeare's Comedies* (London, 1967), p. 40.

less than from their suffering. In the last stages of their ordeal, formality returns and is further heightened: a variety of rhymed verse forms accumulates as, one by one, the lovers enter and fall asleep. Their individuality is at a particularly low ebb, as Puck controls them more directly than ever, even to the point of assuming the men's voices (III. ii. 396–463). The final harmony he creates for them, like the earlier confusion, is seen as the working out of a dance pattern; and more than that, it is the fulfilment of a ritual sense of life, embodied in homely clichés:

> And the country proverb known,
> That every man should take his own,
> In your waking shall be shown.
> > Jack shall have Jill;
> > Nought shall go ill;
> The man shall have his mare again, and all shall be well.
>
> > > (III. ii. 458–63)

Similarly, Theseus sees their coupling in terms of sport and pastime – 'No doubt they rose up early to observe / The rite of May' (IV. i. 129–30) – and as a fulfilment of nature's most basic impulse: 'Good morrow, friends. Saint Valentine is past; / Begin these wood-birds but to couple now?' (IV. i. 136–7). The presence, and the comments, of other characters provide the awareness of convention that the lovers themselves lack, being too caught up in their own experiences. We see love's perceptions as special and limited, and the lovers themselves as lacking in full self-awareness. The magic flower is applied, significantly, to the eye; just as significantly, it is applied while the lover is asleep. And even the final harmony of love, when seen through the homely analogies of Puck and Theseus, is satisfying but nothing to get ecstatic about: 'The man shall have his mare again, and all shall be well' sounds like the voice of a parent comforting a child who has been making a great fuss about nothing. It is certainly not how the lovers themselves would have put it. At the same time, however, we recognize that the lovers *have* got what they want: the law of Athens, so formidable in the first scene, is swept away to accommodate them, and Egeus is reduced to spluttering impotence. In our final attitude to the lovers, there is respect as well as amused detachment.

We recognize, moreover, that they speak about love with some authority: they have been through it, with a vengeance. In this regard we can set them against Peter Quince's amateur dramatic society, who are trying to construct a tale of love and who are completely out of their depth. They belong, quite solidly, to the working-day world: 'Hard-handed men that work in Athens here, / Which never labour'd in their minds till now' (v. i. 72–3); 'A crew of patches, rude mechanicals, / That work for bread upon Athenian stalls' (III. ii. 9–10). Each one has a trade, by which he is identified, and they show a greater interest in the technical problems of placing walls and calculating moonshine than they do in working up convincing emotion (except of course for Bottom, who will throw himself zealously into anything). They seem, in fact, too anxious about decorum to be dealing with anything so erotic as the story of Pyramus and Thisbe: 'You must say "paragon." A paramour is – God bless us! – a thing of naught' (IV. ii. 13–14). Like the characters of *Love's Labour's Lost*, they struggle with one of the most vital problems of expression – how to create a work of art. But if the lovers are so deeply embedded in the experience of love that they are unaware of convention, the mechanicals are so embroiled in the problems of convention that they are quite unconscious of the damage they are doing to the experience the convention should embody.

Yet there is a kind of logic in what they do. They are anxious not to give offence, and so they emphasize the illusory nature of their art – 'we will do no harm with our swords' (III. i. 17). They are also anxious to make the technical side of their work as convincing as possible, to ensure that Wall and Moonshine are real to the audience. Once again, though this time inadvertently, the result is to emphasize the illusory nature of their play. It is easy for critics to lecture them on their failure to understand dramatic illusion;[5] but their stated intention is to give delight without giving offence – 'And, most dear actors, eat no onions nor garlic, for we are to utter sweet breath; and I do not doubt but to hear them say it is a sweet comedy' (IV. ii. 37–9) – and on those terms,

[5] See, for example, R. W. Dent, 'Imagination in *A Midsummer Night's Dream*', *Shakespeare Quarterly*, XV (spring 1964), pp. 123–6; and David P. Young, *Something of Great Constancy* (New Haven, 1966), p. 150.

the play succeeds, though not in quite the way they planned. The effect on the onstage audience (not to mention the offstage one) is like the effect of the lovers' quarrel – it is so much fun to watch that the suffering of the characters does not communicate – except that here the gap between the lovers' feelings and the audience's reactions is more obvious, more broadly comic. Theseus can defend the actors by saying that 'The best in this kind are but shadows' (v. i. 210), but he can also say 'This palpable-gross play hath *well* beguil'd / The heavy gait of night' (v. i. 356–7: my italics). Despite Philostrate's misgivings, this proves to be the ideal entertainment for a nuptial: the dangers that threaten love are systematically destroyed by the way they are presented. The parents who stand in the way of the lovers, though they were originally cast (at I. ii. 50–6), do not appear at all; the wall is 'sweet', 'lovely' and 'courteous' (v. i. 174, 176) – not to mention co-operative, producing a chink on demand; the lion is 'A very gentle beast, and of a good conscience' (v. i. 224). The death of the hero is anything but final, for Pyramus-Bottom rises from the ground as easily as the indestructible hero of a mummers' St George play, or Falstaff at the battle of Shrewsbury. The emotional effect of the play is summed up by Theseus: 'This passion, and the death of a dear friend, would go near to make a man look sad' (v. i. 280–1). And through all this, the actors maintain an unbroken confidence in the rightness of what they are doing: the nervous first-night mistakes so often seen in production are good fun, but have no warrant in the text. As Theseus says of the actors, 'If we imagine no worse of them than they of themselves, they may pass for excellent men' (v. i. 213–14). Far from being disconcerted by the audience's interruptions, Bottom meets them with condescending tolerance:

THESEUS: The wall, methinks, being sensible, should curse again.
PYRAMUS: No, in truth, sir, he should not. *Deceiving me* is Thisby's cue. She is to enter now, and I am to spy her through the wall. You shall see it will fall out pat as I told you; yonder she comes.

(v. i. 180–5)

The actors, like the lovers, inhabit a world of private satisfactions, and seem to a great extent oblivious of what the other characters think of them. But they have chosen an audience that has some experience of the crosses of love, and finds in their version of that experience nothing but a cause of hilarity.

The leading member of that audience is Theseus, and it may appear that he represents some kind of final, objective authority. But his cool, daylight rationality is placed in a context that clearly shows its limits. His scepticism about the visions of 'the lunatic, the lover, and the poet' (v. i. 2–22) is offered with an air of conviction, and is easy to take seriously – until we reflect that in casting doubt on the lovers' story he is denying something we have seen with our own eyes only a few minutes before. More than that, he and Hippolyta have had dealings with the fairies in their younger and wilder days (II. i. 70–80).[6] Neither he – nor, more surprisingly, Hippolyta in her defence of the lovers – appears to recall this simple fact. It is as though, in growing up, they have simply forgotten what they once were, losing clarity of vision in one respect as they have gained it in another. At the end of the scene, the rational sceptic makes an interesting slip: 'Lovers, to bed; 'tis almost fairy time' (v. i. 353). It may be just a casual turn of phrase; or it may be an involuntary acknowledgement of a truth that in his more guarded moments Theseus would deny (like Chesterton's ' "My God", said the atheist'). In any case, his words are borne out as soon as he leaves the stage, as the beings whose existence he has denied once more fill the scene. One final irony should be noticed: in scoffing at fantasy, he also scoffs at art, yet he himself is a figure in a work of art, owing his existence to a poet's imagination and an audience's willingness to suspend disbelief: as G. K. Hunter puts it, 'he himself is just another such "antique fable".'[7]

In his dealings with the lovers in the first scene, Theseus can also be seen as exerting an authority that has no final validity. In preparing to enforce the harsh Athenian law, and urging Hermia

---

[6] See Young, *Something of Great Constancy*, p. 139.
[7] *John Lyly: The Humanist as Courtier* (London, 1962), p. 328. See also Philip Edwards, *Shakespeare and the Confines of Art* (London, 1968), p. 56.

to recognize her father's power, he is counselling patience and submission of a kind that he himself finds difficult:

> but, O, methinks, how slow
> This old moon wanes! She lingers my desires,
> Like to a step-dame or a dowager,
> Long withering out a young man's revenue.

>   (I. i. 3–6)

It seems ironic that as he himself is about to seal an 'everlasting bond of fellowship' (I. i. 85) he is prepared to allow a loveless match to take place. But to do him credit, he enforces the law with evident reluctance: he tactfully leaves the lovers together, and behind the mask of authority we can detect other feelings. In asking Demetrius and Egeus to go with him, he says 'I have some private schooling for you both' (I. i. 116), suggesting that he may want to talk them out of the match. And his words to Hippolyta, 'Come, my Hippolyta; what cheer, my love?' (I. i. 122), suggest a recognition that she too is upset by what is happening. Like the Duke of Ephesus he is trapped by a cruel law 'Which by no means we may extenuate' (I. i. 120); and like that other Duke he brushes the law aside with a wave of his hand once the action of the comedy has taken its course: 'Egeus, I will overbear your will' (IV. i. 176). It is part of the peculiar logic of comedy that rules which seem rigorously binding in the first act suddenly appear trivial when it is time to end the play. The mere sight of the lovers happily paired has become a force stronger than the law of Athens.

Theseus enforces the law with reluctance; Egeus insists on it with a grim fanaticism that makes him the only unsympathetic figure in the play; and a comparison between the two men helps us to see the value of Theseus's kind of authority. In the scene of the lovers' waking, the rich harmony of Theseus's speech on the hounds establishes an atmosphere in which Egeus's jerky, irritable style is utterly out of place:

> Enough, enough, my lord; you have enough;
> I beg the law, the law upon his head.
> They would have stol'n away, they would, Demetrius,

Thereby to have defeated you and me:
You of your wife, and me of my consent,
Of my consent that she should be your wife.

(IV. i. 151–6)

In the text as normally printed, Egeus does not appear in the last scene;[8] his fussy, sterile concern with his own power is the one kind of mentality the play's final harmony can find no room for. Theseus, on the other hand, is allowed considerable authority in the final scene. For all his limits as a commentator on art and love, he is not to be brushed aside as the representative of a worn-out order. His urbanity, common sense and good temper are necessary ingredients in society, as we see when he attempts to soften the conflict between generations, and when he accepts the lovers' union as a *fait accompli*. Throughout the final scene, Theseus and Hippolyta suggest not only mature love but a general principle of balance: he disbelieves the lovers, but she is more open-minded; conversely, he is the more tolerant with the players. Each corrects the other's excesses, but with tact and affection. They are not the play's final spokesmen, for they have no means of comprehending what goes on in the woods; but their cool wisdom is as necessary to the play's total harmony as the desire of the lovers or the earnest good intentions of the clowns.

The fairies, on the other hand, seem to have the range of vision and the freedom of action that the other characters lack. At their first appearance, they are sharply juxtaposed with the plodding, prosaic minds of the mechanicals, and our initial impression is of lightness, speed and freedom:

PUCK: How now, spirit! whither wander you?
FAIRY: Over hill, over dale,
       Thorough bush, thorough brier,
    Over park, over pale,
       Thorough flood, thorough fire,

---

[8] Egeus is omitted from this scene in the Quarto; the Folio gives Philostrate's part to him, but the Quarto arrangement seems more sensible and is normally adopted by editors. Directors often relent and invite him to the party; but the only time I have seen his presence there used creatively was in John Hirsch's production at Stratford, Ontario in 1968, in which Egeus, puffing on a cigar, grunted with crusty approval at Theseus's lecture on the imagination.

> I do wander every where
> Swifter than the moon's sphere;
> And I serve the Fairy Queen,
> To dew her orbs upon the green.

(II. i. 1–9)

At times, the whole created world seems to be their playground: they are, in Mark Van Doren's words, 'citizens of all the universe there is'.[9] But if they have all of space at their disposal, they have only half of time. The lovers and the clowns wander forth freely by day or night; the fairies are more circumscribed, and have to follow the night wherever it goes. They have freedom but no leisure: 'look thou meet me ere the first cock crow' (II. i. 267). If they seem more authoritative, less undermined by irony than the mortals, it may be because they are more conscious of their limits. There is a feeling of urgency as Puck and Oberon try to settle the affairs of the lovers, for they both sense that they are at the limits of their power:

PUCK: My fairy lord, this must be done with haste,
         For night's swift dragons cut the clouds full fast;
         And yonder shines Aurora's harbinger,
         At whose approach ghosts, wand'ring here and there,
         Troop home to churchyards. Damned spirits all,
         That in cross-ways and floods have burial,
         Already to their wormy beds are gone,
         For fear lest day should look their shames upon;
         They wilfully themselves exile from light,
         And must for aye consort with black-brow'd night.
OBERON: But we are spirits of another sort:
         I with the morning's love have oft made sport;
         And, like a forester, the groves may tread
         Even till the eastern gate, all fiery red,
         Opening on Neptune with fair blessed beams,
         Turns into yellow gold his salt green streams.
         But, notwithstanding, haste, make no delay;
         We may effect this business yet ere day.

(III. ii. 378–95)

[9] *Shakespeare* (New York, 1939), p. 77.

Oberon's power takes him as far as sunrise, but no further. This passage defines as well as anything in the play the nature and the limits of the fairy kingdom. They are spirits of the night, but they are not involved with its darkest and most shameful secrets. They are not, like the ghosts of suicides, shut off forever from normality. The flowers, insects, birds and animals of the normal world are theirs also, though they see them with a special intimacy; they can touch the affairs of men, and men know of them. They are spirits, not of the deepest night, but of the border country between night and day, that part of the other world which men too know about. But while Oberon exults in his power to go as far as the sunrise, full daylight is as foreign to his nature as the deepest night. The passage begins and ends with the urgency of time, the limits placed on the fairies by the coming of day.

Even within their normal sphere of action, the fairies' power is not infallible: Puck has no special knowledge, and has to go by appearances: 'Did not you tell me I should know the man / By the Athenian garments he had on?' (III. ii. 348–9). His eyesight, like that of the lovers, can play tricks on him. When he exclaims 'Lord, what fools these mortals be!' (III. ii. 115), we recognize that their folly is the product of his own mistakes, and the laughter is partly against him. But he can fairly claim that Oberon's instructions were inadequate. While the fairies exert an easy control over their own world, in dealing with mortals they are a little out of their depth, and their touch is clumsy. Nor can they avoid emotional problems of their own. When we first see Oberon and Titania the fairy kingdom is in disarray, torn by a civil war over a small boy from the mortal world. At the same time Theseus and Hippolyta, with their own more limited power, have passed through their period of discord:

> Hippolyta, I woo'd thee with my sword,
> And won thy love doing thee injuries;
> But I will wed thee in another key,
> With pomp, with triumph, and with revelling.

> (I. i. 16–19)

Through much of the play the worlds of Theseus and Oberon – rulers, respectively, of the day and night – are opposing and complementary.[10] While other characters mingle, the two rulers never share the stage. In Theseus's city, order and rationality are temporarily dominant, with suggestions of a period of chaos in the past (and with some laws from the past that still need reforming: Egeus invokes a barbaric 'ancient privilege' – i. i. 41). Though the point is not stressed, this is consistent with the familiar legends of Theseus. In the fairy kingdom disorder is temporarily dominant: the mutual reproaches of Titania and Oberon suggest that this is hardly a normal state of affairs: 'Why should Titania cross her Oberon?' (ii. i. 119) But while Shakespeare exploits this kind of contrast all through the play, he can also bring its various worlds together in more intimate and sympathetic contact. In the final scene, with the peace of his own kingdom restored, Oberon uses his blessing to forestall any approaching disorder in the mortal world:

> So shall all the couples three
> Ever true in loving be;
> And the blots of nature's hand
> Shall not in their issue stand.
>
> (v. i. 396–9)

The two worlds, though not intermingled, are finally brought to rest side by side.

The final scene also suggests that it is through the workings of nature that the mortal and immortal worlds come closest together. In love and procreation ('Begin these wood-birds but to couple now?') men become part of the larger harmony of nature, in which the fairies are also included, and over which they have some power. This harmony also touches other human activities: both in work and in social pleasure, man is a creature of the seasons and depends on nature; and just as nature is the medium for transmitting Oberon's final blessing ('With this field-dew consecrate . . .' v. i. 404), so it is the medium by which disorder in the fairy world passes into the human one, affecting both work and social pastime:

[10] Paul A. Olson reminds us that, traditionally, Athens is a city of philosophers and woods are places of unreason. See 'A Midsummer Night's Dream and the meaning of court marriage', ELH, XXIV (March 1957), pp. 106–7.

The ox hath therefore stretch'd his yoke in vain,
The ploughman lost his sweat, and the green corn
Hath rotted ere his youth attain'd a beard;
The fold stands empty in the drowned field,
The crows are fatted with the murrion flock;
The nine men's morris is fill'd up with mud,
And the quaint mazes in the wanton green,
For lack of tread are undistinguishable.

(II. i. 93–100)

As in the final song of *Love's Labour's Lost*, the workings of nature provide a common ground of experience: the fairies discuss a world familiar to the audience, and for a moment they seem closer to us than any of the mortals have been. The flower struck by Cupid's dart has been part of a high, remote experience, which even Puck could not see (II. i. 155–68). But it is still a flower, something small and familiar from the world of nature. In a way, *Pyramus and Thisbe* presents a world more fantastic than that of the fairies, a world where walls move and moons speak. But we laugh it off as an absurdity. The fantasy of the fairy world consists rather in viewing familiar things from a special angle: suddenly flowers, dewdrops and insects seem clearer and more formidable, and we find ourselves engulfed by a world we normally look down on from a height of five or six feet. Then, at the end, the fairies actually invade our world: the references to the 'wasted brands' and the 'dead and drowsy fire' (v. i. 364, 381) remind us of the dwellings of ordinary men. And when Oberon says 'To the best bride-bed will we, / Which by us shall blessed be' (v. i. 292–3) it may strike us that Theseus and Hippolyta will be there already: the two sets of rulers, kept apart throughout the play, are finally juxtaposed in the audience's imagination.

The play suggests that the mortal and immortal worlds are finally separate, and yet very close, divided by a line that is extremely thin but never gives way [11] – not even, as we have seen, when Bottom meets Titania. The mortals who have been affected

---

[11] In two other comedies of the period, *Wily Beguiled* and *Grim the Collier of Croydon*, Robin Goodfellow not only appears to mortals, but is on neighbourly terms with them. Shakespeare's Puck, for all his mischief, is far more detached than this, appearing to mortals – when he appears at all – in an assumed shape.

by that other world feel a sense of deep strangeness, and have to grope to re-establish the normal certainties of life. Lysander, waking up in daylight, grasps the most simple facts only with an effort:

> But as yet, I swear,
> I cannot truly say how I came here,
> But, as I think – for truly would I speak,
> And now I do bethink me, so it is –
> I came with Hermia hither.

(IV. i. 144–8)

The others are equally bewildered, poised between dream and waking:

> DEMETRIUS: These things seem small and undistinguishable,
>   Like far-off mountains turned into clouds.
>   HERMIA: Methinks I see these things with parted eye,
>   When every thing seems double.

(IV. i. 184–7)

We are not sure whether by 'these things' they mean the experiences of the forest or the sight of Theseus and his huntsmen. But as they talk with each other the balance tilts, the immediate present is clearly seen as reality, and the social bonds of the daylight world are re-established. Bottom reverses the process: he wakes with the daylight world on his mind – 'When my cue comes, call me, and I will answer' (IV. i. 197) – and gradually recovers the vision. In both cases, the characters are poised on the border between dream and reality, which is also the border between the fairy world and the mortal one. And while the two worlds are so radically different that each one challenges the reality of the other, turning it into a dream, they are also close enough for a single mind, with an effort, to sense them both at once.

Experiences from one world can even be absorbed into the other. One could say that Cupid's flower does nothing new to the lovers: what we hear of their behaviour in Athens in Act I suggests that there too they were subject to arbitrary and irrational changes of heart, leading to confusion and humiliation.[12] The

[12] See Larry S. Champion, *The Evolution of Shakespeare's Comedy* (Cambridge, Mass., 1970), p. 48.

flower simply provides a comic image of the normal operation of love, intensifying it and speeding it up. And while Demetrius, in one sense, will spend the rest of his life under an enchantment, in another sense what has happened to him is as normal as growing up:

> I wot not by what power –
> But by some power it is – my love to Hermia,
> Melted as the snow, seems to me now
> As the remembrance of an idle gaud
> Which in my childhood I did dote upon.
>
> (IV. i. 161–5)

Just as the passage as a whole is delicately poised between dream and reality, so there is a fine balance here between Demetrius's sense of wonder at what has happened, and his feeling that it is entirely natural. Bottom, of course, has his own way of absorbing the dream into his normal life:

> I will get Peter Quince to write a ballad of this dream. It shall be call'd 'Bottom's Dream,' because it hath no bottom; and I will sing it in the latter end of a play, before the Duke.
>
> (IV. i. 209–12)

The dream cannot be expounded: but it can be turned into material for a performance. One might even say that his transformation in the wood is a comic echo of the versatility he claims as an actor. When Puck, using Bottom's voice, shouts 'Sometime a horse I'll be, sometime a hound, / A hog, a headless bear, sometime a fire' (III. i. 98–9) we may recall Bottom's eagerness to be a lover, a tyrant, a lady and a lion. There are transformations and transformations; and perhaps it is not such a large step after all to go from changing beards to changing heads.

If much of the play's comic life depends on playing different groups of characters off against each other, much of its power to haunt the imagination comes from its suggestion of the ultimate unity of the various worlds it depicts. In a variety of small touches, echoes are set up between one scene and another. Immediately after Hermia awakes in panic from a dream of being attacked by a serpent, we find the mechanicals engaged in taking the terror out of their play, to avoid frightening the ladies. The music and dance of the fairies are followed by the more robust music of the daylight world, the hounds and horns of Theseus; and at the end of *Pyramus and Thisbe* the clowns, like the fairies, show that they too can dance, in their own way. In the final scene, Theseus's earthy jokes about the couples' impatience to get to bed introduce an idea that is picked up and transformed by Oberon's celebration of fertility; just as in Puck's opening words, 'Now the hungry lion roars' (v. i. 360), Snug's apologetic performance sets off an unexpected echo from a more serious world. The various worlds of the play mirror each other, and are ultimately seen as one world, moving in a single rhythm. This feeling is particularly strong from the later forest scenes to the end of the play, as references to time accumulate, and the characters all feel caught in a common rhythm, moving from night into day, and then back again.

Just as each group of characters is placed against the others, so the artistic world they all form together is seen in relation to other kinds of experience, outside the normal scope of comedy. Throughout the play we are made aware of the process of selection by which the comic world is created. The process begins, simply enough, with Theseus's words in the opening scene, 'Turn melancholy forth to funerals; / The pale companion is not for our pomp' (I. i .14–15). Puck and Oberon are careful to draw a distinction between themselves and the 'damned spirits' of the night, but in so doing they remind us of the existence of those spirits (III. ii. 378–95; v. i. 360–79). Titania's lullaby invokes the slimy creeping things of the forest, telling them to keep their distance (II. ii. 9–24). Hermia's dream is frightening enough, but, as in other scenes with the lovers, the formal style with its rhyming couplets helps to cool the terror (II. ii. 145–56). Similarly, the suggestion of bestiality in Titania's affair with Bottom is kept under control by the cool, decorative poetry as she leads him off the stage:

> Come, wait upon him; lead him to my bower.
> The moon, methinks, looks with a wat'ry eye;
> And when she weeps, weeps every little flower,
> Lamenting some enforced chastity.
>
> (III. i. 182–5)

They are going off to bed, but there is nothing torrid about it. The forest might have been a place of unbridled eroticism, but it is not: Lysander and Hermia are very careful about their sleeping arrangements, and Demetrius warns Helena to keep away from him so as not to endanger her virginity (II. i. 214–19). Normally, couples going into the woods mean only one thing, but the lovers of this play are aware of the energies the forest might release, and determined to keep those energies under control. On the other hand the ideal of chastity, in Theseus's reference to Diana's nunnery and in Oberon's description of the imperial votaress who is immune to love, is set aside as something admirable but too high and remote for ordinary people. The play is aware of both extreme attitudes to sex, but steers a civilized middle course appropriate to comedy.

Other possible kinds of art are also referred to, and then banished. Theseus, selecting a play for his wedding night, rejects anything involving satire, eunuchs or the dismembering of poets (v. i. 44–55). Bottom and his crew try to perform a tragedy, and turn it into a glorious farce: the whole machinery of tragedy, Fates, Furies and all, disappears into laughter. More soberly, Oberon refers to some of the smaller miseries produced by the ordinary workings of nature, and banishes them:

> Never mole, hare-lip, nor scar,
> Nor mark prodigious, such as are
> Despised in nativity,
> Shall upon their children be.
>
> (v. i. 400–3)

Throughout the play, we seem to be witnessing a constant process of exorcism, as forces which could threaten the safety of the comic world are called up, only to be driven away. The play stakes out a special area of security in a world full of hostile forces: just as the mortal world is very close to the fairy world, yet finally separate from it, so the comic world of the play is very close to a darker world of passion, terror and chaos, yet the border between them, though thin, is never broken.

But despite the toughness of its defences, the play's world is fragile in another way:

If we shadows have offended,
Think but this, and all is mended,
That you have but slumb'red here
While these visions did appear.
And this weak and idle theme,
No more yielding but a dream,
Gentles, do not reprehend.
If you pardon, we will mend.

(v. i. 412–19)

It is, finally, all an illusion, a dream. Not simply the fairies, or the amateur actors, but the entire company, are seen as 'shadows'.[13] The serpent, a standard image of fear throughout the play, is referred to for the last time: 'the serpent's tongue' (v. i. 422) is now the danger of being hissed by a hostile audience. But even this admission of fragility – the fragility of art itself – also contains an acknowledgement of strength. The dream metaphor is carefully chosen, for throughout the play characters have described as dreams experiences that the audience saw as real and solid. Titania's waking is a case in point:

TITANIA: My Oberon! What visions have I seen!
         Methought I was enamour'd of an ass.
OBERON: There lies your love.

(IV. i. 73–5)

Oberon's demonstration of the reality of the dream is about as direct as it could be. The other dreams have the same reality for the audience, though they may fade in the characters' memories: quite simply, we saw it all happen. *The Taming of the Shrew* moves us into illusion and keeps us there; *Love's Labour's Lost* smashes several illusions and ends before the pieces can be picked up; but *A Midsummer Night's Dream* moves us freely in and out of illusion, giving us a clear sense of both its fragility and its integrity.

How, finally, do we react to this dream? Bottom's warning is

[13] Something like this was suggested at the end of Peter Brook's production for the Royal Shakespeare Company in 1970: the performers took off the cloaks which had distinguished their characters, and faced the audience in a uniform white garb, suggesting that they were all fairies, or (which amounted to the same thing) all actors.

clear: 'Man is but an ass if he go about to expound this dream' (v. i. 202–3). There is no point in rooting through the play for morals or allegories. But Puck's final emphasis on the play's fragility reminds us that we as an audience have some responsibility, and within the play there is a hint of what that responsibility might be:

THESEUS: The best in this kind are but shadows; and the worst are no worse, if imagination amend them.
HIPPOLYTA: It must be your imagination then, and not theirs.
(v. i. 210–12)

The performers of *Pyramus and Thisbe* are severely heckled, but all the same they get a gentler reception than the performers of the Nine Worthies: for one thing, they are allowed to play out their play to the end. For another, their adoption of their parts is accepted, if only for the sake of the joke:

DEMETRIUS: Well roar'd, Lion.
THESEUS: Well run, Thisby.
HIPPOLYTA: Well shone, Moon. Truly, the moon shines with a good grace.
(v. i. 257–60)

The Princess of France was prepared to take her pleasure from the incompetence of the show: 'Their form confounded makes most form in mirth, / When great things labouring perish in their birth' (v. ii. 517–18). Theseus takes a more kindly pleasure in looking behind the performers' incompetence to their good intentions, and if it all amounts to nothing, then

The kinder we, to give them thanks for nothing.
Our sport shall be to take what they mistake;
And what poor duty cannot do, noble respect
Takes it in might, not merit.
(v. i. 89–92)

The audience has the most important role of all. It must, by its own response, give value to things that might otherwise be trivial. If it is to take the illusions of art as a kind of reality, then its perceptions must be, like those of a lover, generous to the point of irrationality: 'Things base and vile, holding no quantity, / Love can transpose to form and dignity' (I. i. 232–3).

Each kind of existence the play shows – the passion of the lovers, the well-meaning bungling of the clowns, the cool order of Theseus and the fantastic disorder of the fairies – is valued for its own sake. Its uniqueness is clearly seen in relation to everything else in the play, and emphasized by the usual comic dislocations. But each element in the play's world, being unique, is also precious, for only by its uniqueness can it contribute to the overall harmony – just as each hound in Theseus's pack, by baying a different note, contributes to the total effect: they are

> Slow in pursuit, but match'd in mouth like bells,
> Each under each. A cry more tuneable
> Was never holla'd to, nor cheer'd with horn,
> In Crete, in Sparta, nor in Thessaly.
>
> (IV. i. 120–3)

As in other plays, an important image is drawn from sport: but this time, we should notice, Theseus values the harmonious chiming of his hounds more than their swiftness in the hunt. And it is, finally, the harmony of the play's vision that gives us most delight.[14]

But the artistic vision itself, which draws these disparate experiences together, is also limited. The epilogue's urbane apology for the triviality of the play picks up other suggestions about art that can be detected throughout. Bottom the actor is the play's greatest fool, yet in a sense he is the character with the most comprehensive vision, who not only sees fairies but greets them with easy familiarity. His versatility as an actor who can play any role (and will, if given half a chance) is a comic image of the dramatist's own power of creation,[15] and when he promises to 'roar you as gently as any sucking dove' (I. ii. 73) he shows the artist's prerogative of rearranging reality. Puck, on the other hand, suggests the

[14] Stanley Wells has drawn the connection between Theseus's speech on his hounds and the total harmony of the play: see his introduction to the New Penguin edition of *A Midsummer Night's Dream* (Harmondsworth, 1967), p. 36.
[15] See John Palmer, *Political and Comic Characters of Shakespeare* (London, 1964), p. 45.

artist's manipulative craft, arranging the mechanics of the plot. He too is a figure of small authority in his own world, a licensed jester and runner of errands who has to have the higher mysteries explained to him. But just as Bottom is the only mortal to speak to the fairies, Puck is the only character to speak to the audience; and this gives him, like Bottom, some identification with the dramatist. Bottom with his innocent egotism and power of fantasy, and Puck with his love of mischief, are both like children;[16] Theseus is the responsible adult. Without him as patron and audience, there would be no performance; but without the artist, for all his childishness, there would be no play.

The understanding of art is necessarily limited; it cuts out a lot of reality in order to create an ordered work. Shakespeare deals with this charge by admitting it, by (paradoxically) suggesting within the play some of the things that have been left out, so that we see the process of selection at work. Art, like love, is a limited and special vision; but like love it has by its very limits a transforming power, creating a small area of order in the vast chaos of the world. The technique of comic dislocation, developed so skilfully in earlier plays, here becomes an instrument of celebration as well as of mockery, and the two are so closely bound together that we can hardly tell which is which. The very qualities we value in Bottom are the ones we find most amusing; and in seeing, and laughing at, the limits of each character's vision, we get a clearer sense of the importance of each. This applies to the work of art itself: at the moment when the play most clearly declares itself to be trivial, we have the strongest appeal to our sympathy for it, and, along with this, the clearest recognition that our own responsiveness is a vital factor in the total harmony:

> Give me your hands, if we be friends,
> And Robin shall restore amends.

(v. i. 426–7)

It is an offer any normal audience is glad to take.

[16] On the childlike qualities of Bottom and the fairies, see, respectively, C. L. Barber, *Shakespeare's Festive Comedy* (Cleveland, 1967), p. 151; and E. K. Chambers, *Shakespeare: A Survey* (Harmondsworth, 1964), p. 69.

6 The Merchant of Venice

The secure harmony of *A Midsummer Night's Dream* is not achieved without some sacrifice. The play itself acknowledges the existence of a darker side of life that has been omitted in order to create a purely comic world; but there is a silent omission that is, in the long run, more significant. An important part of Shakespeare's own comic technique has been temporarily held in abeyance: the extension of a single character over more than one dramatic idiom, the wider range of feeling and awareness displayed (in their different ways) by characters like Julia, Petruchio and Berowne. The characters of *A Midsummer Night's Dream* may be brought into contact with different worlds; but the result is simply to confirm their original natures, not to develop or extend them. Theseus, on hearing of the forest's magic, delivers a rational lecture on the subject; Bottom, actually experiencing it, sees it as more material for one of his own performances. The different groups of characters can harmonize comfortably because the nature of each is securely fixed. But Shakespeare has already shown his interest in characters whose natures expand and develop under pressure, and this leads him to press beyond the achievement of *A Midsummer Night's Dream* into a new and more open dramatic method.

In its broad outlines, *The Merchant of Venice* appears to be an intellectually patterned play – more overtly so, perhaps, than its predecessor. The story of the bond, with its exposure of the inhumanity of mere 'justice', and the story of the caskets, with its neat moralizing about the dangers of appearance, allow for broad, striking theatrical effects and, in combination, generate ideas about right and wrong judgement, worldly and otherworldly wealth, the letter and the spirit – one could go on like that indefinitely. The play is a theme-hunter's delight. It invites broad statements about key ideas: it is a play 'about metals';[1] it concerns 'love's wealth';[2] it presents 'the theme of Justice and Mercy, of the Old Law and the New'.[3] Even the minor plot of Jessica's escape from her father's house appears to carry a broad allegorical significance: the Jew is 'the very devil incarnation' (II. ii. 23) and Jessica herself exclaims 'Our house is hell' (II. iii. 2). From this hell Jessica is brought to Belmont, to Christianity, to salvation. But the play also prompts reflections of a completely different kind: if it were simply an allegory, with each character functioning as part of a thematic pattern, we would not expect to find readers and audiences reacting to its characters as though they were 'people as real as ourselves'.[4] Yet that is precisely what has happened. Critics have lectured the characters for not behaving reasonably, as though they were real people responsible for their own actions, and not creatures of literary artifice: Salerio and Solanio are 'parasites', because they take no action of their own when they see Antonio's danger.[5] Even Portia is guilty of 'mercenary vengefulness' because she does not take the charitable step of showing Shylock his danger from the outset.[6] We may consider that the characters should be judged only by their reactions to choices the play itself offers, and not be seen against the wider range of choices offered by a real world; but the fact remains that, rightly

[1] C. S. Lewis, *Hamlet: The Prince or the Poem* (Annual Shakespeare Lecture of the British Academy: London, 1942), p. 10.
[2] John Russell Brown, *Shakespeare and his Comedies* (2nd edition, revised: London, 1968), pp. 61–75.
[3] Nevill Coghill, 'The basis of Shakespearian comedy', *Essays and Studies*, III (1950), p. 21.
[4] Sir Arthur Quiller-Couch, *Shakespeare's Workmanship* (London, 1927), p. 112.
[5] Sir Arthur Quiller-Couch, introduction to the New Cambridge edition of *The Merchant of Venice* (Cambridge, 1962), p. xxiii.
[6] A. D. Moody, *Shakespeare: The Merchant of Venice* (London, 1964), p. 43. In a similar vein, Harold C. Goddard accuses Portia of deliberately creating unnecessary suspense in the trial scene because she wants 'a dramatic triumph with herself at the center'. See *The Meaning of Shakespeare*, I (Chicago, 1962), p. 109.

or wrongly, the characters in this play do seem to encourage this kind of speculation in a way that the characters of *A Midsummer Night's Dream* (for example) do not. Even Antonio has not been left in his passive role as Shylock's victim; his mind has been read and its inner workings exposed. Graham Midgley concludes that he refuses to resist Shylock's claim because his death will allow him to demonstrate his love for Bassanio; and Shylock's defeat is his defeat too, for 'it has deprived him of the one great gesture of love which would have ended his loneliness and crowned his love with one splendid exit'.[7] Taking a similar view of Antonio, Lawrence W. Hyman sees the trial scene as a contest between Antonio and Portia, competing for Bassanio's love, the one 'with his heart's blood' and the other with her money.[8] Again, these are speculations, depending this time on the existence of an inner drama, a subtext of psychological action beneath the simple workings of the allegory.

We do not speculate in such a way about the characters of a fairy tale, and Granville-Barker's assertion that 'There is no more reality in Shylock's bond and the Lord of Belmont's will than in Jack and the Beanstalk',[9] however it may apply to the stories, does not seem to apply to the characters who move within those stories. We may feel that some of the speculations are unjustified, but we must, I think, admit that the characters have a detailed humanity that makes it impossible for us to see them as simply counters in an allegorical game. It is also generally felt that the physical threat to Antonio, and the intensity of Shylock's emotions, break the immunity, the detachment from real suffering, on which comedy normally depends. Moreover, the range of dramatic idiom in the play is extended beyond that of the earlier comedies, and includes a naturalism of manner – particularly the revelation of feeling beneath apparent small talk – that marks a significant breakthrough.[10] In earlier plays, the characters' feelings were spelled

---

[7] '*The Merchant of Venice*: a reconsideration', *Essays in Criticism*, X (April 1960), p. 131.
[8] 'The rival lovers in *The Merchant of Venice*', *Shakespeare Quarterly*, XXI (spring 1970), p. 112.
[9] Harley Granville-Barker, *Prefaces to Shakespeare*, I (Princeton, 1952), p. 335.
[10] Jonathan Miller's production for the National Theatre in 1970 treated the play as a nineteenth-century problem drama, with realistic sets and (for the

out explicitly in their speeches, with nothing, or very little, left to inference; there was, for the most part, no subtext.[11] This resulted in a clarity and concentration we would not normally think of as naturalistic. But – to take only one example – in the first meeting of Shylock and Antonio, an apparently casual conversation crackles with suppressed animosity:

SHYLOCK: . . . Rest you fair, good signior;
             Your worship was the last man in our mouths.
ANTONIO: Shylock, albeit I neither lend nor borrow
             By taking nor by giving of excess,
             Yet to supply the ripe wants of my friend,
             I'll break a custom. (*To Bassanio*) Is he yet possess'd
             How much ye would?

                                        (I. iii. 54–60)

No enmity is directly expressed; but Shylock's greeting is a little too oily, and rather too long delayed, for Antonio has been on stage for some time. Antonio ignores the greeting, and offers no salutation in return; instead, he plunges directly into business, with a brief, defensive comment about his own principles. After four lines he rudely turns away from the Jew to question Bassanio, as though he could not bear to address his enemy directly, or even look him in the face, for very long. The effect is intensified a few lines later, when Shylock's 'But note me, signior' is met by Antonio's 'Mark you this, Bassanio' (I. iii. 92). And as the usurer begins, slowly and elaborately, to work out the rate, Antonio bursts in with 'Well, Shylock, shall we be beholding to you?' (I. iii. 100). He is impatient to get away, and end a distasteful interview. Then, and only then, do the two men openly acknowledge their hatred (though Shylock has admitted his in an aside,

---

most part) 'natural' acting. Not all of it worked, of course – the casket scenes in particular, reduced to an after-dinner parlour game, lost much of their resonance – but a surprising number of scenes, particularly the early scenes in Venice, responded well to this treatment. The production, while it distorted some of the characters, was none the less valuable in revealing a vein of naturalism in the play's manner covered up by the more romantic productions it normally gets.
[11] There are one or two exceptions to this, which I have noted in earlier chapters: Berowne's attacks on Boyet, for example, may be more an attempt to repair his own self-esteem than appears on the surface. And Theseus's reluctance to enforce the Athenian law is, I think, more implied than directly stated.

earlier in the scene); but the manner of their dialogue has already told us, by implication, everything we need to know.[12]

In the earlier comedies, different groups of characters were smoothly interwoven, and drawn together in a finale in which virtually the whole cast was brought on stage. In this respect the structure of *The Merchant of Venice* is more broken and disjointed: an unusual number of characters – Morocco, Arragon, the Duke, Tubal, Old Gobbo – appear prominently for a scene or two, and are then forgotten. The final act is the most exclusive in Shakespearian comedy: by comparison with those of other plays it is a private affair, and we cannot help being struck by the number of characters who are not there. In place of the formal neatness of the earlier comedies we have a more open and natural structure, with more loose ends. Yet the stories of the bond and the caskets are, in their outlines, as fantastic and stylized as anything in Shakespeare. The experiments of *The Taming of the Shrew* and *Love's Labour's Lost*, in which characters were aware of convention, and consciously employed conventional modes of behaviour, are here extended in a radical way: the stories themselves are shamelessly conventionalized, yet they involve characters who are more realistically conceived than ever. In *The Taming of the Shrew* the two main plots were written in different idioms; but here the different idioms are superimposed on each other throughout the play, and we are asked to respond to them simultaneously. It is a dramatic experiment of considerable daring, and not all the risks come off: the realistic tone of Antonio's first meeting with Shylock does not quite prepare us for the fantastic bond the usurer proposes, and the awkward change of gear is not quite covered by the attempt to pass the bond off as a joke.[13] Similarly, Portia is given

---

[12] Similarly, in the opening scene, we notice the speed with which Salerio and Solanio leave the stage once Antonio and Bassanio have met, and the polite but transparent excuses they give (I. i. 57–61). Even Gratiano breaks off his lecture on melancholy for no apparent reason, and drags Lorenzo away (I. i. 103–4). Bassanio's friends know he has a delicate matter to discuss with Antonio: beneath the casual surface is some very tactful manœuvring.

[13] Bernard Grebanier, in *The Truth about Shylock* (New York, 1962), has shown that contracts in the Middle Ages sometimes included mutilation as a penalty (pp. 161–2); and Elizabethan audiences would be more accustomed than we are to mutilation as a judicial punishment. All the same, great stress is laid *within the play itself* on the fact that Shylock is insisting on a bizarre, unnatural penalty: as Portia says to him, 'Of a strange nature is the suit you follow' (IV. i. 172).

some rather forced jokes to cover her decision to disguise herself as a boy, a decision we accept less easily here than in more purely stylized plays, or plays where the decision comes earlier, as part of the given material. In both cases the motives for the character's action are consistent enough with the rest of his behaviour: the problem is in the dramatic idiom, where a conventionalized action is foisted on us a little too abruptly. But these risks are minor compared with the ultimate risk of the play itself, in which formalized actions are wedded to complex human reality.

In the play's overall design, Venice is a world of money and Belmont a world of love. We may be reminded, at first, of the two cities of Ephesus in *The Comedy of Errors*: a sterile world of material transactions, and a romantic world of fantasy and miracle. But the execution of this design is another matter. The material transactions of Venice are not solely material: they involve human feelings more deeply than does the traffic in chains, ropes and ducats in the earlier play. The love of Antonio and Bassanio expresses itself through money; and there is something painful in Bassanio's embarrassment at asking for a large loan when he has had so much already, and Antonio's hurt reaction to this embarrassment, taking it as casting doubts upon his love:

> You know me well, and herein spend but time
> To wind about my love with circumstance;
> And out of doubt you do me now more wrong
> In making question of my uttermost
> Than if you had made waste of all I have.

(I. i. 153–7)

Money is a sadly inadequate vehicle for the expression of love when it leads to such misunderstandings as this; but it is the only form of expression they have. Even Bassanio's wooing of Portia, 'a lady richly left' (I. i. 161), has a clear financial base, for all his praise of her beauty:

> my chief care
> Is to come fairly off from the great debts
> Wherein my time, something too prodigal,
> Hath left me gag'd.

(I. i. 127–31)

Paradoxically, his voyage to Belmont is both an act of love for Antonio, attempting to recover the money his friend has given him, and an attempt to get clear of him by seeking another source of money and another love. Small wonder, then, that he approaches Antonio cautiously and apologetically (their first conversation, when they are alone, is some irrelevant chat about Gratiano, as though they are both reluctant to broach a painful subject). This dilemma, in one form or another, will haunt Bassanio throughout the play.

Conversely, money is at once the root of the enmity between Shylock and Antonio – 'He lends out money gratis, and brings down / The rate of usance here with us in Venice' (I. iii. 39–40) – and its ultimate means of expression:

> If thou wilt lend this money, lend it not
> As to thy friend – for when did friendship take
> A breed of barren metal of his friend? –
> But lend it rather to thine enemy,
> Who if he break thou mayst with better face
> Exact the penalty.
>
> (I. iii. 127–32)

Shylock offers the bond, ostensibly, as an act of friendship, but its terms express the real relations between the two men. For the Venetians, money is a medium of exchange representing not the goods and services of academic economists, but the passions of love and hate. And by the same token those passions, in Venice, seek out money as their means of expression. Shylock, breeding his gold and silver, is not the only one who treats money as a living thing. The very essence of their lives is material, and when a Venetian loses his money he loses everything:

> Nay, take my life and all, pardon not that.
> You take my house when you do take the prop
> That doth sustain my house; you take my life
> When you do take the means whereby I live.
>
> (IV. i. 369–72)

We expect that from Shylock; but even Antonio can say, when he learns from Portia that his ships are safely returned, 'Sweet lady, you have given me life and living' (v. i. 286).

And yet one of the first ideas introduced in the play – and one
that is discussed at some length – is the instability of wealth.
Salerio describes it as a fragile splendour that can vanish in a
moment:

> Should I go to church
> And see the holy edifice of stone,
> And not bethink me straight of dangerous rocks,
> Which, touching but my gentle vessel's side,
> Would scatter all her spices on the stream,
> Enrobe the roaring waters with my silks,
> And in a word, but even now worth this,
> And now worth nothing?

(I. i. 29–35)

(It is characteristic, too, that even the sight of a church makes
Salerio think of commerce.) With the insecurity of wealth thus
established, there is an anxious sense of need through all the
characters; no one is secure and self-sufficient – each must seek out
and depend on others. Bassanio, before he even thinks of gaining
Portia, must seek out Antonio; Antonio, much as he would like to,
cannot pour forth wealth for his friend; he must seek out Shylock,
and put himself in the hands of his enemy to serve his friend. Even
Shylock claims that he has to depend on Tubal (though that is
probably just the stock patter of his trade). The Venetian state
itself, in a way, needs Shylock: it dare not deny him his 'justice'
since its charter depends on law, and its 'trade and profit . . .
Consisteth of all nations' (III. iii. 30–1). Shylock holds himself
aloof in matters of race and religion, but involves himself in
commerce even with his enemies: 'I will buy with you, sell with
you, talk with you, walk with you, and so following; but I will not
eat with you, drink with you, nor pray with you' (I. iii. 31–3).
But his hatred breaks down even this reservation, and draws him
out of his house to a Christian feast:

> I am not bid for love; they flatter me;
> But yet I'll go in hate, to feed upon
> The prodigal Christian.

(II. v. 13–15)

The early Venetian scenes present a realistic picture of the complexity of human relationships; and part of their naturalism is a sense of restless activity, as characters dart back and forth on errands; but the cumulative effect goes beyond naturalism, as the complex traffic of Venice is set against the comparative stillness of Belmont, and thus takes its place in a more abstract design: while Belmont is a world of security, Venice is a world of need.

It is also a place where the conventional expressions of romantic love have become impossible. In earlier plays, the private, single-minded experience of love was dislocated by being placed against other experiences; here, the dislocation goes so far that the very idea of romantic love is virtually destroyed. Bassanio's comparison of Portia's hair to the golden fleece (I. i. 169–70) is, one might say, not metaphorical enough to be romantic; his concern for the gold *as gold* is all too real. But Bassanio will be seen in another way when he gets to Belmont; the impossibility of Venice as a setting for romantic love is conveyed most clearly in the treatment of Lorenzo and Jessica. Here we have the broad outlines of a very romantic episode: two young lovers elope by night, under the cover of a masque and a banquet, with the girl disguised as a torchbearer. She is escaping, to the accompaniment of music and dancing, from a dark and joyless house; and she is a Jew escaping with a Christian, moving, I have already suggested, from hell to salvation. But this simple outline is so modified by the presentation as to be almost unrecognizable. The involvement of love with money, so characteristic of the Venetian scenes, is essential to this love affair:

JESSICA: I will make fast the doors, and gild myself
            With some moe ducats, and be with you straight.
                                              [*Exit above.*
GRATIANO: Now, by my hood, a gentle and no Jew.
LORENZO: Beshrew me, but I love her heartily . . .
                                       (II. vi. 49–52)

Metaphorically, Jessica is taking love from her father and transferring it to her husband; but the throwing of the casket and the extra detail of her disappearing to get more ducats put the focus on the literal wealth she is stealing. (We may contrast this with the transactions of Antonio, Bassanio and Shylock, where the money is not actually seen on stage until the trial scene, and where the focus is more on its metaphorical function.) And this love is seen as threatened with the instability that threatens money: while Lorenzo's friends wait for the lovers to appear, they comment sardonically (with an echo of earlier speeches about Antonio's merchandise) on the transience of love – the eagerness with which it is pursued and the speed with which weariness sets in:

> How like a younker or a prodigal
> The scarfed bark puts from her native bay,
> Hugg'd and embraced by the strumpet wind;
> How like a prodigal doth she return,
> With over-weather'd ribs and ragged sails,
> Lean, rent, and beggar'd by the strumpet wind!
>
> (II. vi. 14–19)

If Lorenzo were on stage this could be seen as friendly joking; but he is not. His friends appear to be really speaking their minds about love, and the result is to present an unsympathetic context for the elopement.

The masque and the banquet could provide a base of civilized merriment from which to strike at Shylock. But while the news of the masque has its expected function of drawing a torrent of abuse from the usurer, 'The man that hath no music in himself' (v. i. 83), the masque itself never materializes. Lorenzo's friends complain that it has not been properly organized:

GRATIANO: We have not made good preparation.
SALERIO: We have not spoke us yet of torchbearers.
SOLANIO: 'Tis vile, unless it may be quaintly ordered;
            And better in my mind not undertook.

> (II. iv. 4–7)

Jessica adopts her own role in it with reluctance. While other heroines embrace and exploit their male disguises, Jessica exclaims,

> I am glad 'tis night, you do not look on me,
> For I am much asham'd of my exchange;
> But love is blind, and lovers cannot see

The pretty follies that themselves commit,
For, if they could, Cupid himself would blush
To see me thus transformed to a boy.

(II. vi. 34–9)

And the last we hear of the promised revels is a haunting line from
Antonio: 'No masque to-night; the wind is come about' (II. iv. 64).
The elopement is a hurried, furtive affair, accompanied by a
broken ceremony. A stylized presentation might have made it
satisfying; but Shakespeare treats it realistically, as part of the
traffic of Venice; and once again this realism serves the larger
design, for Belmont, not Venice, must be the centre of romantic
love. Not that Lorenzo and Jessica are transformed, even when
they come to Belmont: they are still subject to sardonic commentary, as when Lancelot views the spiritual side of their affair in
material terms: 'This making of Christians will raise the price of
hogs' (III. v. 20).

In *Love's Labour's Lost* romantic love was viewed with critical
detachment; but so too was the mockery that attacked it: both
had to give way to time and death. While these issues are not so
closely connected in *The Merchant of Venice*, it is still worth noting
that Venice is no more a utopia of wit than it is a utopia of
romantic love. Gratiano's joking is tolerated, but seen as ultimately shallow. Bassanio accuses him of speaking

an infinite deal of nothing, more than any man in all Venice.
His reasons are as two grains of wheat hid in two bushels of
chaff: you shall seek all day ere you find them, and when you
have them they are not worth the search.

(I. i. 114–18)

As with Gratiano's own comments on the lovers, if this were said
to his face it might pass off as mere teasing. But Bassanio says this
behind his back, and we are therefore more inclined to take it as a
serious opinion. Certainly we may contrast it with the tributes
paid by other characters to the intelligent fooling of Feste and
Touchstone. Bassanio does not seem very pleased when Gratiano
invites himself to Belmont: 'Why, then you must' (II. ii. 165); and
he tells him in no uncertain terms that he must behave himself:

his mirth is all very well among friends, but might give offence elsewhere (II. ii. 165–74). As we see later, there was no need for Bassanio to worry about Belmont in this respect; but Venice is a place where wit is not always in season. Nor is Gratiano the only offender: the savage jokes of Solanio about Shylock losing his 'two stones' (II. viii. 20, 24), and about his flesh and blood rebelling 'at these years' (III. i. 31), are a shallow and ill-judged response to the usurer's rage. Like the savage jokes of Gratiano himself in the trial scene, they recoil and give us a sympathy for the victim that we might not otherwise have. Lancelot's joking with Old Gobbo is lighter in tone, but bears the same tinge of cruelty: skilfully played, the scene can be amusing, but the roots of its comedy are in blindness and bereavement, and this gives our laughter a slight edge of distaste. In a more purely farcial play we might not be bothered by it; but this play does not allow the detachment of farce. Most important, of course, is Shylock's idea of a joke: his 'merry sport' (I. iii. 140) is a cruel and macabre fantasy of slicing the flesh of his enemy; and the joke (if indeed it is that) soon becomes deadly earnest. But if wit turns sour and cruel in Venice, it flows freely enough in the first Belmont scene. Portia feels a moment of hesitation: 'In truth, I know it is a sin to be a mocker, but . . .' (I. ii. 51). The hesitation is very brief: she subjects her unwanted suitors to a torrent of witty abuse, to which we can respond without hesitation, for her victims are safely offstage, cartoon figures with no reality. And it is the reality of the Venetian figures, Shylock especially, that makes us hesitate in our laughter.

In the early scenes Belmont appears, by comparison with Venice, to be a simple, stylized world, sealed off from the busy traffic of reality, and ruffled only by occasional references to the coming of Bassanio. In Venice the stage is crowded with speaking characters, and scenes are broken by frequent exits and entrances. Belmont is dramatically simple: Portia, Nerissa and the two princes are the only major speakers, and their scenes are for the most part still and static. In place of the complex financial and emotional dealings of Venice there is the single formal problem of the three caskets. If Venice is a world of need, the wealth of Belmont seems secure and immutable. (And one may assume, though the point is not emphasized, that the princes who come to woo

Portia do not, like Bassanio, need the money.) Yet, in the words of Nerissa, 'for aught I see, they are as sick that surfeit with too much as they that starve with nothing' (I. ii. 5-6). Portia's weariness, at the start of her first scene, matches Antonio's melancholy at the start of his. At the centre of the stylized casket game is a living woman, who finds the passive stillness imposed by her formal role more than a little trying:

> The brain may devise laws for the blood, but a hot temper leaps o'er a cold decree; such a hare is madness the youth, to skip o'er the meshes of good counsel the cripple. But that reasoning is not in the fashion to choose me a husband. O me, the word 'choose!' I may neither choose who I would nor refuse who I dislike; so is the will of a living daughter curb'd by the will of a dead father.
>
> (I. ii. 16-22)

At the end of the scene Portia begins to see her father's wisdom when she learns that the first group of unwanted suitors has left rather than face the test. And the casket game does in the end give Portia her will. But our first impression of her is of a natural impatience at being forced into the limiting role of prize in a literary game: we see the human feeling beneath the allegorical pattern.

Our second impression is of cool ironic wit, as she dissects – at length and in detail – her unwanted suitors. Clearly Portia is no remote, romantic heiress. And when the Prince of Morocco comes to woo her, the glamour of his utterance is comically out of place:

> by this scimitar,
> That slew the Sophy and the Persian prince,
> That won three fields of Sultan Solyman,
> I would o'erstare the sternest eyes that look,
> Outbrave the heart most daring on the earth,
> Pluck the young sucking cubs from the she-bear,
> Yea, mock the lion when 'a roars for prey,
> To win thee, lady.   (II. i. 24-31)

As always in Shakespearian comedy, context is important. In heroic tragedy Morocco would cut an impressive enough figure, but here he seems to have wandered into the wrong play. Portia and Nerissa keep their countenances, but we can guess what is in their minds, particularly when Portia tells Morocco that she likes him as well as any of her suitors so far (II. i. 20–2). Morocco is not contemptible, merely oversized and out of place, and many commentators have expressed sympathy for him. The narrow egotism of Arragon is more obviously comic, and his defeat is satisfying in a less subtle way. But again his sense of being a special person might have a certain grandeur in tragedy:

> I will not choose what many men desire,
> Because I will not jump with common spirits
> And rank me with the barbarous multitudes.
>
> (II. ix. 31–3)

In our egalitarian age we laugh more easily at this aristocratic ideal than an Elizabethan audience might have done. But if we think of Portia as being wooed first by Othello and then by Coriolanus, we may be closer to the comic effect Shakespeare is aiming at: the grandeur of a tragic hero, seen in the earthy context of comedy, collapses into bombast. The same thing happens if you try to tell the story of Pyramus and Thisbe in the context of *A Midsummer Night's Dream*.

As Bassanio looks to Belmont to repair his fortunes, so Belmont, in a sense, needs Bassanio. Portia needs to be wooed and won, not by some exotic creature, but by a life-sized figure from a real world. And Bassanio is certainly that. His journey to Belmont is at least as important, and as liberating, as Portia's later journey to Venice. As he approaches, Shakespeare prepares for his victory by ringing the changes on the theme of loss (II. vii–III. i). In Belmont Morocco and Arragon are defeated in a formal, allegorical way, by giving the wrong answer to the riddle. In the swifter world of Venice news of loss comes flooding in from all sides: Shylock has lost his daughter and his money (placed, even in his own speeches, on the same level of importance), and he is losing more money in his fruitless search for her. Money and love, as always, go together, and in this case are lost together. The same thing happens to Antonio, though here the connection is less direct. As we hear the news of disaster to his galleys, we are told also of his parting from Bassanio, which has been withheld from us until now, to take its place in the general tale of loss:

SALERIO: . . . And even there, his eye being big with tears,
          Turning his face, he put his hand behind him,
          And with affection wondrous sensible
          He wrung Bassanio's hand; and so they parted.
SOLANIO: I think he only loves the world for him.

(II. viii. 46–50)

The cumulative effect is to suggest that Salerio's vision, in the opening scene, of the fragility of wealth – 'but even now worth this, / And now worth nothing' (I. i. 34–5) – is coming true. The unstable wealth of Venice, or at least of the chief Venetian characters, is disappearing. And for both Shylock and Antonio loss of love goes with loss of money. The result is to build up expectation of Bassanio's success in a variety of ways: in Belmont two suitors have already lost the game, and our sense of the natural rhythm of such stories leads us to expect the victory of the third; besides, the overinflated rhetoric of those suitors has led us to see the necessity for a different kind of wooer. This establishes what might be called a formal need for Bassanio. In Venice, the disasters to Antonio – and the vengeful passion released in Shylock by his own disasters – suggest the urgency of Bassanio's victory in more realistic terms. (As it turns out, Antonio is rescued not by Portia's money but by Portia herself; but even so, Bassanio's success is a necessary condition.)

Bassanio is the first of Portia's suitors to have a life outside Belmont, to bring with him memories of a world elsewhere. We have seen him prepare his wooing in a bustling, naturalistic sequence:

> You may do so; but let it be so hasted that supper be ready at the farthest by five of the clock. See these letters delivered, put the liveries to making, and desire Gratiano to come anon to my lodging.
>
> (II. ii. 104–7)

And he comes to Belmont, we must not forget, on Shylock's money, borrowed as a business speculation to recover his own losses and repay his friend. Just as we see past Portia's formal role to her personality, we see the realistic underproppings of Bassanio's role as successful suitor. Far from being an embarrassment, our awareness of the practical side of Bassanio's wooing is a necessity: if he is to function as he must in the play's design, he must be a real man, not a pasteboard prince. His very presence releases a new voice in Portia:

> I pray you tarry; pause a day or two
> Before you hazard; for, in choosing wrong,
> I lose your company; therefore forbear awhile.
> There's something tells me – but it is not love –
> I would not lose you; and you know yourself
> Hate counsels not in such a quality.
> But lest you should not understand me well –
> And yet a maiden hath no tongue but thought –
> I would detain you here some month or two
> Before you venture for me. I could teach you
> How to choose right, but then I am forsworn.
> So will I never be; so may you miss me;
> But if you do, you'll make me wish a sin,
> That I had been forsworn. Beshrew your eyes!
> They have o'erlook'd me and divided me;
> One half is yours, the other half yours –
> Mine own, I would say, but if mine, then yours,
> And so all yours.
>
> (III. ii. 1–18)

The confusion, hesitations and sudden outbursts of feeling tell us that for the first time in the play Portia is not in control of herself. Certainly she is no longer content to let the game take its course: the slight impatience with its restrictions we saw in her first scene has been replaced by a deep anxiety, and her need to preserve the decorum of her role first struggles, and then collapses, in the face of her love (III. ii. 24–39). The cool, witty woman of the first scene has become touchingly vulnerable. Her wit is now exercised in a different way, in affectionate joking with Bassanio about his love (III. ii. 24–39): even before he wins her, we hear their voices chiming together, in a manner very different from the formal addresses exchanged by Portia and her othersuitors.

But he must still answer the riddle. And the reason for his success here needs careful examination, for it depends not so much upon logical argument as upon a sense of how convention operates. Morocco's mistake is to make a judgement about Portia: thinking of her in a literary, emblematic way he concludes 'Never so rich a gem / Was set in worse than gold' (ii. vii. 54–5). Arragon's mistake is to make a judgement about himself. In meditating on how much false honour there is in the world (ii. ix. 39–49) he gets very close to what Bassanio later says about the treachery of appearance; but he misses his chance when he declares 'I will assume desert' (ii. ix. 51), and asks for the key of the silver casket. Each of them takes a variety of approaches to the caskets, considering sometimes the metal and sometimes the motto, but at the crucial moment of choice each examines the motto on his chosen casket and draws a logical conclusion from it, about Portia's worth or about his own. But just as one will never solve a crossword puzzle by taking the clues too literally, so Morocco and Arragon have in a sense been too logical:

PORTIA: O, these deliberate fools! When they do choose,
           They have the wisdom by their wit to lose.
NERISSA: The ancient saying is no heresy;
           Hanging and wiving goes by destiny.

                                        (ii. ix. 80–3)

In this exchange, rational thought is set against instinctive wisdom, and the latter is seen as a surer guide. The paradox of Bassanio's success is that he is at once a more down-to-earth character than the other suitors and one whose mind is more finely attuned to the workings of convention. In the speech in which he meditates on his choice, he says nothing about himself as an individual, or Portia as an individual; he ignores all the inscriptions, and thereby avoids the dead-end traps of logical thought. Instead, his mind moves instinctively to the inner logic of the convention: he forgets even love, and he isolates in his mind the single crucial idea – the treachery of appearance – an idea suggested by the caskets themselves, whose appearance gives no clue to their inner reality, and by the accompanying song, with its reminder of the frailty of judgements made by the eye. His speech is not in the least romantic: it consists of cool, slightly bitter commonplaces about the dangers of appearance, and it carries the sense of the insecurity of life that we remember from the world of Venice, and the opening talk of Antonio's ships: 'Thus ornament is but the guiled shore / To a most dangerous sea' (III. ii. 97–8). But there are no explicit personal memories here; the speech is couched in general terms. And Bassanio's cool realism is placed in a highly ceremonial context. If this is the most human of the casket scenes, in the way it releases the feelings of Portia and Bassanio, it is also the most stylized: it is the only one in which music plays, and the song is preceded by a speech from Portia on the emotive power of music to underline loss or victory (III. ii. 43–53). The earlier casket scenes are pedestrian by comparison: only for Bassanio does the casket game become fully ceremonial. The way in which ceremony and reality interact is perhaps suggested by Bassanio's speech when he finds Portia's picture in the casket. He praises it, and then says that his praise is inadequate to the picture, and that the picture is inadequate to the reality. He then turns from the picture to the woman herself (III. ii. 114–29). He contemplates an image of her, as a step to contemplating her directly. Like all ceremonies, the ritual of the caskets embodies a generalized experience, and Bassanio does well to forget the individual reality of his love while he passes through the ceremony (as his rivals fail to do). But at the heart of the ceremony is a living woman. To regard her as the golden fleece, to see her emblematically as Morocco does (and as Bassanio himself does in his first scene – I. i. 168–72) may be a necessary first step, part of the generalization of the ceremony, but it is not the final reality of love. And in the riddle itself we find, again, something human and ordinary at the heart of the convention. The folly of choosing by appearance is a piece of simple, realistic common sense. Where the exotic wooers fail, Bassanio can pierce the heart of the mystery, precisely because he is an ordinary man.

When Bassanio answers the riddle, Portia is released from her static and confining role into the traffic of the world. Gracefully – and with a distinct sense of relief – she surrenders herself to Bassanio:

Myself and what is mine to you and yours
Is now converted. But now I was the lord
Of this fair mansion, master of my servants,
Queen o'er myself; and even now, but now,
This house, these servants, and this same myself,
Are yours – my lord's.

(III. ii. 167–72)

There is more in this surrender than romantic love, seen as an isolated experience. The reference to her house and servants reminds us that love is also a material transaction; though here the material side is secondary, and follows the personal surrender, unlike the tight involvement of money and love in Venice. In the purely romantic ecstasy of the lovers' triumph there has already been a certain caution:

O love, be moderate, allay thy ecstasy,
In measure rain thy joy, scant this excess!
I feel too much thy blessing. Make it less,
For fear I surfeit.

(III. ii. 111–14)

The happiness of this one moment is suspect in its sheer intensity; and soon there is a controlled descent, beginning with the practical surrender of house and servants. The pairing of Gratiano and Nerissa (who now speak for the first time in the scene) provides a comic duplication of the pairing of Portia and Bassanio, and removes some of its uniqueness. It also recalls the earthy side of love – 'swearing till my very roof was dry / With oaths of love'; 'No; we shall ne'er win at that sport, and stake down' (III. ii. 205–6, 217–18). Gratiano's joking finds a more congenial setting here than it does in Venice, and a more attractive function: it opens out the range of experience that is possible in Belmont. And almost immediately that range is opened in a more radical way. Bassanio has brought with him not simply the realism of Venice, but the obligations he incurred there. The entrance of Salerio is like that of Marcade in *Love's Labour's Lost*, breaking in on the secure world of love with grim reality – and not, this time, something merely reported, but a reality the audience has already seen for itself. He enters with a third couple, Lorenzo and Jessica, whose presence, far from contributing to a Noah's Ark ending in the manner of *As You Like It*, sparks memories of the raging Jew, and of the unromantic dramatization of their own mating.

Portia has indeed been released from her static role, and the traffic of the world has invaded Belmont with a vengeance. This is, in fact, a necessary condition of her surrender to Bassanio:

> With leave, Bassanio: I am half yourself,
> And I must freely have the half of anything
> That this same paper brings you.
>
> (III. ii. 250–2)

Her involvement with him includes his more painful involvement with Antonio. Their love cannot be a single, isolated experience, because he is not an isolated man:

> When I told you
> My state was nothing, I should then have told you
> That I was worse than nothing; for indeed
> I have engag'd myself to my dear friend,
> Engag'd my friend to his mere enemy,
> To feed my means.
>
> (III. ii. 260–5)

Portia's impulse to give, released by her love for Bassanio, is quickly extended to meet this new challenge. In marrying him, she has come to share his debt to Antonio, even to the point of delaying the consummation of her own love: 'For never shall you lie by Portia's side / With an unquiet soul' (III. ii. 307–8). Antonio's need must be served first. By implication, Bassanio is not fully won until his debt to his old love is cleared, but there is no jealousy in Portia's eagerness to clear that debt: 'When it is paid, bring your true friend along' (III. ii. 310). One feels that she is eager also to release the wealth of Belmont, so long hoarded up, into the world. But there is, at the same time, a certain naïveté in her confidence in the power of that wealth. When she hears Antonio's debt is three thousand ducats, she exclaims,

> What! no more?
> Pay him six thousand, and deface the bond;

> Double six thousand, and then treble that. . . .
>   You shall have gold
> To pay the petty debt twenty times over.

> (III. ii. 300–9)

She does not yet understand how money is used in Venice. It is not the amount that matters: she could bury Shylock in a heap of ducats without once touching his real need, which is for vengeance. Portia's character has been radically extended from the cool wit of the first scene to the eager, passionate openness of the scene with Bassanio. But it must be extended even further, and more painfully.

Her disguise gives her, like Julia, a masculine freedom of action. But at first she comes to Venice speaking the accents of Belmont, conditioned by the world of easy wealth she has always known. She opposes the free bounty of mercy to Shylock's hard demand for justice:

> The quality of mercy is not strain'd;
> It droppeth as the gentle rain from heaven
> Upon the place beneath.

> (IV. i. 179–81)

But the result of this plea is the most serious instance yet of the device by which a speech is addressed to an uncomprehending listener. Portia speaks of God, heaven and, at the lowest level, of throned monarchs. But Shylock is resolutely a creature of the earth. The most detailed reference he has made to his own tradition is a story of copulating rams. When he speaks of our common humanity, it is in physical terms: 'If you prick us, do we not bleed? If you tickle us, do we not laugh?' (III. i. 54–5). He seeks even his revenge in the most crudely physical terms. Portia's speech on mercy has an easy flow, but its images are somewhat disembodied.[14] Shylock, as is frequently remarked, hoards his words,[15] but his language is as concrete as the scraping sound of the knife on his shoe, and he illustrates his arguments with pungent coarseness:

[14] See Clifford Leech, *The Dramatist's Experience* (London, 1970), pp. 158–9.
[15] See Mark Van Doren, *Shakespeare* (New York, 1939), p. 101; and Theodore Weiss, *The Breath of Clowns and Kings* (London, 1971), p. 126.

> Some men there are love not a gaping pig;
> Some that are mad if they behold a cat;
> And others, when the bagpipe sings i'th' nose,
> Cannot contain their urine. . . .   (IV. i. 47–50)

Portia and Shylock speak with utterly opposing voices; there can be no meeting of minds between them. Her plea for mercy may have won the hearts of the anthologists, but for all the effect it has on Shylock she might as well not have spoken. He cannot be cracked from outside, for his implacable 'humour', as he himself describes it (IV. i. 43), is its own justification, a closed circle of logic – 'Hates any man the thing he would not kill?' (IV. i. 69) – to which no other standard is relevant.

Portia, like Bassanio, must now answer a riddle: she must enter the mind of her adversary, just as Bassanio entered the mind of her dead father and saw the inner logic of the casket game. According to Thomas Marc Parrott, 'In Portia's decision we see the triumph of the spirit over the letter, of equity over legalism.'[16] We see, I think, something more painful and alarming than that. When her appeal to mercy fails, Portia begins to test Shylock, as the caskets had tested her unwanted suitors. In a series of exchanges she establishes that he will not take the money, that he has no surgeon by to staunch the blood (''tis not in the bond' – IV. i. 257), and that he does have the balances to weigh the flesh: in short, that he takes his bond logically and literally, as Morocco and Arragon took the casket mottoes logically and literally. Very well, then: there is one piece of logic he has overlooked. She will use the letter to defeat the letter. When she gives her judgement there is a new tone in her voice, a cold remorseless logic, with a leaden thump on the key words:

> This bond doth give thee here no jot of blood:
> The words expressly are 'a pound of flesh.'
> Take then thy bond, take thou thy pound of flesh;
> But, in the cutting of it, if thou dost shed
> One drop of Christian blood, thy lands and goods
> Are, by the laws of Venice, confiscate
> Unto the state of Venice.   (IV. i. 301–7)

[16] *Shakespearean Comedy* (New York, 1949), p. 139.

She follows up her argument in detail, releasing one by one the full terrors of the law that Shylock had invoked, playing Shylock's own game with a deadly thoroughness that is more than a little alarming. She does in a more purposeful way what Gratiano does more shallowly by flinging Shylock's own words back at him. She leaves it to Gratiano to show triumph, and to the Duke and Antonio to show mercy: she reserves for herself only the impersonal accents of the law. In place of the flowing bounty of her earlier speeches we hear, at the climax of her argument, the hard command: 'Down, therefore, and beg mercy of the Duke' (IV. i. 358). Mercy no longer flows freely: it has to be begged, as Shylock made Antonio and his friends beg. As Bassanio entered and understood the conventions of Belmont, Portia has now entered and understood the special conventions of Shylock's mind, the diabolical game of 'justice'. And she destroys Shylock with the weapon most fatal to convention – parody.

But – apart from the strange moment when Shylock first proposed the bond – we had not previously thought of Venice as a particularly conventionalized world, certainly not when compared with Belmont. It seemed, if less congenial, more natural and realistic. In this respect, however, the balance of the play has now shifted: Venice, in the trial scene, has become a formal world where a simple dramatic issue is at stake. As in the earlier Belmont scenes, a riddle must be solved. We still hear a wide range of voices, from the tense authority of the Duke to the savagery of Gratiano, but the speed and fluidity are gone, and the sense of busy traffic is stilled as a single crucial issue is decided. The enclosure of the action in the court – something new for the Venetian scenes – adds to this effect. Belmont, on the other hand, has acquired a more open and natural dramatic idiom in the immediately preceding scenes, beginning with the arrival of the messengers from Venice. Portia's preparations for her journey have some of the haste and bustle of Bassanio's preparations in the earlier scenes:

> Take this same letter,
> And use thou all th'endeavour of a man
> In speed to Padua; see thou render this

> Into my cousin's hands, Doctor Bellario;
> And look what notes and garments he doth give thee,
> Bring them, I pray thee, with imagin'd speed
> Unto the traject, to the common ferry
> Which trades to Venice.
>
> (III. iv. 47–54)

And just before the trial we have that casual, inconsequential scene with Lorenzo, Jessica and Lancelot. Lancelot's jokes, the preparations for dinner, the seemingly irrelevant detail of the Moor's pregnancy (and where did *she* come from, by the way?) – all these combine to suggest a natural world, going about its independent business, far from the passions of the courtroom.

There may also be, in that scene, some ironic foreshadowing of the trial. Lancelot's complaint that 'This making of Christians will raise the price of hogs' (III. v. 20) may refer forward to Shylock, as well as backward to Jessica. More important, some of Lancelot's joking depends on the excessively literal interpretation of words. Lorenzo remarks,

> I do know
> A many fools that stand in better place,
> Garnish'd like him, that for a tricksy word
> Defy the matter.
>
> (III. v. 58–61)

This is followed immediately by Jessica's praise of Portia; yet we will soon see Portia play Lancelot's game in a far more serious way. These touches, light though they are, may have a slight distancing effect if we can remember them in the trial scene itself, since they place some of the key motifs of that scene in a context that trivializes them. But there is a more daring effect, right at the heart of the trial scene. Portia has just told Antonio to prepare for death, and he and Bassanio are taking a last farewell. The crisis is nearly upon us, when we hear the following:

> BASSANIO: Antonio, I am married to a wife
> Which is as dear to me as life itself;
> But life itself, my wife, and all the world
> Are not with me esteem'd above thy life;

> I would lose all, ay, sacrifice them all
> Here to this devil, to deliver you.

PORTIA: Your wife would give you little thanks for that,
If she were by to hear you make the offer.

GRATIANO: I have a wife who I protest I love;
I would she were in heaven, so she could
Entreat some power to change this currish Jew.

NERISSA: 'Tis well you offer it behind her back;
The wish would make else an unquiet house.

SHYLOCK: (*Aside*) These be the Christian husbands! I have a
daughter –
Would any of the stock of Barrabas
Had been her husband, rather than a Christian!

(IV. i. 277–93)

Like Salerio's arrival in Belmont, this exchange jolts us out of our involvement with the immediate business of the scene, and forces us to see it in a larger context. But here the effect is reversed: we are pulled away from the suffering of the courtroom and reminded of the more comic world of love. As Bassanio speaks, his earnest manner is compromised by our growing realization of the irony of his making the offer in Portia's presence. The effect of his speech hovers between serious concern and laughter; but in the comic symmetry of the following exchanges, and the wry abruptness of the women's replies (especially Nerissa's), the balance quickly tilts towards laughter. Even Shylock makes a joke of it, though his joke is more bitter and takes us back eventually to the serious business of the scene. The defeat of Shylock comes only a few lines later; but this passage has already put us at a slight distance from the trial, and lessened (though not destroyed) the seriousness of our involvement with it, by reminding us that there is a world elsewhere.

It is as well that the trial is thus slightly distanced and conventionalized: it helps us to remember that Portia, in out-Shylocking Shylock, is adopting a necessary but temporary role, not showing us her true face. There is something not only unclean but unreal about the trial, both in Shylock's demand and in the manner of his defeat. At the heart of the casket game is human

reality, reassuringly ordinary and familiar. There is, in the
grimmer game that Shylock plays, human reality of a different
kind, his deep need for vengeance on Antonio; but to satisfy that
need he depends on an impersonal, logical principle, which is no
respecter of persons, and which can be used just as easily against
Shylock as for him. Portia, in her grim parody of Shylock, shows
us what 'justice' really looks like when it is taken to its logical
conclusion. It is a mad obsession with precision:

> if thou tak'st more
> Or less than a just pound – be it but so much
> As makes it light or heavy in the substance,
> Or the division of the twentieth part
> Of one poor scruple; nay, if the scale do turn
> But in the estimation of a hair –
> Thou diest, and all thy goods are confiscate.

> (IV. i. 321–7)

The freeflowing generosity of Portia's normal speech – 'Pay him
six thousand, and deface the bond; / Double six thousand, and
then treble that' (III. ii. 301–2) – is sharply reversed, and becomes
an obsession with increasingly minute measurement. This is more
truly fantastic than anything in the Belmont scenes: like some of
the more unsettling fantasies of Lewis Carroll, it shows what
happens when logical principles are set to work without the
restraints of humanity and common sense. If we are to emerge
from the play with any feeling of reassurance at all, we need to
feel – as I think we do – that this mad trial is not a final vision of
human reality.

All the same, Shylock's hate is real enough, however fantastic
the manner in which he has tried to satisfy it. And that hate has
merely been defeated, not dissipated. The mercy shown him by
the Duke and Antonio makes no more impression on him than
Portia's abstract appeal had done. Moreover, while Shylock can
be ordered off the stage, he remains an immovable part of the
play's vision: he is too vigorous and convincing a figure to be
brushed aside with a wave of the hand, like Egeus, and quickly
forgotten. In fact, we need to remember him if the final scene is
to have its full effect. I have already remarked on the exclusive-

ness – indeed, the privateness – of the comic finale, and I think the vision of harmony it offers is carefully and deliberately restricted. It is right that it should be so, for the play as a whole has shown an uncomfortable world where hate breeds easily and where even love makes painful demands.

Towards the end of *Love's Labour's Lost* and *A Midsummer Night's Dream* there were passages in which the play's central vision was stated in objective terms, apart from the immediate concerns of the characters: the songs of Spring and Winter, an image of mutability, and the description of Theseus's hounds, an image of harmony. At the start of Act V of *The Merchant of Venice*, there is a similar but longer and more elaborate passage. It may seem odd at first glance that Lorenzo and Jessica, so unsatisfying as purely romantic lovers, should be chosen to deliver a rhapsody on the beauty of the night, the music of the spheres and the power of harmony. But that is just the point. In their scene at Belmont just before the trial, they have established a special conversational technique by which, while praising the perfections of others, they joke about their own distance from perfection. Jessica says of Portia:

> Why, if two gods should play some heavenly match,
> And on the wager lay two earthly women,
> And Portia one, there must be something else
> Pawned with the other; for the poor rude world
> Hath not her fellow.
> LORENZO: Even such a husband
> Hast thou of me as she is for a wife.
> JESSICA: Nay, but ask my opinion too of that.
> LORENZO: I will anon; first let us go to dinner.
> JESSICA: Nay, let me praise you while I have a stomach.
>
> (III. v. 70–8)

As soon as they discuss themselves, they become chatty and ironic. And through the opening passage of Act V they teasingly set themselves against higher, unattainable ideals. Their first exchange, on tragic stories of love, is patterned and graceful, but its very patterning makes those tragic tales seem remote. The passage thus creates a comic exorcism of the tragic side of love,

recalling the technique of *A Midsummer Night's Dream* (in fact one
of the tales is that of Pyramus and Thisbe). Then, using the same
patterned dialogue (and burlesquing it in the process) they descend
from these high, remote tales of sorrow and infidelity to a joking
accusation of infidelity here and now:

LORENZO:　　　　　　　In such a night
　　　　　　　Did Jessica steal from the wealthy Jew,
　　　　　　　And with an unthrift love did run from Venice,
　　　　　　　As far as Belmont.
　JESSICA:　　　　　　In such a night
　　　　　　　Did young Lorenzo swear he lov'd her well,
　　　　　　　Stealing her soul, with many vows of faith,
　　　　　　　And ne'er a true one.
LORENZO:　　　　　　　In such a night
　　　　　　　Did pretty Jessica, like a little shrew,
　　　　　　　Slander her love, and he forgave it her.
　JESSICA:　I would out-night you, did no body come;
　　　　　　　But, hark, I hear the footing of a man.

　　　　　　　　　　　　　　　　　(v. i. 14–24)

The pattern is mocked, and then broken. As in the depiction of
Portia's three suitors, we descend from the remote and exotic to
the immediate and human – though here the descent is not so
much reassuring as sharply comic. There can be a sadness, too, in
this descent: Lorenzo's next meditation, on the music of the
spheres, is less stylized, more earnest in tone and admits the imperfections of the here and now with deeper regret:

　Such harmony is in immortal souls,
　But whilst this muddy vesture of decay
　Doth grossly close it in, we cannot hear it.

　　　　　　　　　　　　　　　　　(v. i. 63–5)

When comedy measures itself against the world of tragedy it can
mock it easily enough, for its own vision is essentially different.
But beyond tragedy is the vision of permanent, immutable harmony – a vision that is closer to comedy's own concerns; and here
there is a deeper sadness in measuring the distance between two

imperfect human lovers and the principle of love that orders the universe.

That is as much as Lorenzo and Jessica can give us; but they have seen in Portia a vision of perfection in human terms. And when Portia herself enters the argument is taken one step further:

PORTIA: That light we see is burning in my hall.
           How far that little candle throws his beams!
           So shines a good deed in a naughty world.
NERISSA: When the moon shone, we did not see the candle.
PORTIA: So doth the greater glory dim the less:
           A substitute shines brightly as a king
           Until a king be by, and then his state
           Empties itself, as doth an inland brook
           Into the main of waters. Music! hark!
NERISSA: It is your music, madam, of the house.
PORTIA: Nothing is good, I see, without respect;
           Methinks it sounds much sweeter than by day.
NERISSA: Silence bestows that virtue on it, madam.
PORTIA: The crow doth sing as sweetly as the lark
           When neither is attended; and I think
           The nightingale, if she should sing by day,
           When every goose is cackling, would be thought
           No better a musician than the wren.
           How many things by season season'd are
           To their right praise and true perfection!
                                        (v. i. 89–108)

The importance of context, so vital a part of Shakespeare's comic technique, is here argued explicitly by one of his characters. Context can be used in a variety of ways; but here Portia's argument is that placing too great a beauty against a lesser one, measuring ourselves against standards that are too high, is unjustly belittling, and may blind us to the real beauty of the lesser light. If we concentrate on each experience for its merits, we may find beauty even from the most unlikely sources. (The merry owl of *Love's Labour's Lost* was mildly surprising; here we are asked to think of a sweetly-singing crow!) The argument is confirmed by the atmosphere of the scene as a whole, in which constant references to the beauty of the night and the charm of the music combine to create an image of the harmony that can be achieved even in the fallen world.

This passage, with its hard-won but steady idealism, is still generalized; indeed we may feel that it achieves its confidence only by keeping off the problems of the characters themselves; and the more boisterous, bawdy fun of the ring sequence may seem like a descent to crude realities, away from the vision of harmony. But the ideal is not totally disembodied. It is centred on Portia, the figure of the greatest range and authority in the play: the candle shines from her house; it is her music that sounds. And I suspect that in the ring sequence Portia is applying her attitude of acceptance to the most difficult unresolved dilemma remaining in the play – the conflicting loyalties of Bassanio. The ring embodies those conflicting loyalties: it is Portia's wedding ring, given away at Antonio's insistence, as a sign that his gratitude for his friend's safety outweighs his wife's command:

> My Lord Bassanio, let him have the ring.
> Let his deservings, and my love withal,
> Be valued 'gainst your wife's commandment.
>
> (IV. i. 444–6)

The conflicting demands on Bassanio have been at the bottom of the most striking moments of dislocation in the play, when Salerio brought Antonio's letter to Belmont, and when Portia and Nerissa spoke up for themselves as wives, at the crisis of the trial scene. The whole idea of obligation has been a painful one, conveyed in images of bodily torture:

> Here is a letter, lady,
> The paper as the body of my friend,
> And every word in it a gaping wound
> Issuing life-blood.
>
> (III. ii. 265–8)

The image is rooted in Antonio's grisly debt to Shylock, incurred in serving Bassanio – who wishes at one point that he could repay the debt in similar terms: 'The Jew shall have my flesh, blood,

bones and all, / Ere thou shalt lose for me one drop of blood'
(IV. i. 112–13). The same imagery is used when Portia lectures
Gratiano for having given away his ring, which, she says, was
'riveted with faith unto your flesh' (v. i. 169). Bassanio, not liking
the turn of the conversation, exclaims aside 'Why, I were best to
cut my left hand off, / And swear I lost the ring defending it' (v. i.
177–8). But here the tone is lighter; and throughout the final
scene we are made to see the comic side of Bassanio's dilemma.
The dialogue is patterned and repetitive, Gratiano and Nerissa
add their usual comic symmetry, and when the women claim to
have slept with the youths who had the rings, the laughter becomes broad and earthy. As we saw in the trial scene, there was
always a comic potential in the conflicting demands on Bassanio,
and when he is finally made to face that conflict, a comic idiom is
used. There are one or two hints of serious feeling, as in Bassanio's
pained recollection, 'I was beset with shame and courtesy' (v. i.
217), but for the most part the technique is that of the lovers'
quarrel in *A Midsummer Night's Dream*, keeping us at a distance
from the pain of the dilemma by emphasizing the neatness of its
pattern.[17]

We know, too, that Bassanio's dilemma, so far as it is represented by the giving of the ring, is more apparent than real. He
gave Portia's ring to Portia, and the revelation of this provides a
neat comic resolution. Without wishing to be too solemn about it,
one may suggest that the solution to the comic problem points to
a way of resolving the deeper emotional dilemma: there is no
final contradiction between Bassanio's ties with Portia and his ties
with Antonio. It is the capacity to love that matters, and love can
extend itself beyond a single person. This was suggested earlier in
the play, when Portia saw her obligation to Antonio (whom she
had never seen) as an extension of her love for Bassanio. Being
close friends, she argued, the two men must be similar:

[17] In Terry Hands's production for the Royal Shakespeare Company in 1971,
an attempt was made to present the ring sequence as a serious emotional
dilemma (for example, when Bassanio parted with the ring, Portia burst into
tears). But all through the last scene, there was a distinct feeling that the actors
were fighting the natural rhythm of the dialogue, and I think the experiment,
interesting though it was, demonstrated that the normal comic reading, which
usually works so well, is in fact the right one.

> Which makes me think that this Antonio,
> Being the bosom lover of my lord,
> Must needs be like my lord. If it be so,
> How little is the cost I have bestowed
> In purchasing the semblance of my soul
> From out the state of hellish cruelty!
>
> (III. iv. 16–21)

In the final scene, it is Antonio who gives the ring back to Bassanio, suggesting, emblematically, that he has a share in their happiness.[18] In this way, a personal, emotional dilemma is transformed into a comic plot design, lightened and conventionalized; and in the process its pain is dissipated and it becomes an occasion for happiness. Portia's general idea of seeking happiness in the here and now, even in the most unlikely places, is here applied in practice.

But we are also aware, I think, that happiness can be drawn out of such a situation only if its implications are carefully limited. Antonio's quiet manner in the final scene – 'I am th'unhappy subject of these quarrels' (v. i. 238) – does not suggest a joyful acceptance of his role in the emblematic pattern of harmony. The sexual joking of Gratiano's final speech narrows the implications of love to the two pairs of lovers going off to bed, and Antonio can have no part in this. The restoration of his galleys is an event so mysterious and remote that it carries no emotional weight to match the very real anxiety of his earlier losses:

> PORTIA: . . . Unseal this letter soon;
> There you shall find three of your argosies
> Are richly come to harbour suddenly.
> You shall not know by what strange accident
> I chanced on this letter.
> ANTONIO: I am dumb.
>
> (v. i. 275–9)

---

[18] See Hyman, 'The rival lovers', p. 113. At the end of Sonnet XLII a similar solution is proposed to the love triangle: 'But here's the joy: my friend and I are one; / Sweet flattery! then she loves but me alone.' But here the solution is presented with obvious irony, as a rhetorical trick that carries no real consolation.

There is no direct statement that Antonio is still unhappy, though an actor can suggest this.[19] But the stage is dominated by four lovers (six, if we count Lorenzo and Jessica), and he is the odd man out. Moreover, the satisfactions he is given are so conventionalized that we cannot be sure how much weight they carry in personal terms – very little, if we are to judge by his reticent manner: the character seems a little detached from the conventional pattern in which he is placed. As in *A Midsummer Night's Dream*, the harmony of the comic ending must be achieved by selection; Portia's speeches about finding beauty by shutting out distractions have suggested as much. But while in the other play we were only *told* what had been left out, here we are shown. The play includes many characters – notably Shylock – who have no part in the final scene. Antonio is on stage, but his involvement is limited and his share in the lovers' harmony is dubious. And the comic stylization of the ring sequence, though it functions effectively on its own terms, involves a narrowing of the play's stylistic and emotional range. In short, the play has shown a larger world than it can finally bring into harmony. This sense of instability is reflected in the dramatic idiom. The play's ultimate gamble, I have suggested, is to combine conventionalized action with human reality, naturalistically conceived. This combination produces shifting, unpredictable results, from the trust in convention in the casket scenes to the distaste of the trial scene, in which the conventionalized action suggests an unhealthy narrowing of vision. In the end Shakespeare pulls back from some of the new territory he has explored: the ring sequence, with its patterned teams of lovers, recalls *Love's Labour's Lost* and *A Midsummer Night's Dream* in its comically stylized presentation of the games of romantic love. It presents, in a now familiar way, an image of order coming from apparent disorder: it is a standard comic ending. But such an ending is itself a convention, and in *The Merchant of Venice* that convention, for all its power, is allowed only a limited success in bringing order out of an intractable world. The security the lovers attain is, like the candle that shines from Portia's house,

[19] Tyrone Guthrie's production at Stratford, Ontario in 1955 ended with Antonio alone on stage, still holding the letter with the news of his galleys. As the lights faded, he let the paper fall.

'a good deed in a naughty world', an area of private happiness for those who can achieve it. The gamble of wedding complex characters to formalized action is exciting, but the combination is too volatile to allow more than a limited sense of harmony at the end.

7 Much Ado About Nothing

After the explosive and not fully controlled extension of the range of Shakespearian comedy in *The Merchant of Venice*, *Much Ado About Nothing* suggests a temporary retrenchment. It appears to return to the more modest experiment of *The Taming of the Shrew*, in which different dramatic idioms were played off against each other in the two main plots, with correspondingly different types of characterization – the Bianca plot, with its romantic and conventional intrigue, and the Petruchio plot, lively and unorthodox, dominated by the exploration of character, and mocking the deficiencies of romantic convention. A similar pattern is suggested by the two main plots of *Much Ado*: the Claudio plot is a conventional story, and Shakespeare's version is only one of many. Beatrice and Benedick, on the other hand, are freewheeling, invented characters, whose unorthodox love affair – 'Thou and I are too wise to woo peaceably' (v. ii. 63) – is generally regarded as presenting both a better kind of courtship and a more convincing kind of drama than the stiff orthodoxies of the Claudio–Hero plot. But by now Shakespeare has behind him the experiment of *The Merchant of Venice*, with its more complicated interplay of convention and human reality, and while it is natural that he should now be interested in achieving a tighter control and a more secure harmony, it seems unlikely that he would do this merely by returning to the simple oppositions of the earlier play, effective though they were. To retain some (if not all) of the range and fluidity of

The Merchant of Venice, while at the same time producing something like the harmony of disparate elements that distinguished *A Midsummer Night's Dream* – this, I think, is the experiment of *Much Ado About Nothing*. It has had a more tentative critical reception than some of its fellows, but a good production – and there have been many – creates both an emotional engagement with the characters and a feeling of communal delight at the end. The play can be argued into unity by thematic analysis (usually on deception and self-deception, appearance and reality) but the trick is really done, I believe, in a more directly theatrical way, by an interplay of formality and naturalism.

The opening scenes are relaxed and naturalistic. We watch a bustling stage community going about its business, unwinding after a war. As a community, it has certain forms and ceremonies, but these arise out of a realistic context. There is music and dancing, but they have to be prepared for:

LEONATO: How now, brother! Where is my cousin, your son?
            Hath he provided this music?
ANTONIO: He is very busy about it.

(I. ii. 1–3)

One cannot simply say 'Let music sound' for the air to be filled with harmony. There is a dance, with masks, in which four disguised couples confront each other, toy with mistaken identity and engage in witty repartee (II. i. 73–135). But the result is as far as it could be from the manner of the corresponding scene in *Love's Labour's Lost*: the dialogue (as in most of the early scenes) is in chatty prose, and whereas in the earlier play the couples could exchange lines and it would make little difference, here each encounter is individualized: Don Pedro and Hero are engaging in the opening movement of a courtship, and their exchange builds to the one passage of verse in the sequence, a rhymed couplet ending 'Speak low, if you speak love' (II. i. 85). Balthasar and Margaret engage in a light mock flirtation; Ursula and Antonio base their exchange on the old man's comically unsuccessful attempt to conceal his identity; and, after the inconsequential teasing of these two couples, we have the more pointed and aggressive mutual attack of Beatrice and Benedick. Mistaken identity is only

a pretence, and not just in Antonio's case: while the ladies of
France may totally conceal themselves by changing favours and
donning masks, in the more realistic idiom of this scene a mere
mask is no more effective a disguise than it usually is in real life.[1]

But even in the same scenes there are suggestions of a different
kind of formality as the Claudio–Hero plot gets under way – not
formal actions created by the characters themselves, but a formal
dramatic idiom created by the playwright, within which the
characters move. Claudio's romantic contemplation of Hero is
played off against Benedick's sardonic remarks, creating the now
familiar opposition of romantic lover and realistic commentator.
Discussing Hero, Claudio and Don Pedro slip into patterned,
formal prose, whose rhythm is parodied and then broken by
Benedick, thereby creating – as in *Love's Labour's Lost* – a larger
formal design from the opposition of voices:

> CLAUDIO: That I love her, I feel.
> DON PEDRO: That she is worthy, I know.
> BENEDICK: That I neither feel how she should be loved, nor
> know how she should be worthy, is the opinion
> that fire cannot melt out of me; I will die in it at
> the stake.

(I. i. 197–201)

Claudio is particularly given to formal expression, surrendering to
the conventions of courtship and romantic love, and taking them
as natural. Presented with Hero as his intended bride, he declares

---

[1] While Don Pedro originally intended to pretend he was Claudio, Hero has
been led to expect advances from the Prince (II. i. 56–7), and his broad hint,
'within the house is Jove' (II. i. 82), suggests his real identity. In their opening
exchange, it is clear that Benedick has recognized Beatrice, and she makes no
attempt to conceal her identity (II. i. 108–14). The directness of her counter-
attack leaves, I think, little doubt that she recognizes Benedick. Whether he
realizes he has been recognized is more difficult to judge: talking to Don Pedro
later, he claims Beatrice did not recognize him when she insulted him (II. i. 216);
but this may be an attempt to save face, implying that she would not dare to
attack him so directly if she knew who he was. In soliloquy, he exclaims, 'But
that my Lady Beatrice should know me, and not know me!' (II. i. 180–1); this
could mean either that she claimed a knowledge of his character, yet did not
recognize him; or (and I think this is more likely) that she knew his identity but
was mistaken in his character. She attributes his own harsh words to 'the gentleman that danc'd with her' (II. i. 211–12), but she too may be trying to save face.

'Silence is the perfectest herald of joy: I were but little happy if I could say how much. Lady, as you are mine, I am yours; I give away myself for you, and dote upon the exchange' (II. i. 275–8). Claudio is inside the convention, and this polished, formal speech, with its orthodox idea of surrender in love, is for him an expression of genuine feeling. Taken out of context, it is an attractive speech, at once modest and generous, with a nice balance of feeling and decorum. But its context is Beatrice's line preceding it – 'Speak, Count, 'tis your cue.' This makes the rightness of Claudio's speech look disconcertingly like the rightness of a wind-up toy. Beatrice is outside the convention, and her perspective provides a comically dislocating effect.

The brief passage of confusion in which Don Pedro woos Hero on Claudio's behalf, while the latter is tricked into believing the prince is wooing for himself, is also a conventionalized action, presenting as it does the sort of swift and total deception on which comedy traditionally depends. It is introduced in a formal way: at the end of the dialogue between the masquers the couples go out dancing, and Don John begins to sow mischief – this juxtaposition is in itself a conventional theatrical effect. He pretends he thinks the masked Claudio is Benedick, and asks him to dissuade Don Pedro from his love for Hero. Claudio is taken in. The passage is a sinister variation on the identity games played so lightly by the other characters moments before. Though the point is not followed up, Don Pedro's original plan also involved deception, for he intended to impersonate Claudio (I. i. 283–4). The episode as a whole never comes properly into focus, perhaps because the crucial interview between Don Pedro and Hero takes place offstage; but it seems intended to establish the possibility of a conventional comic deception, even in this realistically conceived world. And it establishes, too, that Claudio is the sort of character who can be taken in by such a deception. Like Proteus he is literary and sententious, and his mind slips easily into patterns. Don Pedro rebukes him for this: 'Thou wilt be like a lover presently, / And tire the hearer with a book of words' (I. i. 268–9). This makes him susceptible to Don John, whose accusation releases in Claudio's mind a collection of literary commonplaces. As Proteus talks himself into deceiving his friend by steadying his mind with sentencious clichés, so Claudio talks himself into abandoning Hero:

'Tis certain so: the Prince woos for himself.
Friendship is constant in all other things
Save in the office and affairs of love;
Therefore all hearts in love use their own tongues.
Let every eye negotiate for itself,
And trust no agent; for beauty is a witch
Against whose charms faith melteth into blood.
This is an accident of hourly proof,
Which I mistrusted not. Farewell, therefore, Hero.

(II. i. 153–61)

Throughout the courtship, misunderstandings and all, Hero herself has hardly anything to say: she is essentially a figure in the pattern, whose chief dramatic function is to stand there and look beautiful. Claudio is characterized, but in a special way: he is at once a figure in a conventional action, and a character with a conventional mind. In moments of relaxation, he engages in casual banter with the others; but in moments of crisis, he thinks and speaks in a formal, sentencious way.

The mixture of dramatic idiom here is potentially as volatile as in *The Merchant of Venice*: out of a naturalistically conceived dramatic world, a courtship develops which follows literary form and therefore seems to change the idiom; but (unlike the courtship of Bianca and Lucentio) it also follows social form, and is therefore compatible with realism. In most romantic comedies parents and friends are not so closely involved, or so sympathetic to young lovers, as they are here; in this respect the courtship reflects Elizabethan realities. And while Claudio's chief interest in Hero is clearly romantic, he can also ask 'Hath Leonato any son, my lord?' (I. i. 256), thus establishing the financial realities of the match.[2] Indeed we may feel that the change to a more

[2] This speech is, however, a touch in passing, a tactful way of introducing the subject of love. Charles T. Prouty describes the Claudio–Hero match as primarily a marriage of convenience, in *The Sources of Much Ado About Nothing* (New Haven, 1950), pp. 43–50; but while that aspect is certainly not forgotten, I think the primary emphasis is on the romantic side. Richard Henze, after reviewing the debate on the nature of the match, sensibly concludes that

conventionalized dramatic idiom is made decisive not by the courtship, but by the deception that threatens to impede it. This is borne out, I think, in the characterization of Don John. While the other characters (even his henchmen, Conrade and Borachio) can relax, he is constantly stiff and formal: he speaks the most heavily patterned prose of the early scenes, recalling at times the rhythms of Lyly. He says to Conrade,

> I wonder that thou, being, as thou say'st thou art, born under Saturn, goest about to apply a moral medicine to a mortifying mischief. I cannot hide what I am; I must be sad when I have cause, and smile at no man's jests; eat when I have stomach, and wait for no man's leisure; sleep when I am drowsy, and tend on no man's business; laugh when I am merry, and claw no man in his humour.
>
> (I. iii. 9–15)

His belief in astrology is interesting: it sets him apart from such freethinking malcontents as Cassius and Edmund. His own character seems arbitrarily determined, even to the point of comic predictability:

BORACHIO: ...I can give you intelligence of an intended marriage.
DON JOHN: Will it serve for any model to build mischief on?

(I. iii. 37–40)

On his way to supper, he mutters 'would the cook were o' my mind!' (I. iii. 62). Where Shylock has specific injuries, and specific plans for revenging them, Don John offers only a generalized and conventional villainy. The suggestions of a quarrel with his brother are never concrete enough to give him a convincing motive for his actions. Shylock's villainy can be understood through its roots in a fully conceived world of business competition and racial tension; Don John's villainy can be understood only in terms of his role in the plot. Claudio is about to get married, and therefore 'Any bar, any cross, any impediment, will be med'cin-

---

'Claudio and Hero have both an arranged marriage and a romantic attachment – the one does not preclude the other'. See 'Deception in *Much Ado About Nothing*', *Studies in English Literature 1500–1900*, XI (spring 1971), p. 192.

able to me. I am sick in displeasure to him; and whatever comes athwart his affection ranges evenly with mine' (II. ii. 4–7). He has, one might say, no *personal* feelings about Claudio and Hero: his villainy is an impersonal force, which identifies in their marriage another impersonal force – happiness – to which it is naturally antagonistic, and which it automatically seeks to destroy. It is not so much a personal as a chemical reaction. (We may contrast this with, for example, Bandello's version of the story, where the slanderer wants the lady for himself.)[3]

Don John affects the play's world in a very special way. Deceiving not only Claudio but Don Pedro as well, he produces a decisive shift to a simplified, arbitrary dramatic idiom:

CLAUDIO: If I see anything to-night why I should not marry her, to-morrow in the congregation where I should wed, there will I shame her.

DON PEDRO: And, as I woo'd for thee to obtain her, I will join with thee to disgrace her.

(III. ii. 110–14)

The style is stiffly patterned, and the expressions of intent are not only arbitrary, but pat and perfunctory. Claudio and Don Pedro are now moving as Don John moves, simply as figures in a story, engaged in conventional roles. They have been drawn away from the relaxed naturalism of the earlier scenes; this is not, as we have seen, much of a change for Claudio, but it is rather startling to find Don Pedro succumbing, neatly balancing his former role as a go-between against his new determination to lend his authority to Hero's rejection. In earlier versions of the story the deception of the groom was more carefully worked out than this: in *Orlando Furioso* the groom is at first sceptical of the slander, and the trick by which he is deceived is described at great length;[4] in *The Faerie Queene* the slanderer is an old and trusted friend.[5] In both cases, the effect is to soften the impact of the groom's decision to reject his bride, and to rationalize his behaviour. But Shakespeare gives

[3] See Geoffrey Bullough, *Narrative and Dramatic Sources of Shakespeare*, II (London, 1959), p. 114.
[4] Ibid., pp. 91–2.
[5] Book II, Canto IV, stanzas xvi–xxxviii.

us only the decision, stark and uncompromising: he does not even bother to show (as he could have done) the trick by which Claudio's senses are deceived. There are no explanations: Shakespeare gives us, in Claudio's decision to reject Hero, only the hard outline of a conventional story.

The rejection itself is also formal and conventionalized. The church scene is, like the trial scene in *The Merchant of Venice*, a big theatrical set piece, broad and striking in its effect. And, like that other scene, it is preceded by more relaxed and naturalistic passages that throw its formality into relief. The most curious of these is Conrade's interview with Borachio, just before they are arrested by the watch. Here Borachio takes us as it were backstage, to show us the grubby inner workings of the plot:

BORACHIO: Therefore know I have earned of Don John a thousand ducats.

CONRADE: Is it possible that any villainy should be so dear?

BORACHIO: Thou shouldest rather ask if it were possible any villainy should be so rich; for when rich villains have need of poor ones, poor ones may make what price they will.

(III. iii. 100–5)

Behind the grand confrontation of the church scene, with its talk of beauty stained and honour lost, is a piece of shabby knavery, done in the dark for money. Borachio's cynical generalizations about rich villains and poor ones remind us that even villainy goes by the laws of the market: for all his posturing and self-dramatization, there is nothing special about Don John. Though the point is less clear, the same might be said of the change in Claudio's feelings:

Seest thou not, I say, what a deformed thief this fashion is, how giddily a' turns about all the hot bloods between fourteen and five and thirty, sometimes fashioning them like Pharoah's soldiers in the reechy painting, sometime like the god Bel's priests in the old church-window, sometime like the shaven Hercules in the smirch'd worm-eaten tapestry, where his codpiece seems as massy as his club?

(III. iii. 120–6)

Conrade complains, we may think with reason, that this has nothing to do with the story Borachio is telling; Borachio denies this, but they are arrested before he can make the point clear (III. iii. 129–32). If the talk of fashion has a point at all, it may be to connect Claudio's unstable affections with a cynical insight into the giddiness of 'all the hot bloods between fourteen and five and thirty'. The change in his feelings, so painful to himself and Hero, is for Borachio nothing more than the way of the world.

Like Lancelot Gobbo's complaint that 'This making of Christians will raise the price of hogs', this odd little scene provides a sardonic perspective on the main action, showing it through the eyes of a minor character. Claudio's denunciation of his bride is also preceded by a scene with Hero herself, providing a different but equally unsettling perspective. Once again we are backstage, as the women bustle about, preparing for the wedding and chatting about Hero's wedding dress:

MARGARET: Troth, I think your other rabato were better.
HERO: No, pray thee, good Meg, I'll wear this.
MARGARET: By my troth's not so good; and I warrant your cousin will say so.
HERO: My cousin's a fool, and thou art another; I'll wear none but this.

(III. iv. 6–11)

There is obvious irony over the scene, particularly in Margaret's bawdy jokes about the wedding night (III. iv. 22–4) which she herself, unwittingly, has just helped to postpone (the talk of fashion may also remind us, if we are quick enough, of the immediately preceding scene with Borachio). But its main point, I think, is its naturalism – including the nervous irritation of Hero, unlike her normal behaviour but quite believable in a bride on her wedding morning, with everyone fussing about her. It re-establishes the easy, natural idiom of the earlier scenes. And this idiom is maintained in the opening of the wedding itself, with Leonato telling the Friar to cut out the formalities and get on with it, and interrupting the ceremony with chatty jokes. When Claudio finally bursts out with his accusation, the effect is not what we might expect, and what we sometimes get in productions – an

elaborate formal ceremony broken up by a spontaneous outburst
of feeling. It is, rather, a natural, easy family affair that everyone
was taking for granted, suddenly and embarrassingly turned into
a melodrama.

Claudio's outburst begins with a riddling exchange with the
bride's father:

CLAUDIO: Stand thee by, friar. Father, by your leave:
            Will you with free and unconstrained soul
            Give me this maid, your daughter?
LEONATO: As freely, son, as God did give her me.
CLAUDIO: And what have I to give you back whose worth
            May counterpoise this rich and precious gift?
DON PEDRO: Nothing, unless you render her again.
CLAUDIO: Sweet Prince, you learn me noble thankfulness.
            There, Leonato, take her back again;
            Give not this rotten orange to your friend;
            She's but the sign and semblance of her honour.
                                                (IV. i. 22–32)

Hero, from being an object of love, becomes an object of clever
rhetorical exercises.[6] Claudio plays on her name: 'O Hero, what
a Hero hadst thou been . . .' (IV. i. 99). He plays also on the contrast (as he sees it) between appearance and reality in her nature:
'But fare thee well, most foul, most fair! Farewell, / Thou pure
impiety and impious purity!' (IV. i. 102–3). The patterning here
becomes painfully artificial, and when Claudio exclaims, 'Out on
thee! Seeming! I will write against it' (IV. i. 55), we may feel that
he has already moved away from natural speech into a rhetorical
exercise in denunciation, based on a set subject. The character's
feelings, it should be emphasized, are real enough to him: in
Elizabethan drama passion is none the less passionate for being
rhetorically expressed. But for the audience, a full emotional
engagement is difficult. After the previous scenes, with their
naturalistic glimpses into the backstage life of the story, Claudio's

---

[6] According to William B. McCollom, 'The role of wit in *Much Ado About
Nothing*', *Shakespeare Quarterly*, XIX (spring 1968), in the church scene 'Claudio's
speeches rely more and more on the verbal tricks recorded in the rhetorical
texts of the time' (p. 167).

speeches – and with them the whole dramatic range of the scene – are sharply limited in effect: the climax is formal and conventional, presenting a generalized image of innocence slandered and love betrayed.

Our engagement with Claudio and Hero as individuals is further restrained by the manner in which our attention is kept off the slandered bride. Her speeches are few and brief, and her main reaction is to faint – a simple theatrical image of grief. Instead of a sustained self-defence by the heroine, Claudio's outburst provokes a variety of reactions from various corners of the stage:

LEONATO: Sweet Prince, why speak not you?
DON PEDRO: What should I speak?
                I stand dishonour'd, that have gone about
                To link my dear friend to a common stale.
LEONATO: Are these things spoken, or do I but dream?
DON JOHN: Sir, they are spoken, and these things are true.
BENEDICK: This looks not like a nuptial.
HERO: True! O God!

                                      (IV. i. 62–7)

Hero's reaction is only one of many; and the most sustained expression of shock comes not from her, but from Leonato, who seems mostly concerned with his own grief. Our attention is thus transferred to a secondary figure, in whom we are naturally less interested than we would be in Hero, but whose feelings are fully dramatized in a way that hers are not. Hero's function, once again, is as a figure in a narrative design. Her role is to wait patiently – even to disappear – until the narrative itself takes its course, and proves her innocent. There is no deep exploration of her own feelings while all this is happening. Furthermore, the scene with Leonato and Dogberry just before the broken wedding reminds us that, even as Hero is rejected, the plot is ticking away in the background, and this knowledge keeps us at some distance from the emotions of the church scene, assuring us that all will be well. This reassurance is greater than in the trial scene of *The Merchant of Venice*, for there, while we may expect Shylock's defeat, we cannot, at the beginning of the scene, see how the trick will be done. In *Much Ado* we know how it will be done, and we know it is only a matter of time; as a result, the comic tone of the play is less deeply threatened.

The Claudio plot could have been resolved in many ways; and Shakespeare's choice of so unlikely an angel of salvation as Dogberry needs to be examined. Much has been made of Dogberry's 'mistaking words'; but the primary source of comedy in the first watch scene is, I think, his peculiar conception of law enforcement. His advice concerning the drunk and disorderly is, 'Why, then, let them alone till they are sober' (III. iii. 42). More serious offences are dealt with in a similar way: 'the most peaceable way for you, if you do take a thief, is to let him show himself what he is, and steal out of your company' (III. iii. 53–5). It would be best, in fact, if they did not arrest anyone, 'for, indeed, the watch ought to offend no man, and it is an offence to stay a man against his will' (III. iii. 74–5). The First Watchman sums up their duties: 'Well, masters, we hear our charge; let us go sit here upon the church bench till two, and then all to bed' (III. iii. 81–3). It is appropriate that Dogberry and the watch should be Don John's nemesis, for they suggest a comically opposing set of values. Where he will go out of his way to cause mischief, even to those who have done him no harm, the watch will go out of their way to be inoffensive, no matter how they are provoked. But the most important aspect of their role, I think, is their utter detachment from the issues and feelings – even from the facts – of the plot they accidentally unravel. Shakespeare is at pains to see that Don John's mischief is undone not by a change of heart in the erring characters, or by the intelligent intervention of Hero's friends, but by the impersonal workings of the plot, the machinery of accident and coincidence unintentionally set in motion by the clowns.

Shakespeare emphasizes this by showing the futility of attempts at intervention by characters close to Hero. In the church scene itself Beatrice and Benedick, more practical than the others, try to establish the facts: it is Beatrice who first suggests the obvious, 'O, on my soul, my cousin is belied!' (IV. i. 146), and this leads Benedick to try first (and unsuccessfully) to establish an alibi (IV. i. 147), and then, more shrewdly, to identify Don John as the culprit (IV. i. 188–9). But none of this can prove Hero's innocence. The Friar has a theory:

When he shall hear she died upon his words,
Th'idea of her life shall sweetly creep
Into his study of imagination,
And every lovely organ of her life
Shall come apparell'd in more precious habit,
More moving, delicate, and full of life,
Into the eye and prospect of his soul,
Than when she liv'd indeed.   (IV. i. 223–30)

This indeed helps to change the lover's mind in Bandello's version of the story;[7] but the news of Hero's death has no visible effect on Claudio. Nor are he and Don Pedro much moved by Leonato's challenge; and that challenge, in any case, hovers between pathos and comic futility, tilting towards the latter with Antonio's blustering intervention, 'He shall kill two of us, and men indeed; / But that's no matter; let him kill one first' (v. i. 80–1). The scene would be more simply affecting if it involved one old man instead of two. Benedick's challenge is more serious and impressive, but even that has no real effect in terms of the romantic plot; its main function is within its own plot. The agent of salvation must, in the end, be Dogberry; and Dogberry's intervention is, in its own way, as impersonal as Don John's. Questioning Conrade and Borachio, he pursues a generalized idea of villainy: 'Masters, it is proved already that you are little better than false knaves, and it will go near to be thought so shortly' (IV. ii. 19–21). He has no notion of what their crime is: casting about for accusations, he lights first on 'perjury', then on 'burglary' (IV. ii. 37–46); his most specific idea is that they have slandered Don John. But the real offence, the one that rouses in him the full wrathful majesty of the law, is that of calling him an ass (IV. ii. 69–80). He pursues that crime right to the end, and in his final scene, while the plot is unravelled, with Claudio and Don Pedro repentant and Leonato contriving the reunion of the lovers, Dogberry takes no notice of the other characters' feelings, still brooding on the fact that he has been called an ass (v. i. 238–40, 290–3).

Yet, as Borachio declares, 'What your wisdoms could not discover, these shallow fools have brought to light' (v. i. 220–1). The

[7] See Bullough, *Narrative and Dramatic Sources*, pp. 122–3.

Claudio–Hero plot is unravelled accidentally, by a character who is not concerned with it (he has, we should notice, no part in the final scene) and does not even understand what he is doing. The solution is therefore a matter of plot design, with no psychological or moral overtones. Claudio's change of heart is produced, not by the news of Hero's death, or by the rebukes of Leonato and Benedick, but by the discovery that his bride was innocent after all – in other words, by setting the machinery of the action into reverse. His repentance is simple and direct: 'Sweet Hero, now thy image doth appear / In the rare semblance that I lov'd it first' (v. i. 237–8). It is also, we should notice, conventionalized – a matter of form and image, just as his renunciation was. His acceptance of Leonato's offer of a new wife is also simple and direct, and equally conventionalized. It is a formal gesture of reconciliation – and, behind that, a formal restoration of what he has lost. He accepts his new bride so readily, not because he is a cad, but because he is a character in a conventionalized action.

We may feel, however, that this conventionalized action has forced him into making a series of gestures we would find unpleasant if they occurred in real life.[8] We may feel, in fact, that the whole treatment of the Claudio–Hero plot presents the same unhealthy narrowing of feeling and motive we observed in the trial scene of *The Merchant of Venice*; that, set beside the psychological reality of Beatrice and Benedick, the conventionalized story of Claudio and Hero, with its simple pattern of courtship, betrayal and restoration, is not merely artificial, but distastefully so. It is frequently suggested that the reality of the subplot in some way 'shows up' the melodrama of the main plot.[9] This, I think, is true

[8] Critics have often reacted to Claudio in this way, either attacking or exonerating him for his behaviour, and often producing strangely contradictory readings of the church scene. According to John Russell Brown, *Shakespeare and his Comedies* (2nd edition, revised: London, 1968), in that scene Claudio 'can scarcely bring himself to say the necessary words' (p. 115). On the other hand, we are told by Bertrand Evans, in *Shakespeare's Comedies* (London, 1967), that Claudio's attack on Hero 'has an exuberance that borders on sadism' (p. 81). Evans sums up a sustained attack on Claudio (pp. 80–6) by calling him a 'sadistic prig' (p. 92).

[9] See, for example, E. K. Chambers, *Shakespeare: a Survey* (Harmondsworth, 1964), p. 106; and Kenneth Muir and Sean O'Loughlin, *The Voyage to Illyria* (London, 1937), p. 117.

up to a point; and Shakespeare has achieved this effect by his usual device of dislocation. If the play were conventional through-out, Claudio's behaviour would not bother us; but such devices as the naturalistic passages before the church scene force us to see Claudio against a wider range of feeling and a more flexible dramatic idiom. Other characters are not so exclusively creatures of the plot as he is – and their reactions, whether it be the indig-nation of Beatrice or the cynical detachment of Borachio, lead us to judge him from a realistic perspective, as someone blind, foolish and cruel. I have already noted that he appears in the earlier scenes not just as a creature of convention, but as a conventional man – and we see in the church scene the dangers of being such a man. As Lucentio and the conventions he followed were mocked together, so Claudio and the conventions he follows are judged together, and found wanting – up to a point.[10]

But only up to a point. When the mechanism of the story is thrown into reverse, an important change takes place in the handling of convention. Instead of being set against an unsym-pathetic background of realism, the Claudio story is allowed to expand its range of reference in a way that strengthens our acceptance of it. In the scene at Hero's tomb, external forms – the music, the ceremony, the mourning poem – are made to carry the weight of Claudio's grief. It is the most formal scene in the play, and if it is well staged (as there is no excuse for it not to be) it may lead us to feel that formal expressions of feeling have their own kind of value. So, too, do arbitrary patterns of action. At the end of the scene, night changes slowly to day as Don Pedro speaks:

> Good morrow, masters; put your torches out;
> The wolves have prey'd; and look, the gentle day,
> Before the wheels of Phoebus, round about
> Dapples the drowsy east with spots of grey.
> Thanks to you all, and leave us. Fare you well.
> CLAUDIO: Good morrow, masters; each his several way.

[10] W. H. Auden, in *The Dyer's Hand* (London, 1963), sums up the dangers of Claudio's dependence on convention: 'He falls into the trap set for him because as yet he is less a lover than a man in love with love. Hero is as yet more an image in his own mind than a real person, and such images are susceptible to every suggestion' (p. 518).

DON PEDRO:　Come, let us home, and put on other weeds;
　　　　　　 And then to Leonato's we will go.
　CLAUDIO:　And Hymen now with luckier issue speed's
　　　　　　 Than this for whom we rend'red up this woe.

　　　　　　　　　　　　　　　　　　　(v. iii. 24–33)

– and we are launched into the final scene. If the story's move
from grief to joy is an arbitrary pattern, so too are the cycles of
nature – and here the two are imaginatively connected. Don
Pedro's speech, like the songs of Winter and Spring in *Love's
Labour's Lost*, is one of those moments when the characters' experiences are connected with the impersonal rhythms of nature. At
crucial moments – such as birth, marriage and death – we surrender our individuality and become part of a pattern, and one of
the functions of conventionalized stories is to remind us of that.

Moreover, if Hero's role as a creature of the action makes her
helpless in the church scene, it gives her a special impressiveness
in the finale. The Friar, urging patience, has predicted 'But on
this travail look for greater birth' (IV. i. 213) and the hint offered
here (so like the Abbess's view of the ending of *The Comedy of
Errors*) is expanded in the final sequence. The unmasking of Hero
– and this time the mask really *does* conceal – is delicately touched
with hints that a miracle of resurrection has taken place:

　　HERO:　And while I liv'd I was your other wife;
　　　　　　　　　　　　　　　　　　[*Unmasking.*
　　　　　　 And when you lov'd you were my other husband.
　CLAUDIO:　Another Hero!
　　HERO:　　　　　　　　Nothing certainer.
　　　　　　 One Hero died defil'd; but I do live,
　　　　　　 And, surely as I live, I am a maid.
DON PEDRO:　The former Hero! Hero that is dead!
　LEONATO:　She died, my lord, but whiles her slander liv'd.

　　　　　　　　　　　　　　　　　　　(v. iv. 60–6)

As in Demetrius's attempt to explain what happened to him in the
forest, there is a delicate balance between natural experience and
miracle. In the end, the formality of the Claudio plot brings its
own kind of satisfaction. In restraining the characters' individuality, reducing our emotional engagement and concentrating in-

stead on the story as a formal pattern, Shakespeare has at first shown us the unattractive side of convention, the unhealthy narrowing of experience into mechanical clichés. But the surrender of individuals to an impersonal pattern of action – in this case, the pattern of regeneration and rebirth – can also show the workings of a benign force beyond individual will. Very often, as Stephen Fender puts it, 'The ending of a comedy seems more perfect than anything the characters could have achieved working on their own.'[11] In lesser comedies this unmerited happiness can seem an empty contrivance; but in *Much Ado* Shakespeare characteristically links it with an undeniable reality – the regenerative power of nature. And – particularly in the theatre, where the basic rhythms of the story work on us more powerfully than they do in the study – the ending not only delights but convinces.

The story of Beatrice and Benedick, however, appears at first to delight and convince us by very different means. The focus of attention is more on character than on formal action, more on personality than on plot. The manner of their scenes is open and natural, and depends for much of its effect on the existence of a subtext (something the Claudio–Hero plot does not have). We can see this most clearly, I think, if we compare one of their exchanges with a set of wit between Berowne and Katharine in *Love's Labour's Lost*:

BEROWNE: Your wit's too hot, it speeds too fast, 'twill tire.
KATHARINE: Not till it leave the rider in the mire.
BEROWNE: What time o' day?
KATHARINE: The hour that fools should ask.
BEROWNE: Now fair befall your mask!
KATHARINE: Fair fall the face it covers!
BEROWNE: And send you many lovers!
KATHARINE: Amen, so you be none.
BEROWNE: Nay, then I will be gone.

(II. i. 119–27)

The exchange is tight, fast and formal. It is essentially a game, in which each player is concerned with returning the other's volleys

[11] *Shakespeare: A Midsummer Night's Dream* (London, 1968), p. 47.

(tennis is the obvious analogy, in view of the simple back-and-forth movement; one imagines the audience's heads moving like those of the spectators at Wimbledon). Each player is concerned to match the idea – and the rhyme – of the other; apart from a simple competitive instinct no feelings are engaged, and Berowne's final shot is also a simple, sporting acknowledgement of defeat. If we compare this with the opening combat between Beatrice and Benedick, we find tight rhymed verse replaced by flexible prose; we find also that beneath the exchange of ideas we can detect a deeper interplay of minds. Benedick strikes a pose, presenting an obvious target and deliberately drawing Beatrice's fire:

BENEDICK: ... But it is certain I am loved of all ladies, only you excepted; and I would I could find it in my heart that I had not a hard heart, for, truly, I love none.

BEATRICE: A dear happiness to women! They would else have been troubled with a pernicious suitor. I thank God and my cold blood, I am of your humour for that: I had rather hear my dog bark at a crow than hear a man swear he loves me.

BENEDICK: God keep your ladyship still in that mind! So some gentleman or other shall 'scape a predestinate scratch'd face.

BEATRICE: Scratching could not make it worse, an 'twere such a face as yours were.

BENEDICK: Well, you are a rare parrot-teacher.

BEATRICE: A bird of my tongue is better than a beast of yours.

BENEDICK: I would my horse had the speed of your tongue, and so good a continuer. But keep your way a' God's name, I have done.

BEATRICE: You always end with a jade's trick, I know you of old.

(I. i. 105–24)

At first, Beatrice is on the attack, with Benedick simply presenting a target. She shows a relaxed, easy superiority, even condescending to ironic agreement with him. But when he suddenly returns her fire, she is thrown off balance, and in her anxiety to fight back her wit coarsens and she becomes simply rude. She is like Dr Johnson: if her pistol misses fire, she knocks you down with the butt end of it. The passage ends with a rapid, almost desperate skirmish, as each one tries to get the last word at whatever cost. This is a game in which the players are so deeply engaged that their instincts are no longer purely sporting ones: beneath the wit we sense two minds at work, each one probing the other's defences, each afraid of losing the other's respect. There is insecurity, even anxiety, beneath the aggressiveness.

Their wit is seen as a special manner consciously adopted, not a natural mode of expression. When they meet in the dance, they attack each other's wit, Benedick accusing Beatrice of having hers 'out of the "Hundred Merry Tales"' (ii. i. 113) and Beatrice describing Benedick as 'the Prince's jester, a very dull fool' (ii. i. 120). The latter attack really hurts, for he complains to the prince about it vehemently and in detail, as though seeking reassurance (ii. i. 213–32). While Claudio and Hero slip naturally into their roles, taking them as normal, Beatrice and Benedick engage in a different kind of role-playing, conscious of their roles and a little anxious about them:

> But that my Lady Beatrice should know me, and not know me! The Prince's fool! Ha! It may be I go under that title because I am merry. Yea, but so I am apt to do myself wrong; I am not so reported; it is the base, though bitter disposition of Beatrice that puts the world into her person, and so gives me out. Well, I'll be revenged as I may.
>
> (ii. i. 180–6)

In particular, Benedick's role as a misogynist is consciously adopted, as we see when Claudio asks his opinion of Hero: 'Do you question me, as an honest man should do, for my simple true judgment; or would you have me speak after my custom, as being a professed tyrant to their sex?' (i. i. 142–5). When Claudio replies that he wants Benedick's 'sober judgment' (i. i. 146) all he gets is a passage of compulsive joking, tricky and evasive. If the effect of Claudio's love is to 'tire the hearer with a book of words' (i. i. 269), we may feel that Beatrice and Benedick (particularly the latter) are also trapped by a convention of behaviour – though in this case it is more naturalistically conceived, a convention they have constructed for themselves as a protective shell to cover feelings of insecurity. Anti-romantic wit is seen, not as a fixed and absolute attitude, but as a temporary pose.

They are, of course, satiric about the conventional behaviour of others. Benedick complains about the way love has reduced Claudio to a series of predictable gestures, and his language to 'so many strange dishes' (II. iii. 19). Beatrice mocks the social convention of the arranged marriage, insisting (like Katherina the shrew) on the importance of the woman's will:

> Yes, faith, it is my cousin's duty to make curtsy, and say 'Father, as it please you.' But yet for all that, cousin, let him be a handsome fellow, or else make another curtsy and say 'Father, as it please me.'
>
> (II. i. 44–7)

Each of them draws up a prescription for the ideal mate, with the clear implication that such an ideal is impossible, and that this is an excuse for avoiding matrimony (II. i. 6–34; II. iii. 23–31). The dedication demanded by the rituals of courtship would be justifiable only if the loved one were utterly perfect – and the loved one never is. In presenting a satiric perspective on the conventional affair of Claudio and Hero, Beatrice and Benedick are of course adopting conventional roles of their own, and taking their place in a larger formal design. Yet while Claudio and Hero are secure in their positions in the larger design, the same cannot be said of Beatrice and Benedick. Their role in the long run is not simply opposition to romantic love: at the end of the dialogue of masked dancers, music sounds for the dance itself, and we hear the following:

BEATRICE: . . . We must follow the leaders.
BENEDICK: In every good thing.
BEATRICE: Nay, if they lead us to any ill, I will leave them at the next turning.

> (II. i. 132–5)

In the play as a whole, Beatrice and Benedick do indeed 'follow the leaders' – the leaders being Claudio and Hero. They do so for their own reasons, and using their own judgement – but they follow all the same. According to David L. Stevenson, 'they are dramatized as testing the antiromantic roles they are actually playing against their sense of what it would be like to be a Hero or a Claudio, to fall into the words and phrases and stances of institutionalized romance.'[12] Attacking the experience of the orthodox lovers, they also display a curiosity about it and, one suspects, a kind of envy for those whose feelings can be so simple.

If the other lovers can be mocked for being predictable, the claim of Beatrice and Benedick to originality is also open to mockery. As in *A Midsummer Night's Dream*, each plot provides a comic perspective on the other. As Claudio and Hero move towards marriage in their way, Beatrice and Benedick do the same in theirs. The subtext is used to suggest their real desire for each other: quite simply, they protest too much about their refusal to marry. In the midst of a tirade against Beatrice, Benedick suddenly cries out, 'I would not marry her' (II. i. 223), to which the appropriate reply would be 'Nobody asked you, sir, she said'. Beatrice's fantasy about leading apes in hell is light and amusing, but we may wonder if it is a little too carefully developed, as though she is trying to cheer herself up (II. i. 33–41). Both of them are prone to Freudian slips, like Beatrice's 'I am sure he is in the fleet; I would he had boarded me' (II. i. 124–5); and Benedick's 'Is it not strange that sheeps' guts should hale souls out of men's bodies? Well, a horn for my money, when all's done' (II. iii. 54–6). The scene in which Claudio and Hero are formally engaged is also the scene where Beatrice's desires are most clearly suggested. She makes a joke of her continuing spinsterhood: 'Thus goes every one to the world but I, and I am sunburnt; I may sit in a corner and cry "Heigh-ho for a husband!"' (II. i. 286–8), and she jokes with Don Pedro about marrying him. We suspect that she is cheering herself up; indeed she comes very close to admitting pain behind the gaiety:

DON PEDRO: ... out o' question, you were born in a merry hour.

---

[12] Introduction to the Signet edition of *Much Ado About Nothing* (New York, 1964), p. xxxvii. It is worth noting that the one scene in which Hero takes a decisive, leading role is the scene in which Beatrice is tricked into love (III. i).

BEATRICE: No, sure, my lord, my mother cried; but there
was a star danc'd, and under that was I born.
Cousins, God give you joy!

(II. i. 299–303)

The ensuing dialogue is at first glance rather odd:

LEONATO: Niece, will you look to those things I told you of?
BEATRICE: I cry you mercy, uncle. By your Grace's pardon.

[*Exit Beatrice.*
(II. i. 304–7)

The motive for the exit seems incredibly vague, unless we assume
that Leonato senses Beatrice's feelings are getting too close to the
surface, and is tactfully giving her a chance to withdraw – a
chance she is glad to take. When she is gone, the others talk of her
gaiety, but now they seem to be talking about it a little too much,
overstressing something they had thought was obvious in order to
cover a growing suspicion that this gaiety may not be all it seems.
Seen against this background, Don Pedro's sudden interjection,
'She were an excellent wife for Benedick' (II. i. 317), takes on
added point. He is not suggesting the match just for the fun of it:
he sees it as filling a need.[13]

Not only do they 'follow the leaders', but the manner in which
they are brought together is in some ways more conventionalized
than the courting of Hero. Apart from the use of a disguised go-
between, that affair reflects the realities of Elizabethan matchmaking. But Beatrice and Benedick are brought together in a
more theatrical way, by a trick. The eavesdropping scenes are an
amusing reversal of the conventional use of such scenes, where (as
in *Love's Labour's Lost* and *Twelfth Night*) the eavesdroppers share
the audience's laughter at the figure in the centre of the stage.
Here the eavesdropper himself is the unwitting butt of laughter.
But the convention, though turned on its head, is no less con-

---

[13] At one point Beatrice talks as though there had been a previous affair between them, and Benedick had played her false (II. i. 248–51). I would not like
to build too much upon this, since such a brief mention of so important a fact
might be a sign of incomplete revision; but if it is to be taken seriously, it could
be seen as one more indication of naturalism in the conception of the characters,
giving them a life outside the action of the play. On the latter point, see David
Lloyd Stevenson, *The Love-Game Comedy* (New York, 1946), pp. 212–13.

ventional for that. Eavesdropping as a technical device is employed with unusual frequency all through the play.[14] And perhaps one reason for this is to play on the very familiarity of the device, to emphasize what a reliable comic trick it is. Claudio – typically – uses stock images to connect the gulling of Benedick with other kinds of sport (as, in *The Taming of the Shrew*, the gulling of Sly is connected with hunting): 'O, ay; stalk on, stalk on; the fowl sits' (II. iii. 86); 'Bait the hook well; this fish will bite' (II. iii. 100). And Don Pedro suggests that, like Sly, Beatrice and Benedick will be turned into actors in a play created by the other characters for their own amusement: 'The sport will be when they hold one an opinion of another's dotage, and no such matter; that's the scene I would see, which will be merely a dumb show' (II. iii. 197–9). There is formal patterning even in the tone of the two scenes. In the scene with Benedick, an anti-romantic mood is firmly set. The atmosphere suggested by Claudio's 'How still the evening is / As hushed on purpose to grace harmony!' (II. iii. 36–7) is not, it seems, borne out by the song:

DON PEDRO: By my troth, a good song.
BALTHASAR: And an ill singer, my lord.
DON PEDRO: Ha, no; no, faith; thou sing'st well enough for a shift.
BENEDICK: An he had been a dog that should have howl'd thus, they would have hang'd him; and I pray God his bad voice bode no mischief.

(II. iii. 70–6)

Benedick's voluble complaints, and the fact that Don Pedro is no more than polite, lend some justification to the persistent stage practice of burlesquing the song.[15] The effect is to banish from the scene any suggestion of an easy, obvious romanticism, and to provide instead a clear hard light. The tone of Beatrice's scene, however, is quite different. While the other scene is in prose, this

[14] See John Dover Wilson, *Shakespeare's Happy Comedies* (London, 1969), pp. 128–9.
[15] In Michael Langham's production at Stratford, Ontario in 1958, and in Franco Zeffirelli's production for the National Theatre in 1965, the song was treated as a parody of the more florid type of operatic singing.

one contains a cool, decorative poetry unusual for the play. It affects even the conventional image of trickery:

> The pleasant'st angling is to see the fish
> Cut with her golden oars the silver stream,
> And greedily devour the treacherous bait.
> So angle we for Beatrice; who even now
> Is couched in the woodbine coverture.   (III. i. 26–30)

If the scenes were too much alike, the effect of the second would be anti-climactic; but the hard, practical masculinity of the one scene and the more graceful, feminine tone of the other are useful in another way: Benedick is seen against a community of men, Beatrice against a community of women. One is reminded of the exclusively masculine (and feminine) celebrations that precede a wedding, and of the arrangement of attendants at the wedding itself. The effect is to emphasize the sexual differences which it is the business of marriage to harmonize. The unorthodox lovers are seen as part of a familiar pattern of life.

As so often in Shakespeare's comedies, there is reality at the heart of the convention – the reality of general human experience. But there is another kind of reality as well. The trick plays upon the individual psychologies of Beatrice and Benedick. Each is accused of pride, of cruelty and of being unworthy of the other's love. In particular they are attacked for the very wit they have used as a means of keeping the distance between them. Don Pedro accuses Benedick of having 'a contemptible spirit', and the most he will grant him is that 'He doth, indeed, show some sparks that are like wit' (II. iii. 166, 170–1). Ursula says of Beatrice's wit, 'Sure, sure, such carping is not commendable' (III. i. 71). The role of wit-cracker that each has played is attacked. And the love for which that wit was a substitute is emboldened by the news that, if offered, it would be returned. What we may, I think, imagine as the inner wish of each of them is thus fulfilled, and the barriers they have erected to protect themselves from the disappointment of that wish come tumbling down. Benedick's eagerness to be deceived confirms this suggestion: 'I should think this a gull, but that the white-bearded fellow speaks it; knavery cannot, sure, hide himself in such reverence' (II. iii. 109–11). Benedick would not

take such a factor seriously if he were not eager to believe what he
hears and willing to take any excuse to do so.

So far, their minds work identically; but in the soliloquies that
follow each deception, an important difference is revealed. Benedick moves uneasily into his new role, testing ways of defending
it against the mockery of his friends, and trying to square it with
his earlier behaviour:

> I may chance have some odd quirks and remnants of wit
> broken on me because I have railed so long against marriage;
> but doth not the appetite alter? A man loves the meat in his
> youth that he cannot endure in his age. Shall quips, and sen-
> tences, and these paper bullets of the brain, awe a man from the
> career of his humour? No; the world must be peopled. When I
> said I would die a bachelor, I did not think I should live till I
> were married.
>
> (II. iii. 214–22)

Against these anxious rationalizations, Beatrice's surrender is
direct and simple:

> What fire is in mine ears? Can this be true?
> Stand I condemn'd for pride and scorn so much?
> Contempt, farewell! and maiden pride, adieu!
> No glory lives behind the back of such.
> And, Benedick, love on; I will requite thee,
> Taming my wild heart to thy loving hand;
> If thou dost love, my kindness shall incite thee
> To bind our loves up in a holy band;
> For others say thou dost deserve, and I
> Believe it better than reportingly.
>
> (III. i. 107–116)

She adopts her new role as completely as Claudio or Hero; and
the formal style, so different from Benedick's tentative prose,
reflects this[16] (the speech has the form of a sonnet with the first

[16] M. C. Bradbrook offers a different explanation, suggesting that this declaration is rhymed so that a fully personal acknowledgement of love can be held
back until the church scene. See *Shakespeare and Elizabethan Poetry* (Harmondsworth, 1964), p. 163. But I will argue that what happens in that scene is not
quite so simple as a declaration of love.

quatrain removed; this, and the speech at Hero's tomb, are the only cases of alternate rhyme in the play). Her nature at this point is more simple and decisive than his, and one reason is that his loyalties are more complicated: he is keeping one eye on the masculine community, wondering what they will think of him. This difference is borne out in the following scenes, when they confront their friends (III. ii. 7–66; III. iv. 34–84): both are off balance, unable to maintain their old roles; but of the two Benedick is the more thoroughly nonplussed, and is quite unable to defend himself against the jokes of his companions.

This is not yet a simple love affair; and the church scene bears this out. After the formal, rhetorical and utterly predictable passion of Claudio, the exchange between Beatrice and Benedick is full of surprises. Contrary to the pattern of their soliloquies, it is Benedick who manages a simple declaration of love, and Beatrice who hedges, defending herself with compulsive joking in the old manner:

BENEDICK: I do love nothing in the world so well as you. Is not that strange?
BEATRICE: As strange as the thing I know not. It were as possible for me to say I lov'd nothing so well as you; but believe me not, and yet I lie not; I confess nothing, nor I deny nothing. I am sorry for my cousin.
BENEDICK: By my sword, Beatrice, thou lovest me.
BEATRICE: Do not swear, and eat it.

(IV. i. 266–73)

She is holding something back; and when her defences finally crumble, more than just her love is released:

BEATRICE: I love you with so much of my heart that none is left to protest.
BENEDICK: Come, bid me do anything for thee.
BEATRICE: Kill Claudio.
BENEDICK: Ha! Not for the wide world.
BEATRICE: You kill me to deny it. Farewell.

(IV. i. 284–9)

The contrast between Claudio's formal tirade and this exchange – spontaneous, explosive and unpredictable – is striking, to say the least. The first part of the church scene went exactly as we might expect, with its characters moving in the roles dictated by the story. But here the characters reveal themselves as more complicated than we thought. Just as the formal mating of Claudio and Hero provoked the more psychologically determined mating of Beatrice and Benedick, so now the formalized suffering of the one love affair provokes psychological complications in the other. Beneath their differences, the two stories can be seen as moving in fundamentally the same way: love must pass through an ordeal. But the way the ordeal is dramatized is radically different.

The affair of the challenge, with the lover performing a task set by his lady, is of course a convention of romantic literature.[17] But like the comic convention of eavesdropping, it reveals a lot about the characters' minds. The behaviour of Claudio and Don Pedro provokes in Beatrice a scathing contempt for the masculine world of Benedick's friends:

> Princes and Counties! Surely, a princely testimony, a goodly count, Count Comfect; a sweet gallant, surely! O that I were a man for his sake! or that I had any friend would be a man for my sake! But manhood is melted into curtsies, valour into compliment, and men are only turn'd into tongue, and trim ones too. He is now as valiant as Hercules that only tells a lie and swears it. I cannot be a man with wishing, therefore I will die a woman with grieving.
>
> (IV. i. 312–20)

Three times, in this scene, Beatrice wishes she were a man (IV. i. 303–4, 314, 319). In more stylized comedies, heroines extend their power of action through male disguise. Denied this outlet, Beatrice turns to Benedick – and for a moment he fails her. Her reply to his refusal is 'I am gone though I am here; there is no love in you' (IV. i. 291–2). It is as though, in the first shock of revealing their love to each other, both had suddenly retreated, Benedick taking refuge in his friendship for Claudio, Beatrice in her loyalty to

---

[17] See Karl F. Thompson, 'Shakespeare's romantic comedies', *Publications of the Modern Language Association of America*, LXVII (December 1952), p. 1089.

Hero. It is part of the realism of the scene that Benedick cannot surrender an old friendship as swiftly or easily as Claudio can renounce his love. But, paradoxically, this touch also unites the two plots, showing Benedick, like Claudio, in danger of throwing away his love. One might also suggest that behind Beatrice's command lies something deeper than her loyalty to Hero: a need to test Benedick, to force him to choose between his masculine loyalties and his love, and to prove that he has true manhood, as opposed to the false manhood she sees in his friends. Before the church scene there was no need for her to make such a demand, and she could be confident in her love; but the behaviour of the prince and Claudio forces this test. We have seen already, in a comic way, how involved Benedick is with his friends, and how this makes him hesitate in his expressions of love. Beatrice's first attacks on him, in the opening scene, suggest a resentment of his ties with men:

BEATRICE: ...Who is his companion now? He hath every
          month a new sworn brother.
MESSENGER: Is't possible?
BEATRICE: Very easily possible: he wears his faith but as the
          fashion of his hat; it ever changes with the next
          block.

(I. i. 59–63)

There is a hint of jealousy in this. And in the same scene she has questioned his valour: 'I pray you, how many hath he kill'd and eaten in these wars? But how many hath he kill'd? For, indeed, I promised to eat all of his killing' (I. i. 35–7). Don Pedro, in the eavesdropping scene, also jokes about Benedick's cowardice: 'in the managing of quarrels you may say he is very wise, for either he avoids them with great discretion, or undertakes them with a most Christian-like fear' (II. iii. 173–6). If one is teasing a man, this is an easy accusation to make, and it need not be taken too seriously;[18] all the same, in proving the truth of his love, Benedick must also prove that the jokes about him are not true. It is a sign that he and Beatrice are moving out of the realms of conventional

[18] Elsewhere, speaking more seriously, Don Pedro describes Benedick as 'of noble strain, of approved valour, and confirm'd honesty' (II. i. 342–3).

wit, and facing the reality of their natures more seriously. At the bottom of this episode lies a conventional love story pattern: Benedick must prove his worthiness as a lover by proving his manhood. This is something more basic – more primitive, even – than the conventions of the Claudio plot. But it is worked out largely in psychological terms, through a subtle examination of the tensions and uncertainties of the characters' minds.

We are now confronted by that crucial factor in Shakespearian comedy – the larger world of experience outside the private world of love. Here, as in *Love's Labour's Lost*, the lover must prove himself by a venture into this outside world – in this case, risking his life and cutting off old friendships in an affair concerning another woman's honour. This means, also, moving temporarily outside the shelter of the normal world of comedy into a world of deeper and more painful feelings. In the scene of Benedick's challenge, the licence of comedy is temporarily suspended: both love and wit are held in abeyance as Benedick goes about his serious business. The joking of his friends is tasteless and embarrassing, and Benedick gives it a cold reception:

CLAUDIO: We had lik'd to have had our two noses snapp'd
           off with two old men without teeth.
DON PEDRO: Leonato and his brother. What think'st thou?
           Had we fought, I doubt we should have been too
           young for them.
BENEDICK: In a false quarrel there is no true valour.

(v. i. 115–20)

Their relationship has in the past been dominated by wit; but when Claudio asks Benedick to adopt his old role and cheer them up – 'Wilt thou use thy wit?' – Benedick replies 'It is in my scabbard; shall I draw it?' (v. i. 124–5). And a few lines later: 'You are a villain; I jest not' (v. i. 143). Through the rest of the scene the prince and Claudio continue to joke, but Benedick is the unsympathetic listener *par excellence*, and the jokes acquire a nervous, rattling quality against the icy dignity of his replies. Finally, when he leaves, they are forced to admit the truth they have been trying to avoid:

DON PEDRO: He is in earnest.

  CLAUDIO: In most profound earnest; and I'll warrant you for the love of Beatrice.

(v. i. 186–8)

They released that love themselves, by a comic trick. But the implications of that love have gone far beyond anything they could have imagined. They have tended to regard Benedick as their puppet, teasing him for the feelings they have tricked him into. But that simply comic view of Benedick will not do any longer.

The play is enriched by this brief excursion outside the normal bounds of comedy, showing us that Beatrice and Benedick are capable of more than love and wit. But this is established just firmly enough to increase our respect for them as they return to the comic world, and is not developed enough to destroy the play's ultimate immunity from the harsher facts of life. The suspension of comedy is only temporary. By a neat compromise Benedick is allowed to prove his valour without actually drawing blood – thanks to Dogberry. As always, the Beatrice–Benedick story follows the contours of the other plot and is in some measure controlled by it. As Claudio is restored to Hero, Benedick is restored to Beatrice; and wit returns, but this time with a different nature and a new function. The old wounding aggressiveness is gone. Benedick's is now 'A most manly wit . . . it will not hurt a woman' (v. ii. 14–15). His skirmish with Margaret is merely a light echo of the competitive wit of the earlier scenes, and his ensuing exchange with Beatrice shows them using a different technique altogether:

BENEDICK: Thou and I are too wise to woo peaceably.

BEATRICE: It appears not in this confession: there's not one wise man among twenty that will praise himself.

BENEDICK: An old, an old instance, Beatrice, that liv'd in the time of good neighbours; if a man do not erect in this age his own tomb ere he dies, he shall live no longer in monument than the bell rings and the widow weeps.

BEATRICE: And how long is that, think you?

BENEDICK: Question: why, an hour in clamour, and a quarter in rheum.

(v. ii. 63–72)

They are now mutually exploring the same idea, and the idea itself is a general one. They are no longer eyeing each other with the old anxious watchfulness but, secure in their love, they are turning their eyes together to the outside world. Behind the lighter and more detached tone there is a new peace of mind. Wit was always, in them, the partial enemy of love, and it was temporarily surrendered during the testing of love. When it returns, it is transformed. They are still playing the game of wit, but this time it is purely for the fun of it, for they have come to terms with themselves and with each other.

They have also come to terms with the conventions of romantic love. There is a fine balance struck between the continuing individuality of their natures and the comically unoriginal situation of being in love. Claudio says of Benedick, in effect, what Benedick has said of him: 'If he be not in love with some woman, there is no believing old signs' (III. ii. 36–7). Like Lorenzo and Jessica, Benedick comically sets himself against the great lovers of the past:

> Leander the good swimmer, Troilus the first employer of panders, and a whole bookful of these quondam carpet-rogues, whose names run yet smoothly in the even road of a blank verse, why, they were never so truly turn'd over and over as my poor self in love. Marry, I cannot show it in rhyme; I have tried; I can find out no rhyme to 'lady' but 'baby' – an innocent rhyme; for 'scorn,' 'horn' – a hard rhyme; for 'school,' 'fool' – a babbling rhyme; very ominous endings. No, I was not born under a rhyming planet, nor I cannot woo in festival terms.
>
> (v. ii. 27–37)

He is characteristically satiric about literary expressions of love; all the same, love is a real experience for him, and he is sufficiently in the grip of its conventions to try some literary expression of his own. His anti-romantic nature persists in asserting itself, but all the same he tries. In the final scene, where Hero is ceremonially restored to Claudio, the relationship of Beatrice and Benedick is also touched with ceremony: Beatrice, like Hero, enters masked, and unmasks at the sound of Benedick's voice (v. iv. 72–3). There follows a light, formal recapitulation of the relationship between the two sets of lovers: Beatrice and Benedick teasingly pretend to love each other 'no more than reason' and 'in friendly recompense' (v. iv. 74, 77, 83); then their two love sonnets are revealed by Claudio and Hero, the pretence of reluctance (never very serious) collapses, and Benedick stops Beatrice's mouth with a kiss. For all their individuality, Beatrice and Benedick have been caught in the conventional expression of love; and we are reminded that Claudio and Hero are the leaders of this particular dance.

At first glance, the contrast between the two plots of *Much Ado About Nothing* is striking, perhaps overemphatic. Yet they diverge from a common beginning, in which a realistic dramatic mode is touched with hints of form and ceremony. And in the end they come together in a finale which begins with high formality, then moves towards a more natural and open manner. In Hero's unmasking, a miraculous vision of a spirit returned from the dead is also an ordinary woman; and the Friar concludes, 'Meantime let wonder seem familiar, / And to the chapel let us presently' (v. iv. 70–1). We return to a more familiar social ceremony. The concluding speeches (except for the messenger's brief reminder of Don John) are in brisk, naturalistic prose. The final words, Benedick's 'Strike up, pipers', are a call for a dance: we are given, once more, a ceremonial image of order; but as in the early scenes the ceremony arises from a naturalistic context. A ceremonial view of life and an awareness of life as it really is are not, in the end, incompatible. This works in two ways. The action of the Claudio plot, by its very formality, is seen as connected with the basic, familiar rhythms of life. And the love affair of Beatrice and Benedick – so naturalistically conceived, so determined by individual character – is seen, at bottom, as a matter of convention. In praising its psychological reality we should not overlook how much the pleasure it gives depends on the essential, impersonal rhythms it shares with the other story. It is, in the end, a richer experience because it satisfies in more than one way; but the simpler, bolder outlines of the Claudio plot are a necessary buttress for it. In *Much Ado About Nothing*, as in *The Merchant of Venice*, the range of dramatic idiom is wide, from a bold dependence on pure convention to an equally striking naturalism. But here the vision is steadier, and the final image of harmony is less exclusive. We are made to see that however individual we are we are ultimately bound by the rhythms of life, and we must follow the leaders. The play asserts more confidently than its predecessor the idea of human reality at the heart of convention: and in that way, besides being a notable achievement in its own right, it prepares for the triumph of *As You Like It*.

8 As You Like It

At the start of *As You Like It*, we overhear what seems to be a casual conversation between a young man and a servant. But as we listen, it occurs to us that the situation unfolded in the dialogue, that of a young man oppressed by a wicked older brother, is familiar from old tales; and the fact that there are three brothers increases this feeling. At the same time we are bound to protest that Adam must already know everything Orlando is telling him. What looks at first like a realistic conversation is in fact a blatant theatrical trick: the machinery of exposition is unashamedly exposed. Yet throughout the opening scene the manner of the dialogue continues to be as natural and easy as in any of the realistic scenes of *The Merchant of Venice* or *Much Ado About Nothing*. And throughout the play this double-exposure effect persists: the characters converse in a convincingly natural manner within situations that are clearly the product of theatrical artifice. With some exceptions, it is not so easy to identify scenes as largely stylized or largely naturalistic. In place of the sharper confrontations between one idiom and another that we found in the two preceding plays, we are given a smoother, subtler blend.

The villains of the piece illustrate this. Shylock, though he has a conventional role in the comic structure, impresses us finally as a piece of realistic character drawing; Don John is all convention. But with Oliver and Duke Frederick it is harder to say where we stand. When Oliver himself seeks to understand his own conduct there is a fusion of psychology and arbitrary villainy:

I hope I shall see an end of him; for my soul, yet I know not why, hates nothing more than he. Yet he's gentle; never school'd and yet learned; full of noble device; of all sorts enchantingly beloved; and indeed, so much in the heart of the world, and especially of my own people, who best know him, that I am altogether misprised.

(I. i. 146–51)

'I know not why' – if he were purely an arbitrary villain, he would not have asked the question. And in his envy of his brother's grace and popularity he does find an explanation of a kind. It is partly the villain's natural tendency to destroy anything finer than himself: but while in Don John this remained an impersonal principle, in Oliver it acquires a more personal edge. There is a further explanation hinted in Orlando's 'Come, come, elder brother, you are too young in this' (I. i. 48–9): Oliver's petulant manner in the first scene – so different from the quiet gravity of his first appearance in the forest – suggests that he is indeed a spoiled young man who simply needs to grow up. The equivalent character in Lodge's *Rosalynde* has a more obvious motive for his actions – their father's will bequeathed him less than his younger brother, and his actions are rooted in envy and greed;[1] but Oliver's conduct, while less openly explained, is at least partly understandable.

In Frederick's nature there is a similar fusion of the arbitrary and the explicable. He is not simply a cardboard tyrant: through most of his first scene he behaves quite decently, pitying Orlando, trying to dissuade him from his rash venture with Charles, and insisting 'You shall try but one fall' (I. ii. 183). Though we hear of his censorship of foolery (I. ii. 73–83), we hear also that Touchstone is 'the roynish clown, at whom so oft / Your Grace was wont to laugh' (II. ii. 8–9). More important, we are told that his affection for Rosalind is (or has been) as great as Celia's (I. i. 101–2), and that it was his idea, not Celia's, to keep Rosalind at court when her father was banished: 'It was your pleasure, and your own remorse' (I. iii. 66). Yet he is also moody and irrational,

[1] See Geoffrey Bullough (ed.), *Narrative and Dramatic Sources of Shakespeare*, **II** (London 1968), p. 165.

given to acting on impulse: he is twice described as 'humorous' (I. ii. 245; II. iii. 8). We see this when, in response to a friendly inquiry, he hears the name of Orlando's father: suddenly his genial manner disappears, and the man snaps on the mask of the tyrant. As with Oliver, there is envy of a more popular man – 'The world esteem'd thy father honourable' (I. ii. 204) – compounded, one may suppose, by the recollection that Sir Roland was a favourite of the banished duke. We see here the natural insecurity of the usurper. Frederick projects these feelings on to Celia, claiming that she should be jealous of Rosalind's popularity, as he is now, on her behalf (I. iii. 73–81). LeBeau, however, sees the Duke's motives as inadequate, and presents him as an arbitrary villain:

> But I can tell you that of late this Duke
> Hath ta'en displeasure 'gainst his gentle niece,
> Grounded upon no other argument
> But that the people praise her for her virtues
> And pity her for her good father's sake.

(I. ii. 256–60)

Certainly Lodge's usurper has a more calculated political motive for banishing Rosalynde: if she stays at court she may marry and produce an heir who would be a rival claimant for the kingdom.[2] In Shakespeare, the political motive is there but is less carefully stated, more purely impulsive: 'Thou art thy father's daughter, there's enough' (I. iii. 54). All the same, while Shakespeare has reduced the rational explanations of villainy that Lodge offered in *Rosalynde*,[3] and while his villains have a clearly conventional role in the comic structure, he has made them understandable. Their arbitrary actions spring from irrational, insecure personalities. There is even a hint of pathos, of human vulnerability, in their envy of those more popular than they are. This may be why, unlike Shylock and Don John, they are capable of repentance. Shylock was too firmly grounded in a world of tension and hatred to be saved, Don John too purely and simply a villain. As Sylvan

[2] Ibid., p. 176.
[3] See Sylvan Barnet, 'Strange events: improbability in *As You Like It*', *Shakespeare Studies*, IV (1968), p. 122.

Barnet has pointed out, the sheer instability of Frederick and Oliver makes them open to reform.[4]

Frederick's reform is almost entirely conventional, and since it takes place offstage, we never have to come to grips with its psychological implications – though there are enough hints of Frederick's better side in the early scenes to let us do this if we wanted to. But the reformed Oliver appears before us, and we are made aware not just of his role in the story but of his nature as a character. The new gravity and calm of his manner suggest that he has grown up; the example set by Orlando's forgiveness might be thought to have had some effect; but Shakespeare convinces us of his reform in a more daring and unusual way, by a manipulation of dramatic idiom. Through his own account, Oliver's experience becomes a carefully constructed narrative: he describes the setting, as a writer would do, and describes himself as a character in the story:

> Under an oak, whose boughs were moss'd with age
> And high top bald with dry antiquity,
> A wretched ragged man, o'ergrown with hair,
> Lay sleeping on his back.
>
> (IV. iii. 103–6)

The measured gravity, the literary detachment, keep the speaker himself at a distance from the experience. Like Aegeon's tale in *The Comedy of Errors* it is essentially non-dramatic, something related, not experienced – even more so, for Oliver tells his story in the third person. Then at the end the character in the story and the man who stands before us are suddenly fused, and separated again:

> . . . in which hurtling
> From miserable slumber I awak'd. . . .
> 'Twas I; but 'tis not I. I do not shame
> To tell you what I was, since my conversion
> So sweetly tastes, being the thing I am.
>
> (IV. iii. 130–1, 134–6)

There are hints in the story of a Christian allegory – a man fallen beneath a tree, threatened by a serpent, is saved by a hero who

[4] Ibid., p. 127.

sheds his own blood[5] – but I think these serve primarily to increase the air of literary contrivance. Oliver moves into a story, and comes out a new man. His deliberately split roles as speaker and character reflect an equivalent split in his nature, detaching what he was from what he is: 'A wretched ragged man' went to sleep under the tree, but 'I awak'd'. The manipulation of literary convention thus fuses with a familiar human experience: we can be so changed by time and circumstance that when we recall our past actions they seem like those of a different person.

Analysis makes heavy weather of this; but here, as throughout the play, the blending of convention and human reality is so light, swift and subtle that we accept the fusion as natural. It is the art that conceals the art, and more than that it is a way of extending our sense of human possibilities, of suggesting that the distinction between ordinary experience and the conventionalized actions of storybook characters may be a false one. Orlando reacts to his brother's oppression with the impulses of a hero and the confusion of an ordinary man: 'I will no longer endure it, though yet I know no wise remedy how to avoid it' (I. i. 21–2). He carries suggestions of Hercules, queller of giants, serpents, and lions;[6] but the mythical level of the action is carefully restrained: for one thing, the giant he overthrows is an ordinary goodnatured man who wrestles for his professional credit and, pitying Orlando's youth, does not want to harm him. He decides to be rough only when deluded by Oliver into believing that his own life is in danger. This goes some way to blur the mythical simplicity of the wrestling sequence. And the fact that the wrestling takes place onstage suggests that we are meant to be as interested in Orlando's professional technique as in his heroic role. In the forest, while Orlando may write like a Petrarchan lover, Rosalind insists he does not look like one (III. ii. 342–55) – and he has, as Harold Jenkins points out, 'the very human trait of unpunctuality'.[7]

Orlando and Rosalind fall in love at first sight, in the prescribed manner; but there is more to it than the arbitrary hurling of

[5] These suggestions are elaborately developed by Richard Knowles, 'Myth and type in *As You Like It*', *ELH*, XXXIII (March 1966), pp. 11–13.
[6] See ibid., p. 5.
[7] '*As You Like It*', *Shakespeare Survey*, VIII (1955), p. 47.

Cupid's dart, which might hit anyone – or the arbitrary working of Puck's flower, which has its effect no matter whose eyes it is applied to, and no matter whom (or what) the victim first sees. Rosalind and Celia have attempted, at Frederick's request, to dissuade Orlando from wrestling with Charles; he will not take their advice:

> But let your fair eyes and gentle wishes go with me to my trial; wherein if I be foil'd, there is but one sham'd that was never gracious; if kill'd, but one dead that is willing to be so. I shall do my friends no wrong, for I have none to lament me; the world no injury, for in it I have nothing: only in the world I fill up a place which may be better supplied when I have made it empty.

ROSALIND: The little strength I have, I would it were with you.

    CELIA: And mine, to eke out hers.

(I. ii. 166–76)

It is clear only after the wrestling that Rosalind has fallen in love, but she seems impressed by Orlando's simple dignity in his misfortunes, and it may well be that between them there is not just arbitrary love but sympathy and fellow feeling: Rosalind too is 'one out of suits with fortune' (I. ii. 225). As in *Much Ado*, the roots of love are suggested through the subtext, before love is openly declared.

The forest of Arden is itself the product of a fusion of conventions. At times it suggests the playwright's native landscape, at other times the forest of classical pastoral: Warwickshire is notably deficient in lions and olive trees, yet this forest has both.[8] The mingling of conventions is to a great extent dependent on the mixed nature of the characters themselves: we hear of the olive trees, for example, once in a scene with Phebe (III. v. 74) and once in the scene of Oliver's conversion (IV. iii. 76) – the scene that also gives us the serpent and the lion. The native population of Arden is mixed indeed: for one kind of wedding, the forest can produce an Elizabethan hedge-priest, Sir Oliver Martext, whose very name suggests the real problems the church has always faced in country parishes; for another kind of wedding, it can produce

[8] See E. C. Pettet, *Shakespeare and the Romance Tradition* (London, 1949), p. 90.

Hymen himself. There is one shepherd, Corin, whose language, pungent and concrete, is rooted in his occupation, and who experiences the hard facts of social and economic reality: 'But I am shepherd to another man, / And do not shear the fleeces that I graze' (II. iv. 73–4). There is another shepherd, Silvius, who 'little cares for buying anything' (II. iv. 85), and whose language has no particular roots in rural experience (pleading with Phebe, he uses a very urban image, drawn from public executions – III. v. 3–6). There is nothing in the play to suggest that Silvius knows one end of a sheep from the other, and when he and Phebe are played with yokel accents it always sounds wrong. The female population is equally mixed: there is Phebe, a shepherdess who can quote Marlowe in a gracefully allusive manner: 'Dead shepherd, now I find thy saw of might: / "Who ever lov'd that lov'd not at first sight?"' (III. v. 80–1). And there is Audrey, a country wench (a very distinct breed from the shepherdess) who finds the very word 'poetical' hard to understand (III. iii. 14–15). These figures represent not simply different types of character, but different types of dramatic idiom. Yet they mingle freely – Corin and Silvius are first seen together – and no one coming to Arden remarks on the incongruity.

This may be because they themselves enjoy considerable imaginative freedom in the forest. The liberty of the mind that allows Shakespeare to mix dramatic styles is not only part of the play's manner, but part of its matter as well. We are often assured by critics that Arden is a place of testing and education,[9] as though there were something suspect about pure holiday. But I do not feel this is a prominent issue: the characters may learn, perhaps, that the property of rain is to wet and fire to burn, and that if a cat will after kind, so be sure will Rosalind. But they are not under the severe and obvious pressure to learn that characters experience in, for example, *The Taming of the Shrew* and *Love's Labour's Lost* (where the cast includes a sprinkling of pedants, to emphasize the point). Rosalind may tease Orlando about his Petrarchanisms, but unlike Berowne he is never shown repenting, and there is never any doubt that Rosalind wants him, bad verses and all. I think the

[9] See, for example, Jay L. Halio, ' "No clock in the forest": time in *As You Like It*', *Studies in English Literature 1500–1900*, II (spring 1962), pp. 206–7.

keynote of the forest scenes is rather an imaginative freedom to
explore ideas and play roles – on one's own terms, and for one's
own amusement. There is a quality of relaxation, even in the way
the forest is introduced. In *A Midsummer Night's Dream* we are
firmly removed from the court, kept in the wood, and then just as
firmly returned. Here, the forest fades into the play gradually,
overlapping with lingering scenes in the court. The fact that the
play opens in Oliver's orchard helps to blur the transition, suggesting that Shakespeare envisaged property trees as a permanent
feature of the stage. The forest is introduced by a line at the end of
a court scene, Celia's 'Now go we in content / To liberty, and not
to banishment' (I. iii. 133–4), and in the scene that follows immediately we get some idea of what that liberty means. You can
be master of your own mind in this forest in a way that is impossible in the enchanted wood near Athens. Duke Senior uses
this freedom to draw philosophy from the weather and the landscape; and he lets his mind play over country and town, drawing
them together imaginatively:

> Come, shall we go and kill us venison?
> And yet it irks me the poor dappled fools,
> Being native burghers of this desert city
> Should, in their own confines, with forked heads
> Have their round haunches gor'd.
>
> (II. i. 21–5)

Corin would never talk like this: to see the slaughter of animals as
pitiful is the prerogative of the town-bred man. The countryman's
view needs to be harder, and narrower.

Jaques, in his speech on the wounded deer, elaborates the incident into a fantasy about a bankrupt citizen, and releases his
imagination to range even more freely than the Duke's:

> Thus most invectively he pierceth through
> The body of the country, city, court,
> Yea, and of this our life, swearing that we
> Are mere usurpers, tyrants, and what's worse,
> To fright the animals and to kill them up
> In their assign'd and native dwelling-place.
>
> (II. i. 58–63)

Affected it may be; but it shows also the free play of a civilized mind, unconfined by court or country. And while the Duke realizes the practical necessities of forest life, he is not limited by them; hearing that Jaques is in his moralizing vein, he postpones his hunting to seek him out (II. i. 66–8). The playful elaboration of Jaques's fantasy, and the Duke's philosophizing, give us our first real taste of Arden; and the emphasis throughout is not on the tough, simple life Arden provides for the natives (Corin is the spokesman for that) but rather on the fresh material it offers for the courtly figures to exercise their wits upon. At his first appearance, Orlando insists that mere rustic simplicity is not for him, and that Oliver's refusal to educate him like a gentleman is a disgrace (II. i. 7–10). When he meets Ganymede, he remarks 'Your accent is something finer than you could purchase in so removed a dwelling' (III. ii. 318–19), and this is clearly something that attracts him to the youth. Pure rusticity is of no more value to the courtly figures than it is to Guiderius and Arviragus in *Cymbeline*, who also complain of lack of breeding.

Similarly the trouble with Frederick's court is that it is not civilized enough: it is a place where wits like Touchstone are suppressed, and denied their traditional privilege of attacking folly:

CELIA:	Prithee, who is't that thou mean'st?
TOUCHSTONE:	One that old Frederick, your father, loves.
CELIA:	My father's love is enough to honour him. Enough, speak no more of him; you'll be whipt for taxation one of these days.
TOUCHSTONE:	The more pity that fools may not speak wisely what wise men do foolishly.
CELIA:	By my troth, thou sayest true; for since the little wit that fools have was silenced, the little folly that wise men have makes a great show.

(I. ii. 73–82)

Duke Senior is more civilized in this respect, tolerating and even encouraging the satire of Jaques; and Touchstone enjoys as much licence as he wants in Arden. The court is also a place where 'breaking of ribs' is considered 'sport for ladies' (I. ii. 123). The

oppression of the court is not a matter of whips and jackboots, but
something more attuned to the spirit of the play – a stifling of
genuine fun, and a crude idea of what constitutes sport; bad
manners and bad taste, as opposed to the civilized liberty of
Arden.

This oppression affects Rosalind and Orlando: their love
dialogue at the court is hesitant, groping, and shy:

ROSALIND: He calls us back. My pride fell with my fortunes;
              I'll ask him what he would. Did you call, sir?
              Sir, you have wrestled well, and overthrown
              More than your enemies.

CELIA: Will you go, coz?

ROSALIND: Have with you. Fare you well.

                          [*Exeunt Rosalind and Celia.*

ORLANDO: What passion hangs these weights upon my tongue?
              I could not speak to her, yet she urg'd conference.
              O poor Orlando, thou art overthrown!
              Or Charles or something weaker masters thee.

                          (I. ii. 241–9)

Here, as in *The Two Gentlemen of Verona*, love is more an oppressive
than a liberating power – they both feel 'overthrown' by it. Both
are tongue-tied: in the following scene Rosalind has 'Not a word
. . . to throw at a dog' (I. iii. 2–3). The atmosphere of the court,
in which both are 'out of suits with fortune' and Orlando in particular is denied his full development, may have something to do
with this. But all this changes when the characters come to the
forest. Throughout the opening scenes, Celia is the woman with
the wit and initiative, and Rosalind merely follows along. It is
Celia who suggests going to the forest; but once the notion of disguise is introduced, Rosalind starts developing her own ideas, and
using her own wit (I. iii. 102–18). And the change anticipated
here becomes decisive in the forest, where Rosalind, wearing the
disguise, comes into her own, and the earlier balance between the
women is reversed. Orlando finds both his tongue and his spirits
in Arden. Comforting old Adam, he uses wit to rise above mis-
fortune:

Thy conceit is nearer death than thy powers. .... I will be with thee presently; and if I bring thee not something to eat, I will give thee leave to die; but if thou diest before I come, thou art a mocker of my labour. Well said! thou look'st cheerly; and I'll be with thee quickly.

(II. vi. 7–13)

Berowne feared it was impossible 'To enforce the pained impotent to smile' (v. ii. 842); but Orlando does it. This achievement is in tune with a play in which wit is not simply an aggressive weapon (though it can be that) but a liberation of the mind. And Orlando the lover also finds his tongue, in surprisingly ornate, patterned verse – like Beatrice's confession, a sonnet with the first quatrain removed (III. ii. 1–10). Those who journey to Arden may arrive dog-tired and hungry, but after the first shock of physical deprivation they recover quickly, and seem, if anything, more fully alive than before.

The freedom of the forest provides a chance for those dislocating confrontations of different characters that provide one of Shakespeare's favourite comic effects. Harold Jenkins has written of the play's 'piquant but seemingly casual juxtapositions', and of 'the ease and rapidity with which pairs and groups break up, re-form, and succeed one another on the stage'.[10] The play is unusually rich in such moments since, freed for the most part from the demands of developing an intrigue, Shakespeare can concentrate on juxtapositions of different minds and experiences purely for their own sake. One is tempted to say that the main action of the play takes place in its language, for confrontations of characters mean, as usual, confrontations of style. Up to a point the effect is that of *A Midsummer Night's Dream* – a series of mutual dislocations, rather than one controlling view that compromises all the others. In the earlier play, however, each group of characters was allowed, in turn, to take over the stage, and the dislocations were provided more by the sheer presence of other groups than by their direct intervention – the fairies watching the lovers, the lovers

[10] '*As You Like It*', p. 50. See also Mary Lascelles, 'Shakespeare's pastoral comedy', in John Garrett (ed.), *More Talking of Shakespeare* (London, 1959), p. 81.

watching the clowns. In that respect *As You Like It* is a more active play, full of brisk local skirmishes:

> ROSALIND: Jove! Jove! this shepherd's passion
> Is much upon my fashion.
> TOUCHSTONE: And mine; but it grows something stale with
> me.
> CELIA: I pray you, one of you question yond man
> If he for gold will give us any food;
> I faint almost to death.
>
> (II. iv. 56–61)

Here, two views of love are quickly juxtaposed – Rosalind's rhymed, romantic contemplation and Touchstone's wry, prosaic dismissal – and both are broken in on by the voice of Celia, who (like Speed) is uninterested in love or indeed anything that is not edible. Once the characters have been established, their mere physical juxtaposition will do the trick – as when Orlando rushes out, crying, 'Run, run, Orlando; carve on every tree / The fair, the chaste, and unexpressive she' (III. ii. 9–10) and Touchstone and Corin enter at once, without a scene break; or when the first meeting of Orlando and Rosalind in the forest is succeeded by the first scene with Touchstone and Audrey. In reading the play one's visual imagination must be always alert: at II. vii. 74–90, for example, as Amiens sings 'Blow, blow, thou winter wind', this song of 'man's ingratitude' and 'benefits forgot' is set against the stage picture of Orlando and Adam sharing the Duke's banquet – an image of courtesy, loyalty and generosity, a small island of comfort under the freezing sky.

Touchstone is particularly useful for moments such as this, for he has a natural tendency to react against the person he is speaking with. Against Silvius's dreamy, disembodied view of love –

> If thou rememb'rest not the slightest folly
> That ever love did make thee run into,
> Thou hast not lov'd.
>
> (II. iv. 31–3)

– he offers concrete experience, seen with cynical detachment:

I remember, when I was in love, I broke my sword upon a stone and bid him take that for coming a-night to Jane Smile; and I remember the kissing of her batler, and the cow's dugs that her pretty chopt hands had milk'd. . .

(II. iv. 43-7)

But the other shepherd finds Touchstone in a different vein. Corin's mind is simple, direct, and practical. He knows that 'the property of rain is to wet, and fire to burn; that good pasture makes fat sheep; and that a great cause of the night is lack of the sun' (III. ii. 23-6). Faced with a mind as concrete as this, Touchstone's mind at once reacts by using words with a deliberate vagueness that allows him to play verbal tricks:

Why, if thou never wast at court thou never saw'st good manners; if thou never saw'st good manners, then thy manners must be wicked; and wickedness is sin, and sin is damnation. Thou art in a parlous state, shepherd.

(III. ii. 37-40)

The most frequently discussed juxtapositions, however, involve Jaques and Orlando: when Orlando's heroic posture, with drawn sword, is deflated by Jaques's cool wit; and when in turn Jaques's view of old age as mere senile collapse is set against Orlando's entrance with old Adam. For the shrewdest discussion of these and similar moments we are indebted to Harold Jenkins, and it is worth recalling his warning that 'Shakespeare seeks no cheap antithesis'.[11] There is no simple partisan laughter at any one figure; rather, we are gently reminded of the incompleteness of each character's view seen in isolation. No one attitude can be taken as absolute or final, for truth can always wear another face: it is dangerous to laugh too simply even at Silvius, for while Touchstone is unimpressed by him, Rosalind sees in his experience a reflection of her own (II. iv. 41-2, 56-7).

A sense of the relativity of experience is implied by these comic juxtapositions, as it was in *The Comedy of Errors*. But here it is more than implied: it is directly stated. Time, says Rosalind in her set piece on the subject, moves at different paces for different people:

[11] '*As You Like It*', p. 49.

it all depends on your point of view (III. ii. 290–312). This may be one significance of the play's title. When Touchstone and Corin discuss the merits of court and country life, no objective reality emerges. Touchstone says of the country:

> In respect that it is solitary, I like it very well; but in respect that it is private, it is a very vile life. Now in respect it is in the fields, it pleaseth me well; but in respect it is not in the court, it is tedious.
>
> (III. ii. 15–18)

A single quality can be a virtue or a fault, depending on one's point of view. Corin has a similar idea about good manners: 'Those that are good manners at the court are as ridiculous in the country, as the behaviour of the country is most mockable at the court' (III. ii. 41–3). But lest we should settle too comfortably in the idea that at least the difference between court and country is a fixed truth, Touchstone insists that from some points of view they are identical: shepherds' and courtiers' hands are both greasy, and while the one is smeared with tar the other is no less disgustingly smeared with civet (III. ii. 47–61). No fixed attitude to court or country emerges from this debate, unless it be the idea that everything is relative. But to state this idea so clearly – more clearly than in any previous comedy – is to bring it out into the open, and that makes it vulnerable. A Shakespearian comedy is a very dangerous place for an abstract idea to be wandering loose. And the idea that all experience is relative, that everything depends on your point of view, is no safer than any other.

In order to see how this idea is dealt with, we need first to examine the function of role-playing in the comedy. If a character's attitude is not final or absolute when seen against the world at large, possibly it is not final or absolute even for himself. There is often an element of pose in the statements the characters make, as others are quick to point out:

JAQUES: What stature is she of?

ORLANDO: Just as high as my heart.

JAQUES: You are full of pretty answers. Have you not been acquainted with goldsmiths' wives, and conn'd them out of rings?

ORLANDO: Not so; but I answer you right painted cloth, from
whence you have studied your questions.

> (III. ii. 253–9)

Touchstone's set piece on time is certainly a calculated performance. We are told that he

> laid him down and bask'd him in the sun,
> And rail'd on Lady Fortune in good terms,
> In good set terms – and yet a motley fool.

> (II. vii. 15–17)

Nor is Touchstone the only one to employ 'good set terms'.
Jaques's speech on the seven ages of man begins with a cliché and
ends with a self-consciously rhetorical climax (II. v. 31–3). So does
Duke Senior's lecture on the uses of adversity, with its balanced,
alliterative conclusion:[12]

> And this our life, exempt from public haunt,
> Finds tongues in trees, books in the running brooks,
> Sermons in stones, and good in everything.
> I would not change it.
>
> AMIENS: Happy is your Grace
> That can translate the stubbornness of fortune
> Into so quiet and so sweet a style.

> (II. i. 15–20)

Amiens seems to be congratulating the Duke on a fine performance
as much as on his ideas. It is not entirely mischievous, I think, to
wonder how many times Duke Senior's followers have heard this
speech before. And the ease with which he returns to the 'envious
court' is notorious: the value of the simple life is an idea to be
entertained, not a final commitment.

But not all the characters simply toy with attitudes, retaining
the ultimate detachment the Duke seems to achieve: some are
fully absorbed in the roles they play. Silvius and Phebe, in the
parts of suffering lover and disdainful beauty, show no awareness

---

[12] See Robert T. Price, 'The moral languages of *Rosalynde* and *As You Like It*',
Studies in Philology, LXVIII (April 1971), p. 172.

that their behaviour is conventional. But Corin says of them (with a rare departure from his usual earthy style) :[13]

> If you will see a pageant truly play'd
> Between the pale complexion of true love
> And the red glow of scorn and proud disdain,
> Go hence a little, and I shall conduct you,
> If you will mark it.
>
> (III. iv. 47–51)

Rosalind picks up the suggestions of the word 'pageant': 'I'll prove a busy actor in their play' (III. iv. 54). For a moment, we remember Puck, and – though Rosalind becomes more personally involved in this pageant than Puck does in the 'fond pageant' of the Athenian lovers – the general effect is similar: Silvius and Phebe are absorbed in their roles, unconscious of the entertainment they provide for their onstage audience. Touchstone is more aware of his audience; yet in a different way he too is trapped by his role. He cannot turn off his professional, joking manner, and it is remarkable how often we find him 'wasting his sharpness on the desert air':[14] some of his most elaborate performances are directed at Corin, Audrey and William, who are all in varying degrees too slow to appreciate them. His particular line is a knowing cynicism – pleasant enough when he is entertaining Jaques or the ladies, who can feed him the right kind of questions and enjoy his performance. But he cannot adjust to his mental inferiors, and with them his manner varies between condescension and outright bullying. There is even something compulsive in his attack on William: 'By my troth, we that have good wits have much to answer for: we shall be flouting, we cannot hold' (v. i. 11–12). He never drops his professional manner, and as a result we never know – for example – whether his cynicism about Audrey is real or merely teasing.[15] The character is defined, and limited, by the formal role of the flouting jester.

Jaques presents a more complicated case. Behind the pose of

[13] It is typical of the play's openness of manner that even Corin, at one point, is made to talk like Silvius.

[14] D. J. Palmer, 'As You Like It and the idea of play', *Critical Quarterly*, XIII (autumn 1971), p. 244.

[15] See ibid.

melancholy we detect a genial interest in humanity. His lecture on the seven ages has a light, jocular tone that works against the cynicism of its content. And he seems gregarious by nature: 'I prithee, pretty youth, let me be better acquainted with thee' (IV. i. 1–2); 'Will you sit down with me, and we two will rail against our mistress the world, and all our misery' (III. ii. 261–2). He collects people, prizing Touchstone in particular as a rare item.[16] But while unlike the jester he allows us glimpses of the man behind the mask, he has no real freedom beyond his adopted role. We see this when he wishes to change his part, becoming not a light entertainer specializing in melancholy, but a fully-fledged satirist reforming the world. The Duke brings him sharply to heel, claiming that he would do

> Most mischievous foul sin, in chiding sin;
> For thou thyself hast been a libertine,
> As sensual as the brutish sting itself;
> And all th'embossed sores and headed evils
> That thou with licence of free foot hast caught
> Wouldst thou disgorge into the general world.
>
> (II. vii. 64–9)

This sharp and surprisingly serious rebuke contrasts with the Duke's usual indulgence of Jaques – 'I love to cope him in these sullen fits' (II. i. 67). And it reveals more of Jaques than we might have expected to learn: a comic figure does not usually have a past. Jaques is tolerable as an entertainer if he keeps his satire light; but that satire has no value as a moral corrective, for it reflects merely his own experience of corruption. The Duke is telling him, in effect, that he can be tolerated only if he does not claim to be taken too seriously. Jaques's reply, offering the conventional argument that satire is general and not aimed at particular individuals, evades the Duke's charge; but for the rest of the play we hear nothing more of Jaques the reformer of the world. We have now seen that the lightening of his cynicism by conscious role-playing is a necessary tactic to preserve the social acceptability his gregarious nature requires. Like the type figures

[16] See John Palmer, *Political and Comic Characters of Shakespeare* (London, 1964), p. 393.

of his most famous speech, he has a part, and – like it or not – he must play it.

Arden gives Touchstone and Jaques freedom to exercise their wits, but that freedom is finally limited by their own adopted roles. Rosalind's disguise as Ganymede, on the other hand, is genuinely liberating. For one thing, there is a clear distinction between the role and the character behind the role; a different name, a different sex. This is not to say that Ganymede and Rosalind are utterly different beings, and that nothing Ganymede says can be taken as Rosalind's serious view. It is not so simple as that. Ganymede is part of Rosalind's nature, but clearly not the whole; rather the role is a device allowing Rosalind a freedom of comment impossible in a conventional love affair, while at the same time freeing her from any final commitment to Ganymede's point of view. Like the women of *Love's Labour's Lost* she can be properly scathing about her lover's attempts at poetry: 'O most gentle pulpiter! What a tedious homily of love have you wearied your parishioners withal, and never cried, "Have patience, good people"' (III. ii. 145–7). This is before she knows who wrote the verses; but even in direct conversation with Orlando she can be satiric about the way love is expressed in literature, poking fun at both the conventions of love poetry and the great love stories of the past:

> The poor world is almost six thousand years old, and in all this time there was not any man died in his own person, videlicet, in a love-cause. Troilus has his brains dash'd out with a Grecian club; yet he did what he could to die before, and he is one of the patterns of love. Leander, he would have liv'd many a fair year, though Hero had turn'd nun, if it had not been for a hot midsummer-night; for, good youth, he went but forth to wash him in the Hellespont, and, being taken with the cramp, was drown'd; and the foolish chroniclers of that age found it was – Hero of Sestos. But these are all lies: men have died from time to time, and worms have eaten them, but not for love.
>
> (IV. i. 83–95)

While in *Pyramus and Thisbe* tragedy was dismissed as irrelevant, here it is rejected as untrue. Rosalind's speech is controlled by a cool sense of the world as it really is – men *do* die, but not for love.

But the paradox is that despite the conviction with which the satire is spoken, and the realism that appears to control it, the satire is itself conventional, just as Berowne's renunciation of rhetoric was conventional (and rhetorical). Ganymede claims to have learned his views on love from 'an old religious uncle', an ex-courtier disillusioned with love and women (III. ii. 320–6). This figure is also identified as the 'great magician' who can produce a bride for Orlando (v. iv. 32–3). He is, one imagines, first cousin to Frederick's 'old religious man', a literary stock figure. Ganymede's view of love is thus second-hand, orthodox and not always in tune with the facts: contemplating Orlando, he cannot imagine him as a lover, for 'There is none of my uncle's marks upon you' (III. ii. 342). In thus identifying the satiric role as conventional, Rosalind preserves herself from any final commitment to it, just as Ganymede swears 'by all pretty oaths that are not dangerous' (IV. i. 169). In confessing her love directly – which she does over and over – she can be as extravagant as the old tales she mocks: 'his kissing is as full of sanctity as the touch of holy bread' (III. iv. 12–13). After Ganymede has been particularly active, with an extended attack on women, love and marriage, Rosalind hastens to redress the balance:

ROSALIND: O coz, coz, coz, my pretty little coz, that thou didst know how many fathom deep I am in love! But it cannot be sounded: my affection hath an unknown bottom, like the Bay of Portugal.

CELIA: Or rather, bottomless; that as fast as you pour affection in, it runs out.

ROSALIND: No; that same wicked bastard of Venus, that was begot of thought, conceiv'd of spleen, and born of madness; that blind rascally boy, that abuses everyone's eyes because his own are out – let him be judge how deep I am in love. I'll tell thee, Aliena, I cannot be out of the sight of Orlando. I'll go find a shadow, and sigh till he come.

CELIA: And I'll sleep.

(IV. i. 184–96)

Rosalind veers between frank confession and self-mockery, trying hard to keep her balance as her feelings are released. Celia meets her confession with pure mockery, and then with ostentatious indifference; her interventions help us to distinguish between the satire of the totally immune and the satire of a woman genuinely in love but trying to keep her poise. Celia's manner is cool, detached and simple; Rosalind's is more complex, showing a wry awareness of her own extravagance while insisting on that extravagance as the only adequate expression of her feelings. The play's open, flexible manner is nowhere better illustrated, or more eloquent.

Just as the satirist tries to restrain the lover even when the mask is off, so the lover is always compromising the satirist. The mask has a habit of slipping: 'By this hand, it will not kill a fly' (iv. i. 98); 'By my life, she will do as I do' (iv. i. 141). The cry of 'Alas, dear love, I cannot lack thee two hours!' (iv. i. 159) sounds genuine; Rosalind has been caught off guard by Orlando's sudden decision to leave, and she hastily covers the mistake by turning it into self-parody: 'Ay, go your ways, go your ways. I knew what you would prove; my friends told me as much, and I thought no less' (iv. i. 162–4). Not only that, but Rosalind uses the freedom provided by the disguise to solicit love shamelessly: 'Come, woo me, woo me; for now am I in a holiday humour, and like enough to consent. What would you say to me now, an I were your very, very Rosalind?' (iv. i. 61–3). She even goes through a mock wedding – she wants to say the words, if only in jest. When she offers to cure Orlando, we sense the real relationship between the satiric posture and the love beneath it:

> . . . at which time would I, being but a moonish youth, grieve, be effeminate, changeable, longing and liking, proud, fantastical, apish, shallow, inconstant, full of tears, full of smiles; for every passion something, and for no passion truly anything, as boys and women are for the most part cattle of this colour; would now like him, now loathe him; then entertain him, then forswear him; now weep for him, then spit at him; that I drave my suitor from his mad humour of love to a living humour of madness; which was, to forswear the full stream of the world

and to live in a nook merely monastic. And thus I cur'd him; and this way will I take upon me to wash your liver as clean as a sound sheep's heart, that there shall not be one spot of love in't.

ORLANDO: I would not be cured, youth.

ROSALIND: I would cure you, if you would but call me Rosalind, and come every day to my cote, and woo me.

(III. ii. 376–91)

Rosalind's description of the giddiness of women and the madness of love is extravagant, freewheeling and somewhat disembodied, a rhetorical playing with ideas. It is controlled, or rather appears to be controlled, by the practicality inherent in the comic image of the sound sheep's heart. But Orlando's blunt reply brings the whole house of cards tumbling down. The madness of love is just what he wants; the giddiness of womankind could not matter less. And with Rosalind's rejoinder we see where the real centre of control lies. Under the cover of attacking love, she wishes to act out her own desires. She does not want Orlando to be cured, any more than he does himself. Her last speech, like Orlando's, is very simple and direct, and through it, step by step, her caution vanishes as each request comes nearer to the heart of her desire. There is a similar though more complex effect in the mock courtship scene itself:

I will be more jealous of thee than a Barbary cock-pigeon over her hen, more clamorous than a parrot against rain, more new-fangled than an ape, more giddy in my desires than a monkey. I will weep for nothing, like Diana in the fountain, and I will do that when you are dispos'd to be merry; I will laugh like a hyen, and that when thou art inclin'd to sleep.

ORLANDO: But will my Rosalind do so?

ROSALIND: By my life, she will do as I do.

(IV. i. 133–41)

Once again the satiric posturing is extravagant and self-conscious, a game of language with no firm conviction behind it. And once again its extravagance is emphasized by the blunt statements that follow it; there is the same feeling that Rosalind, encouraged by

Orlando, is bringing herself under control. Her 'By my life, she will do as I do' is ambiguous. Perhaps she implies the real Rosalind will not be like this. But more likely she is warning him – more likely still, reassuring him – that he is not marrying a remote Petrarchan beauty but a real woman. In any case her basic reason for indulging in the fantasy is clear: she is imagining herself married to Orlando.

Rosalind has the range of feeling and expression we observed in some of the major figures of previous comedies. But she has more control over the wide possibilities of her nature than Berowne, with his unstable veering between self-indulgence and self-contempt, or Portia, who is forced into imitating Shylock somewhat against the grain of her nature. She is closer to Petruchio, who turns one possibility of his nature – noisy bullying – into a comic performance, and thus exorcizes it to clear the way for domestic peace. Everything is relative, it all depends on your point of view – that idea depends on the comic confrontations of different figures, each of whom is locked in a fixed position, whether consciously like Jaques, or unconsciously like Silvius. Rosalind can take us beyond that idea by including in her nature several points of view. She can encompass the romanticism of Silvius, the realism of Touchstone, and even at times Corin's awareness of the working-day world. Having various attitudes at her command, she is in a position to pick and choose among them. 'It all depends on your point of view' – but if one is not to be paralysed by inactivity, one has to decide which point of view is worth acting on. On the question of love, Rosalind finally stands with Orlando: 'I would not be cured.' The satiric point of view cannot be forgotten, for that would be to deny an important part of her nature. But it can be put in its place by being turned into a performance, acted out and thus exorcized. This could be seen as a last fling before the surrender of marriage – Rosalind giving free play to her individuality before, like Millamant, dwindling into a wife. But the satiric view of love is as conventional, as unoriginal, as the acceptance of it. Rosalind's freedom is rather her power to choose between conventions, to decide that one is to be treated as a game, and the other taken seriously. Unlike Jaques and Touchstone, she turns only part of her nature into a performance, and thus maintains the control and flexibility they lack. And this process of selection in Rosalind's nature is reflected in the play as a whole: beneath the shifting surface of *As You Like It* is a firm acceptance of the conventions of love.

As we saw in *Love's Labour's Lost*, love's dependence on conventional expression makes it vulnerable to mockery. This is also true in *As You Like It*: Orlando's verse is bad enough, and Touchstone's parody shrewdly points out its reliance on an over-easy rhyme scheme. But unlike the ladies of the earlier comedy, Rosalind can see the folly of the expression without questioning the truth of the love. The reason for this is suggested in Phebe's first encounter with Ganymede. She pokes fun at Silvius for using a shopworn poetic convention:

Now I do frown on thee with all my heart;
And if mine eyes can wound, now let them kill thee.
Now counterfeit to swoon; why, now fall down;
Or, if thou canst not, O for shame, for shame,
Lie not, to say mine eyes are murderers.

(III. v. 15–19)

Like the ladies of *Love's Labour's Lost*, she mocks the convention by taking it too literally. But a few lines later she sees Ganymede and is forced to acknowledge the truth behind the cliché, 'the wounds invisible / That love's keen arrows make' (III. v. 30–1). The problem of love's dependence on convention, stated in *Love's Labour's Lost*, is here resolved in a manner characteristic of Shakespeare's comedies: by the test of experience. Love poetry deals in conventions and is therefore easy to mock – but in fact the behaviour love forces on us is predictable and conventional; when you fall in love, one of the things you surrender is your originality. Therefore the sheer predictability that makes love poetry so open to ridicule is also a guarantee of its accuracy. In the end, Silvius remains untouched, Phebe is converted; and even the mockery of Celia – for whom love is 'to make sport withal; but love no man in good earnest' (I. ii. 23–4) – is swept away, as she meets her nemesis in Oliver.

Much of the comic effect of *As You Like It* comes, as we have seen, from a swift interplay of perspectives. But that is not the play's final effect. In the forest scenes we seem for a while to be suspended beyond time, enjoying an endless afternoon. The only movement is a back-and-forth shuttling as the various characters wander in, confront each other and wander out again. But just as there is a controlling attitude behind the interplay of perspectives, so in the play as a whole there is a steady forward motion behind the apparent casualness. We can trace through the play two main ways of seeing time. One is the Jaques–Touchstone view of inevitable decay:

> And so, from hour to hour, we ripe and ripe,
> And then, from hour to hour, we rot and rot;
> And thereby hangs a tale.
>
> (II. vii. 26–8)

Jaques's set piece on the seven ages of man is essentially an elaboration of this view. Rosalind, in her satiric vein, shares it. The great mock courtship scene (IV. i) imitates the progress of a love affair through time, from disdain to acceptance to a re-enactment of the marriage service, and then to the disillusion of marriage itself. Man's life is linked with the seasons, and the process is seen as one of decay: 'No, no, Orlando; men are April when they woo, December when they wed; maids are May when they are maids, but the sky changes when they are wives' (IV. i. 130–3). This is the realist's view, and the satirist's view. But this view is part of the self-conscious role-playing of all three characters, and thus its seriousness is compromised. In the play itself we detect a different, less mechanical view of the changes of time, one that is embodied not in any one speech, but in the whole movement of the play.

The early scenes are dominated by a sense of an old order lost. The idea is centred on old Adam, whom Orlando addresses as the last survivor of better days:

> O good old man, how well in thee appears
> The constant service of the antique world,
> When service sweat for duty, not for meed!
> Thou art not for the fashion of these times,
> Where none will sweat but for promotion,
> And having that do choke their service up
> Even with the having; it is not so with thee.
>
> (II. iii. 56–62)

Orlando looks back to a world of decent order and harmony, as opposed to the new world of self-seeking individualism. Oliver is very much a 'new man': 'What's the new news at the new court?' (I. i. 89). And certainly in the new world order is neglected: old Sir Roland's will is ignored, the rightful Duke is banished, and the court is dominated by a moody individual whose whims enslave everyone else. Connected with this contrast between an idealized past and a corrupt present is the curious obsession with fathers that runs all through the early scenes. Rosalind and Orlando both brood over their lost fathers. When attacked first by Oliver and then by Frederick, Orlando seems more concerned to defend his dead father's dignity than his own (I. i. 51–3; I. ii. 211–13). Rosalind cannot be merry, 'unless you could teach me how to forget a banished father' (I. ii. 3–4). And Adam, set upon by Oliver, exclaims 'God be with my old master! / He would not have spoke such a word' (I. i. 75–6).

But while passages like this may seem to confirm the idea of decay through time, the old order is not dead; it is recoverable in the forest of Arden. When Charles the wrestler describes the banished Duke's court, he speaks of it as though the past has come to life again:

> They say he is already in the Forest of Arden, and a many merry men with him; and there they live like the old Robin Hood of England. They say many young gentlemen flock to him every day, and fleet the time carelessly, as they did in the golden world.
>
> (I. i. 105–9)

Instead of seeing time as inevitable decay, this suggests that time's progress may be circular: the golden age we nearly always associate with the past can be recovered. This is also suggested in Le-Beau's 'Hereafter, in a better world than this, / I shall desire more love and knowledge of you' (I. ii. 263–4). And when Orlando comes to the forest these hints of the recovery of the old order are fulfilled. His appeal to the order and decency of the past meets with a responsive voice from the Duke:

> If ever you have look'd on better days,
> If ever been where bells have knoll'd to church,

>   If ever sat at any good man's feast,
>   If ever from your eyelids wip'd a tear,
>   And know what 'tis to pity and be pitied,
>   Let gentleness my strong enforcement be;
>   In the which hope I blush, and hide my sword.
> DUKE: True is it that we have seen better days,
>   And have with holy bells been knoll'd to church,
>   And sat at good men's feasts, and wip'd our eyes
>   Of drops that sacred pity hath engend'red;
>   And therefore sit you down in gentleness,
>   And take upon command what help we have
>   That to your wanting may be minist'red.
>
>   (II. vii. 113–26)

The Duke knows just what Orlando means; the young man has in a sense come home. The incantatory repetitions give a posed, formal dignity to this moment. Like Orlando's address to old Adam, it is quiet, serious and free from the usual comic dislocation. It is also the last occasion in the play on which there is an appeal to the golden past. Having found a community where the old decency and order are maintained, the characters no longer find it necessary to look backwards. After the scene of the Duke's banquet, old Adam disappears from the play; he is not even referred to. His disappearance, like that of Lear's fool, is unexplained in plot terms, but in both cases the character's dramatic function has been fulfilled, and he is no longer needed.

In this respect the pivot on which the play turns is Rosalind's line 'But what talk we of fathers when there is such a man as Orlando?' (III. iv. 34–5). The characters turn from nostalgia for the security of a father-dominated world to the decision to create their own kind of order in marriage. Here again, time is seen not as the medium of decay but as the medium of fulfilment. In the final movement of the play, there is an urgent drive forward. A transition from winter to spring is marked in the songs, and is frequently brought out in production.[17] 'It was a lover and his lass' offers the traditional *carpe diem* theme, urging us to 'take the

[17] See Arthur Colby Sprague and J. C. Trewin, *Shakespeare's Plays Today* (London, 1970), pp. 78–80.

present time ... For love is crowned with the prime' (v. iii. 28–30). As usual in Shakespearian comedy, human actions are connected with the rhythms of nature, and this song prepares us for the comic finale by providing the play's clearest images of spring and fertility.[18] This is matched by the mating instinct that overtakes the characters in the final act, from Audrey's growing impatience with Touchstone's delays (v. i. 1–4) to Rosalind's description of Oliver and Celia: 'They are in the very wrath of love and they will together. Clubs cannot part them' (v. ii. 36–8). By common consent, Rosalind and Orlando bring their satiric games of courtship to an end:

ROSALIND: ... Why, then, tomorrow I cannot serve your turn for Rosalind?
ORLANDO: I can live no longer by thinking.
ROSALIND: I will weary you then no longer with idle talking.
(v. ii. 45–8)

The bawdy overtones of 'serve your turn'[19] are deliberate; we are moving towards the practical realities of love. In the process, Ganymede disappears; like old Adam, he has served his purpose. It is not just that Rosalind removes the disguise; it is rather that this aspect of her nature is gradually withdrawn, and the change is therefore subtler than the simple removal of a mask. When she faints at the sight of the bloody napkin even Oliver will not believe she is 'counterfeiting' (IV. iii. 164–70); the disguise has slipped dramatically, and will never be so secure again. The napkin itself suggests a genuine love token, the lover proving his valour for his lady. And when Rosalind makes her last appearance as a boy in the final scene, both the Duke and Orlando, for the first time in the play, remark that Ganymede looks a bit like Rosalind (v. iv. 26–9). When she appears as herself in the finale, it is not just the winding up of a comic intrigue, but the end of a gradual transition from the games of satire to the ceremonies of love.

[18] In Peter Wood's production at Stratford, Ontario in 1959, the scene began with Touchstone and Audrey sniffing the air; most of the production had been set in winter, and this was the first day of spring. The song itself was treated as the first stage of the finale, with more and more characters entering at each verse, and joining in.
[19] Cf. *Love's Labour's Lost*, I. i. 277–8.

But as satire fades away, so too does the purely romantic contemplation of love. The litany of the four lovers in v. ii marks the
transition. Silvius, chief spokesman for the romantic view, gives it
a final, definitive statement, and the others join in, acknowledging
the truth it has for them:

> It is to be all made of fantasy,
> All made of passion, and all made of wishes;
> All adoration, duty, and observance,
> All humbleness, all patience, and impatience,
> All purity, all trial, all observance;
> And so am I for Phebe.

PHEBE: And so am I for Ganymede.
ORLANDO: And so am I for Rosalind.
ROSALIND: And so am I for no woman.

(v. ii. 87–95)

But the patient yearning suggested here would be sterile if not
matched by action; and in the atmosphere of growing urgency at
the end of the play, action cannot be delayed much longer.
Rosalind, having joined in the litany, suddenly becomes impatient with it:

> Pray you, no more of this; 'tis like the howling of
> Irish wolves against the moon. (*To Silvius*) I will
> help you, if I can. (*To Phebe*) I would love you if I
> could. – Tomorrow meet me all together. (*To Phebe*)
> I will marry you if ever I marry woman, and I'll be
> married tomorrow. (*To Orlando*) I will satisfy you if
> ever I satisfied man, and you shall be married to-
> morrow. (*To Silvius*) I will content you if what
> pleases you contents you, and you shall be married
> tomorrow. (*To Orlando*) As you love Rosalind, meet.
> (*To Silvius*) As you love Phebe, meet; – and as I
> love no woman, I'll meet. So, fare you well; I have
> left you commands.

SILVIUS: I'll not fail, if I live.
PHEBE: Nor I.
ORLANDO: Nor I.

(v. ii. 102–15)

In turning from verse to prose, she turns from romantic contemplation to realistic action; but the prose is still patterned and formal, and the responses of the other characters echo the rhythm of the earlier litany. The ceremonial idiom is broken only to be redirected. In Rosalind's speech, the ceremonial and the practical come together; and thus we could say that the realism of Ganymede has also been broken only to be redirected. The result, in the final scene, is an image of love that is ceremonial but not disembodied, and practical but not satiric.

A recurring idea in Shakespearian comedy is the naturalness of magic: we saw this in the resurrection of Hero, and in the operation of the fairies in *A Midsummer Night's Dream*. Here, something natural – the reappearance of Rosalind in her true form – is given overtones of mystery, overtones which are in turn restrained by our knowledge of the facts:

> Believe then, if you please, that I can do strange things. . . .
> it is not impossible to me, if it appear not inconvenient to you,
> to set her before your eyes tomorrow, human as she is, and
> without any danger.
>
> (v. ii. 55, 60–3)

This anticipates the careful way Paulina prepares the watchers at Hermione's statue for the miracle to come. The distinction between magic and natural events is blurred – just as, throughout the play, conventionalized action and familiar human behaviour have been fused. Hymen's entrance – and according to the Folio, this is not the rationalist editor's 'person presenting Hymen' but, quite simply, Hymen[20] – is the high point of miracle in the play. But while we are told –

> Then is there mirth in heaven,
> When earthly things made even
> Atone together . . .
>
> (v. iv. 102–4)

– we are also reminded that "Tis Hymen peoples every town' (v. ii. 137). There may be a similar double perspective in Jaques's 'There is, sure, another flood toward, and these couples are

[20] See Barnet, 'Strange events', p. 122.

coming to the Ark' (v. iv. 35–6), which suggests both animal coupling and the working of a divine plan.

Nor is the formality of the conclusion completely smooth: even in the formal greetings exchanged when Rosalind enters there is a slight breaking of the rhythm with Phebe's 'If sight and shape be true, / Why then, my love adieu!' (v. iv. 14–15). And Hymen's address to the couples also contains small changes of rhythm, suggesting that while the four couples are bound into one pattern, there are lingering differences among them:

> Here's eight that must take hands
> To join in Hymen's bands,
>   If truth holds true contents.
> You and you no cross shall part;
> You and you are heart in heart;
> You to his love must accord,
> Or have a woman to your lord;
> You and you are sure together,
> As the winter to foul weather.
>
> (v. iv. 122–30)

Each pair of lovers is, in fact, different, and represents a different way of viewing marriage. Orlando and Rosalind are the most comprehensive: they are brought together, as we have seen, partly by conventional love at first sight and partly by personal sympathy. They are both aware of the conventions of love, but not dependent on convention alone: when Jaques says to them 'Nay, then, God buy you, an you talk in blank verse' (iv. i. 28–9), the joke is finally against him, for they talk in prose. And we should notice that Orlando can be no less playfully ironic in his Petrarchanism than Rosalind herself:

ROSALIND: Well, in her person, I say I will not have you.
ORLANDO: Then, in mine own person, I die.

> (iv. i. 81–2)

Their submission to love is fully mature, including as it does an awareness of love's laughable side. Celia and Oliver present a similar balance, but within a narrower range: their love depends purely on the convention of love at first sight, with no attempt to rationalize it;[21] but at least Oliver is prepared to acknowledge possible objections, even while sweeping them aside: 'Neither call the giddiness of it in question, the poverty of her, the small acquaintance, my sudden wooing, nor her sudden consenting, but say with me, "I love Aliena"' (v. ii. 5–7). Silvius and Phebe remain purely conventional – as they need to do if Phebe's disappointment in Ganymede and her surrender to Silvius are to be satisfying. If either character had psychological depth, we would be tempted to ask awkward questions; as it is, their relationship (like that of Claudio and Hero) is worked out in terms of narrative design, and their affair is formally cemented with a couplet: 'I will not eat my word, now thou art mine, / Thy faith my fancy to thee doth combine' (v. iv. 143–4). In their reliance on convention they represent one part – and an important one – of the larger harmony embodied in Rosalind and Orlando. Touchstone and Audrey represent another part: 'I press in here, sir, amongst the rest of the country copulatives, to swear and to forswear, according as marriage binds and blood breaks' (v. iv. 53–6). Both Hymen and Jaques seem to agree with Touchstone that this marriage is headed for trouble, presumably since it is more a coupling of bodies than a marriage of true minds. All the same, the sexual level they represent is vital: one of Rosalind's first references to Orlando is to 'my child's father' (i. iii. 11), and she and Celia joke about putting a man in her belly (iii. ii. 188–90). Oliver and Celia have 'made a pair of stairs to marriage which they will climb incontinent, or else be incontinent before marriage' (v. ii. 35–6). Even Silvius's love is not totally disembodied: there may be the usual pun when he vows to have Phebe 'Though to have her and death were both one thing' (v. iv. 17), and less equivocally Jaques commends him to 'a long and well-deserved bed' (v. iv. 184).

The image of marriage at the end is thus a complex one, bringing together a rich variety of attitudes. And the new world of marriage is fused with the old world of decency and order represented by the Duke: Rosalind greets her father and her husband with the same words, 'To you I give myself, for I am yours' (v. iv.

110–11). There is a harmony of different generations suggested
here, quite different from the conflict of youth and age so frequently found in comedy (and invoked in this play by Silvius,
who accuses Corin of being too old to understand love – II. iv. 21–
30). The harmony of the ending finally includes more than the
joining of the sexes in marriage: it involves a full restoration of
social order in the broadest terms. The Duke promises that

> every of this happy number,
> That have endur'd shrewd days and nights with us,
> Shall share the good of our returned fortune,
> According to the measure of their states.
>
> (v. iv. 166–9)

The last line in particular suggests a respect for the social decorum
we saw so rudely violated earlier in the play. The old values,
recovered in the forest, will now return to the court. Just as the
play toys with and rejects the satiric view of love, so (through the
speeches of Touchstone and Jaques) it has toyed with the realist's
view of time as a linear movement to inevitable decay, but chosen
in the end to focus on that one moment of happiness when we
seem to have cheated time, when a new world and an old come
together in permanent harmony, 'mirth in heaven'.

But though Ganymede has disappeared, Jaques and Touchstone are still on stage. Each wins his own kind of satisfaction as a
performer in the final scene. Touchstone, the professional, gets to
play for his biggest audience, gives them his most elaborate
routine (on the degrees of the lie), and wins 'the only "encore" in
Shakespeare'.[22] Jaques, like Antonio, is left out of the Noah's Ark
procession; but unlike Antonio he has his own pleasures to fall
back on. With a splendid flourish – 'What you would have / I'll
stay to know at your abandoned cave' (v. iv. 189–90) – he stalks
off the stage, on his way to add Frederick to his collection of interesting people. But each in his own way acknowledges the authority of love – Touchstone by surrendering to it, though with much
ironic grumbling; Jaques by distributing good wishes before he
goes. His speech imitates Hymen's, though he acknowledges the
broader implications of the ending by including the Duke. For

[22] Brian Vickers, *The Artistry of Shakespeare's Prose* (London, 1968), p. 219.

once the satiric mask is dropped, and his friendly interest in people comes into the open:

> (*To the Duke*)
> You to your former honour I bequeath;
> Your patience and your virtue well deserves it.
> (*To Orlando*)
> You to a love that your true faith doth merit;
> (*To Oliver*)
> You to your land, and love, and great allies;
> (*To Silvius*)
> You to a long and well-deserved bed;
> (*To Touchstone*)
> And you to wrangling; for thy loving voyage
> Is but for two months victuall'd.
>
> (v. iv. 180–6)

Admittedly he cannot resist a final dig at Touchstone, but his prophecy is not much worse than Hymen's own. In the closing moments of the play Jaques is almost as prominent as Rosalind, and the balance between these two figures suggests the balance of the play itself, with satire stating its case but finally deferring to love.

But in Shakespearian comedy the duplication of a gesture is liable to make that gesture comic (as in the eavesdropping scene of *Love's Labour's Lost*). And Jaques in duplicating Hymen's speech may be, consciously or unconsciously, getting in a last kick for satire after all. Four couples is a high average, even for Shakespearian comedy. The only other play where there are so many is *A Midsummer Night's Dream*, and there they are never all on stage together. The ending is not merely ceremonial but artificial, and the sardonic comments on the Touchstone–Audrey match remind us that not all marriages are made in heaven. The play's final image of harmony may be serious enough, but is it credible? Do we, perhaps, feel a final detachment from it, as something belonging to art alone? Here Shakespeare employs a comic device he has not used since *A Midsummer Night's Dream* – the awareness *within the play* that the play itself is an artifact. The blatant exposition in the first scene is rather like that of the play-within-the-play in *The*

Taming of the Shrew, and has the same distancing effect. Phebe's references to Marlowe, and Jaques's 'Nay, then, God buy you, an you talk in blank verse' (IV. i. 28–9) both threaten the dramatic illusion. There is a more subtle effect in an early scene:

LEBEAU: There comes an old man and his three sons –
  CELIA: I could match this beginning with an old tale.

(I. ii. 104–5)

We could also match this beginning with *As You Like It*. These suggestions come to a head in the epilogue, where Rosalind's 'If I were a woman . . .' (l. 15) reminds us of the boy actor. The choice of a female character to deliver the epilogue is peculiar, as she herself admits (in *All's Well That Ends Well*, another play dominated by a heroine, the epilogue is spoken by the King). But the choice of Rosalind is deliberate. Throughout the play she is the character who makes the most creative use of role-playing, the one who is most careful to see the relation between performance and reality. And as in the play itself the conventions of love could be mocked while the love was accepted as real, so in the epilogue the play is admitted to be an illusion (and perhaps not even a good play), but the final effect is different from Puck's urbane apology for something 'No more yielding but a dream':

I charge you, O women, for the love you bear to men, to like as much of this play as please you; and I charge you, O men, for the love you bear to women – as I perceive by your simp'ring none of you hates them – that between you and the women the play may please.

(Epilogue, 10–15)

The play is an artifact, an illusion, and that is freely admitted – but all we have to do is look at the audience to see the truth of its final vision of humanity walking to the Ark in pairs. This may be one more reason for the play's title. One recalls the famous moment in Gogol's *The Government Inspector*, when the Mayor wheels on the audience and demands 'What do you think you are laughing at? You are laughing at yourselves!' But here, the moment of recognition is without bitterness.

Not that the image of love presented here is particularly digni-

fied. The 'simp'ring' of the men – and the possibly bawdy suggestion of 'between you and the women the play may please'[23] –
seem a long way from Hymen's 'mirth in heaven'. But even for
Hymen, mirth in heaven depends on 'earthly things'. And there is
no point in standing on one's dignity where love is concerned: in
the words of the song,

> Take thou no scorn to wear the horn;
> It was a crest ere thou wast born.
> > Thy father's father wore it;
> > And thy father bore it.
> The horn, the horn, the lusty horn,
> Is not a thing to laugh to scorn.
>
> > > > (IV. ii. 13–18)

The physical level of love is the common one, the one we can all
understand, and it dominates the epilogue: 'If I were a woman, I
would kiss as many of you as had beards that pleas'd me, complexions that liked me, and breaths that I defied not' (ll. 15–17).
This is the one clear bond between the play and the audience's
own experience of life. It is also the one aspect of love whose power
a satirist like Touchstone is prepared to admit, and the one interest shared by all four couples. If this play is peculiarly successful
in showing the reality behind convention, this may be because it
sees convention is strongest where it embodies recognizable, predictable experiences: in love in particular, all the clichés come
true. Dispensing with the sort of intrigue he used in *The Merchant
of Venice* and *Much Ado About Nothing*, Shakespeare avoids the distasteful narrowing of experience produced by such conventions as
Shylock's bond and Don John's plotting. Instead, he concentrates
on a convention – the Noah's Ark ending – which allows us in the
audience to feel that we are not merely spectators but participants.
We are entitled to poke fun at it if we wish. The liberty of Arden
will admit almost any point of view. But if we do laugh, we must
also recognize that, like Rosalind when she played Ganymede, we
are laughing at ourselves.

[23] See D. J. Palmer, 'Art and nature in *As You Like It*', *Philological Quarterly*,
XLIX (January 1970), p. 30.

9 Twelfth Night

As You Like It and *Twelfth Night* are often seen as the twin peaks of Shakespeare's achievement in romantic comedy, yet within the conventions of the genre they could hardly be more different. It is as though the later play was created by taking the major impulses behind its predecessor and throwing them into reverse. While *As You Like It* was almost without conventional comic intrigue, *Twelfth Night* bristles with plot complications. Instead of enjoying the freedom of the forest, with the organic cycles of nature in the background, the characters are enclosed in houses and formal gardens, and in the background is not the familiar countryside but the implacable, mysterious sea. Instead of the swift, decisive matings and friendly courtship games of the earlier play, we have unrequited love (a minor motif in *As You Like It*) expressing itself through unreliable messengers. Not since *The Two Gentlemen of Verona* has there been such emphasis on the pains rather than the pleasures of love; not since *Love's Labour's Lost* have we been so aware that love's means of expression are unreliable. It is as though the ground won in the intervening plays – and most notably in *As You Like It* – has been deliberately surrendered.

A civilized liberty was the keynote of the earlier play. *Twelfth Night* is, by comparison, strictly divided into compartments. In the earlier play, prose and verse mingled freely, and both could be used for moments of casual naturalism, or moments of formality.

Here there is a stricter division, and a tighter logic – prose for comic or naturalistic effects, verse for formal and romantic ones. This reflects a firmer separation of romantic and comic figures: the plotlessness of *As You Like It* allowed a casual mingling; in *Twelfth Night* each set of characters has a plot to tend to, and is largely kept within the confines of that plot. When a character from one plot becomes involved in the other, the effect is not so much to unify the play as to create a comic shock. Viola among the clowns, and Malvolio trying to be a lover, are both laughably out of their depth. There is also a sharp division between the two households that dominate the play. Orsino's is dramatically simple – a single figure surrounded by attendants, who except for Viola are functional and characterless – and even Viola is utterly dedicated to her master. Olivia's household is dramatically more open and complex: there is a fully developed life below stairs, largely unconcerned with Olivia's problems, and even the attendants who appear with their mistress, Malvolio and Maria, spend most of the action engaged in their own affairs.

The 'dykes that separate man from man', upon which, according to W. B. Yeats, 'comedy keeps house',[1] are nowhere more apparent in Shakespeare's comedies than they are in *Twelfth Night*. In plays like *A Midsummer Night's Dream* and *As You Like It* the confrontation of different minds was mostly stimulating and entertaining – a celebration of human variety. In *Twelfth Night*, however, we see the other side of this vision: each individual is locked in his own private understanding, and his ability to escape from himself and share experiences with others is limited. That did not matter so much in *A Midsummer Night's Dream* and *As You Like It*, where the comedy created a broad, secure community, and our delight sprang from watching each individual take his place in that community, all of them contributing to a larger vision. But here the sense of community is weaker. Instead, we are aware of each character as an individual, out on his own, the lovers trying to make contact but with limited success, and the comic figures either openly hostile or forming relationships based on temporary expediency. If the frequent comparisons between

---

[1] 'The tragic theatre', *Essays and Introductions* (London, 1961), p. 214.

Twelfth Night and Jonsonian comedy have any basis,[2] it may be in this sense of sharply distinguished individuals adrift in a fragmented world, each with his own obsession. Certainly individual characters come more clearly into focus than in any previous comedy of Shakespeare's, and the sense that they can be bound together in a common experience is weaker. The play ends not with a dance or a procession of couples trooping off to bed, but with the solitary figure of Feste, singing of the wind and the rain. And this image of solitude echoes and reverberates throughout the play.

The solitude of the lovers results from their experience of unrequited love, an experience that leaves them frustrated and restless. Our first impression of Orsino is of a character in search of an attitude, full of emotion but with no satisfactory outlet for emotion, nothing around which to shape it. He calls for music, savours it, then suddenly finds it tiresome. His unrequited love for Olivia may appear to be the centre of his life, but even in the first scene his attitude to that love shifts uneasily:

> O spirit of love, how quick and fresh art thou!
> That, notwithstanding thy capacity
> Receiveth as the sea, naught enters there,
> Of what validity and pitch soe'er,
> But falls into abatement and low price
> Even in a minute.
>
> (I. i. 9–14)

The life-giving suggestions of 'quick and fresh' are suddenly replaced by an image of annihilation. Here as throughout Shakespeare, the sea suggests both destruction and new life; in Orsino's mind, however, the ideas are held not in balance but in confusion. This shifting quality persists throughout the first scene:

> O, when mine eyes did see Olivia first,
> Methought she purg'd the air of pestilence!

[2] See, for example, Paul Mueschke and Jeannette Fleischer, 'Jonsonian elements in the comic underplot of *Twelfth Night*', *Publications of the Modern Language Association of America*, XLVIII (1933), pp. 722–40; and Herbert Howarth, *The Tiger's Heart* (London, 1970), pp. 102–19.

> That instant was I turn'd into a hart,
> And my desires, like fell and cruel hounds,
> E'er since pursue me.
>
> (i. i. 19–23)

An image of cleansing is succeeded by images of guilt and danger; again, the shift is rapid and illogical, with no coherent attitude behind it. When he hears of Olivia's vow he seizes on it, surprisingly, as a source of hope:

> How will she love when the rich golden shaft
> Hath kill'd the flock of all affections else
> That live in her; when liver, brain, and heart,
> These sovereign thrones, are all supplied and fill'd,
> Her sweet perfections, with one self king!
>
> (i. i. 35–9)

For a moment he seems confident and self-assertive, in the role of the dominant, masculine lover; but then he cries 'Away before me to sweet beds of flow'rs: / Love-thoughts lie rich when canopied with bow'rs' (i. i. 40–1) – and once more his love collapses into passive self-indulgence. The love of Olivia dominates his life, or so he thinks. But no clear image of that love, or of Olivia herself, emerges from this scene. There may be some point in Viola's question, 'Is he inconstant, sir, in his favours?' (i. iv. 6). The speed with which 'Cesario' becomes a favourite suggests that the impulse of love, seeking an outlet, has fixed on the nearest thing that looks like a woman (for that is how Orsino describes his new servant – i. iv. 29–33). When Feste sums him up the sea is invoked once again, this time to suggest a restless, pointless wandering:

> Now the melancholy god protect thee; and the tailor make thy doublet of changeable taffeta, for thy mind is a very opal. I would have men of such constancy put to sea, that their business might be everything, and their intent everywhere; for that's it that always makes a good voyage of nothing.
>
> (ii. iv. 72–7)

What we see in Orsino is an unfulfilled nature – to add another image to Feste's – prowling to and fro like a caged animal.

He and Olivia are both locked up in their respective houses. At

first she is dedicated to the self-punishing routine of mourning for
her brother:

> But like a cloistress she will veiled walk,
> And water once a day her chamber round
> With eye-offending brine.
>
> (I. i. 28–30)

Again, we notice the sense of enclosure, with the suggestion this
time of circles traced out in a prison yard. But Olivia, no less than
Orsino, is restless, and will not settle to a routine. If her mourning
were serious, she would not accept Feste's daring joke about her
brother's soul so easily as she does. And while she has vowed not
to accept Orsino's messages, Malvolio's description of the messenger, laying insulting emphasis on his youth, is enough to make
her change her mind. But while she finds an object for her love, it
is an unresponsive one, and Olivia becomes trapped in a situation
beyond her control, one in which there is no right course of action.
In III. i, we see her trying various approaches to Cesario, dropping
broad hints but urging him to speak first:

> To one of your receiving
> Enough is shown; a cypress, not a bosom,
> Hides my heart. So, let me hear you speak.
>
> (III. i. 117–19)

– then pretending indifference: 'Be not afraid, good youth; I will
not have you' (III. i. 128); then pathetically trying to turn the
conversation round again: 'I prithee tell me what thou think'st of
me' (III. i. 135). Finally, her reserve collapses in a frank and
passionate declaration (III. i. 146–53). She knows she has compromised herself and betrayed her dignity by offering love so
frankly to an inferior, and one who is unwilling to accept her; but
she is powerless to control her feelings:

> I have said too much unto a heart of stone,
> And laid mine honour too unchary out;
> There's something in me that reproves my fault;
> But such a headstrong potent fault it is
> That it but mocks reproof.
>
> (III. iv. 191–5)

By the normal standards of courtship, a woman who is the active wooer is in a false position, and she makes embarrassing mistakes. In her first meeting with Cesario she offers him money, which he indignantly rejects, yet we see her later, prepared to make the same mistake again: 'How shall I feast him? What bestow of him? / For youth is bought more oft than begg'd or borrow'd' (III. iv. 2-3). Her dependence on Malvolio to deliver what is in effect her first message of love is symptomatic of her dilemma: he makes the message as insulting as he can, adding the unnecessary touch of hurling the ring to the ground, and claiming (falsely) that this was part of Olivia's orders. Olivia's love can find no satisfactory outlet, no reliable means of expression. It is, like Orsino's, a passion that leaves her trapped and unfulfilled.

The lovers are confined by circumstance as much as by their own natures: so long as their love is misdirected, they find no relief or satisfaction. The figures of the comic plot are trapped in another way – by limited, clearly defined comic personalities. In Sir Toby Belch's opening pun, 'Confine? I'll confine myself no finer than I am' (I. iii. 9), there may be an extra significance of which he is not aware. To be occasionally drunk may be the sign of a free spirit; to be consistently drunk is not. Sir Toby may challenge the restrictions of Olivia's household, but he is too bound by his addiction to the bottle to put genuine liberty in their place. Even his respect for his niece finds alcoholic expression: 'I'll drink to her as long as there is a passage in my throat and drink in Illyria. He's a coward and a coystrill that will not drink to my niece till his brains turn o'th' toe like a parish-top' (I. iii. 35-8). Sir Andrew, with the fuddled good sense of which he is occasionally capable, sees how their lives have been restricted:

SIR TOBY: ... Does not our lives consist of the four elements?

SIR ANDREW: Faith, so they say; but I think it rather consists of eating and drinking.

SIR TOBY: Th'art a scholar; let us therefore eat and drink.

(II. iii. 9-12)

Sir Toby's only answer is to accept the charge and open another bottle. Sir Andrew yearns for better things: he imagines for him-

self the full life of the courtier, soldier and scholar: dancing, duel-
ling, masques and revels. He envies the fool's singing voice, and
Cesario's gift with words; and he will, if goaded, try almost anything once. But the aspirations of Sir Philip Sidney are wedded to
the capacities of Sir Andrew Aguecheek. However earnestly he
may try to improve himself, he suffers a comic paralysis of will;
his weakness ties him to the more decisive character of Sir Toby,
and he is confined in Sir Toby's narrow world of eating and drinking. He is occasionally let out on his chain – as when Sir Toby
encourages his efforts at dancing or wooing – but only for his
companion's amusement.[3] Sir Toby has the capacities of a gentleman – he is shrewd, witty and not afraid of swordplay; but
his talents have no outlet. He has come to terms with life, but
in a way that belittles and restricts him. Sir Andrew has the
ambition but not the capacity; both are trapped by their own
natures – comically, but, the more we look at them, pathetically
too.

It is more difficult to see pathos in Malvolio – in his early
scenes, at least. He too is in the prison of his ego, but for him it is a
gorgeous palace. His egotism kills his capacity for ordinary
pleasure: 'O, you are sick of self-love, Malvolio, and taste with a
distemper'd appetite' (I. v. 85–6). He takes no pleasure, that is,
if it is provided by anyone else – by Feste, for example. But he is an
endless source of pleasure to himself. Like Orsino, he leads a
fantasy life, 'practising behaviour to his own shadow' (II. v. 15).
In the long soliloquy of the letter scene the stiff constraint of his
ordinary manner disappears, and he becomes urbane and expan-
sive, revelling in the details of his dream. In fact Malvolio is fully
happy only when he is alone; his prickly manner at other times is
his reaction to the presence of other people, whose very existence
is an irritating intrusion: 'Go off; I discard you. Let me enjoy my
private' (III. iv. 84–5). Malvolio is the most obviously solitary
figure in Illyria; but his solitude is also a striking comic variant on
the confinement suffered by Orsino and Olivia, indulging fantasies of love that cannot be gratified, and the restriction of

[3] In David William's production at Stratford, Ontario in 1966, Sir Toby
cracked a whip as Sir Andrew danced; their relations were those of trainer and
performing animal.

personality that lies behind the gregariousness of the drunken knights.

The fascination with the power – and the dangers – of language that runs through Shakespeare's comedies appears again in *Twelfth Night*. Here, as in *Love's Labour's Lost*, the emphasis is on the dangers. The foibles of the characters are shown through the way they misuse words, and are trapped by words.[4] Orsino turns everything into verbal fantasies, to feed his desire for sensation. Even an invitation to healthy activity produces a pun:

CURIO: Will you go hunt, my lord?
ORSINO: What, Curio?
CURIO: The hart.
ORSINO: Why, so I do, the noblest that I have.

(I. i. 16–18)

Instead of hunting, he develops an elaborate conceit of himself as Actaeon. For Orsino, all activities (including love itself) are swallowed up by the language that expresses them, and the result is a life of words alone, with no hope of action. Sir Toby plays tricks with such simple terms as 'late' and 'early' in order to give himself an excuse to keep on drinking:

SIR TOBY: ... Not to be abed after midnight is to be up
               betimes; and 'diluculo surgere' thou know'st –
SIR ANDREW: Nay, by my troth, I know not; but I know to be
               up late is to be up late.
SIR TOBY: A false conclusion! I hate it as an unfill'd can.
               To be up after midnight and to go to bed then is
               early; so that to go to bed after midnight is to go
               to bed betimes.

(II. iii. 1–8)

Sir Andrew sees the truth of the matter – one imagines him picking his way, slowly and carefully, to the conclusion that to be up late is to be up late. But Sir Toby can talk rings around him, and create a fantasy world where the cry of 'Time, gentlemen, please'

---

[4] On the treatment of language throughout the play, see Terence Eagleton, 'Language and reality in *Twelfth Night*', *Critical Quarterly*, IX (autumn 1967), pp. 217–28. Eagleton stresses the power of language to create an illusory world, divorced from reality.

is never heard. Malvolio also creates a fantasy world, and bends language to this purpose. The one point in Maria's letter that does not seem to co-operate must be made to co-operate: 'M, O, A, I. This simulation is not as the former; and yet, to crush this a little, it would bow to me, for every one of these letters are in my name' (II. v. 125–7). When convinced of Olivia's love, he takes even 'fellow' as a term of endearment (III. iv. 72–3). Sir Andrew's futile aspirations include a desire to be eloquent, and he anxiously collects words that he thinks will help: ' "Odours," "pregnant," and "vouchsafed" – I'll get 'em all three all ready' (III. i. 87–8). He does not notice the irony with which Viola used the words. His problem is not so much that he creates his own private world from language – rather, that his feelings of verbal inadequacy make him susceptible to the fantasies of others, Sir Toby in particular. He is always trying to catch up – 'Is that the meaning of "accost"?', 'What's your metaphor?', 'What is "pourquoi" – do or not do?' (I. iii. 55, 67, 86). For all these characters, language is not a means of escaping from the private self, and making contact with others; it is rather a means of defining the self and confirming its private-ness – one more barrier erected against the realities of the world outside.

It is not so much that words are inherently unreliable, as in *Love's Labour's Lost*. It is more that words, honest enough if let alone, can be made corrupt by those who use them. Feste and Viola, who both depend on words – one as a professional wit, the other as a messenger of love – see the dangers of the medium on which they rely:

FESTE: . . . To see this age! A sentence is but a chev'ril glove to a good wit. How quickly the wrong side may be turn'd outward!

VIOLA: Nay, that's certain; they that dally nicely with words may quickly make them wanton.

FESTE: I would, therefore, my sister had no name, sir.

VIOLA: Why, man?

FESTE: Why, sir, her name's a word, and to dally with that word might make my sister wanton. But indeed words are very rascals since bonds disgrac'd them.

VIOLA: Thy reason, man?

FESTE: Troth, sir, I can yield you none without words, and words are grown so false I am loath to prove reason with them.

(III. i. 10–23)

This special awareness of language sets Feste and Viola somewhat apart, as characters with an extra measure of insight. And to some extent they are free from the constraints of circumstance and personality that afflict the others. They can move, as no one else can, from one household to another; and they can extend their natures by playing roles, while keeping the role and the inner personality distinct: 'I am not that I play' (I. v. 173); 'I wear not motley in my brain' (I. v. 51–2).

Both characters show, in their different ways, a sensitivity to the people they deal with. Feste in his role as commentator and entertainer has to understand the minds of his audience, and tune his speech to their moods – as Viola also does in a less calculating way, when she speaks of love to Olivia and Orsino. It is Viola, in fact, who sees most clearly this aspect of the fool's art:

> He must observe their mood on whom he jests,
> The quality of persons, and the time;
> And, like the haggard, check at every feather
> That comes before his eye.

(III. i. 59–62)

He knows already what amateurs like Berowne must learn – the importance of his audience. We see him, before risking his satire on Olivia's mourning, testing the air: 'I must catechize you for it, madonna. Good my mouse of virtue, answer me' (I. v. 57–8). From this point of view, Malvolio is the sort of audience every comedian dreads, for he knows just how much depends on him, and he refuses to co-operate: 'Look you now, he's out of his guard already; unless you laugh and minister occasion to him, he is gagg'd' (I. v. 81–2). But the others, at one time or another, fall under Feste's spell, and in this respect he goes some way towards drawing together the broken world of Illyria. He can unite Sir Toby and Sir Andrew into a silent, appreciative audience by singing to them of love; he can rouse Olivia and Orsino to laughter. On the rare occasions when he takes a direct part in the action, it is to bring people together: he fetches Olivia to her first meeting with Sebastian, and he delivers the letter that clears up the confusion surrounding Malvolio. But these direct interventions are rare. If his role as entertainer gives him freedom of movement, it also gives him a certain detachment. One reason for his absence in the early stages of the trick against Malvolio may be that he cannot be part of a team, taking sides with one faction against another. Foolery – which 'does walk about the orb like the sun' (III. i. 36) – is too universal for that. When he does join in the trick, impersonating Sir Topas, he plays for both sides, taking instructions from Malvolio as well as Sir Toby. An important condition of his professional freedom is that he does not become too closely involved with any member of his audience. His role, in the end, is both liberating and confining.

In Viola we see an intuitive, outgoing sympathy, an ability to share in the predicaments of others: her involvement is greater than Feste's, for she lacks his professional detachment. Like Olivia, she begins by mourning for a brother, and when she hears of the Countess's grief, she exclaims 'O that I serv'd that lady' (I. ii. 41). But her sympathy for both Olivia and Orsino finally depends on a shared experience of unrequited love. When Orsino tells her 'It shall become thee well to act my woes' (I. iv. 25), he is speaking more truly than he knows, for she feels for him what he feels for Olivia – and what, ironically, Olivia feels for her. E. K. Chambers writes of Viola, 'With the specific of simple truth she purges the pestilence of artifice and rhetoric.'[5] On the contrary, she uses the rhetoric of love for all it is worth. She makes her first serious contact with Orsino by demonstrating that she can speak his language:

ORSINO: . . . How dost thou like this tune?
VIOLA: It gives a very echo to the seat
        Where Love is thron'd.
ORSINO: Thou dost speak masterly.
        My life upon't, young though thou art, thine eye
        Hath stray'd upon some favour that it loves.

                             (II. iv. 19–23)

---

[5] *Shakespeare: A Survey* (Harmondsworth, 1964), p. 41.

He takes her eloquence as a sign of love, and whatever we may feel about this as a general principle, he is right in this case. But despite her eloquence, her outgoing sympathy and the freedom created by her role as Cesario, that role (like Feste's) finally imposes limits on her. We see her power, and the restrictions on that power, in two crucial interviews – one with Olivia and one with Orsino.

When Viola comes to Olivia's house as the messenger of Orsino's love, barrier after barrier falls. Sir Toby is ordered away from the gate, and replaced by the more formidable Malvolio; but when Malvolio reports his attempt to keep Viola out, the messenger sounds so interesting that she is admitted after all. In the interview itself the process continues: Viola is left alone with Olivia; and then Olivia unveils. Step by step, but rapidly, Viola is allowed to take liberties that would have seemed unthinkable at the beginning of the scene. This progressive removal of inhibition is reflected in the way language is used. At first we may wonder how seriously Viola is taking her own mission:

> Most radiant, exquisite, and unmatchable beauty – I pray you tell me if this be the lady of the house, for I never saw her. I would be loath to cast away my speech; for, besides that it is excellently well penn'd, I have taken great pains to con it.
>
> (I. v. 160–4)

She emphasizes that she is putting on an act, and thus calls into question the sincerity of her words; she denies the reality of Orsino's love, for reasons we can guess – 'Whoe'er I woo, myself would be his wife' (I. iv. 41). Olivia responds in the same spirit, asking 'Are you a comedian?' (I. v. 171). Like the ladies of *Love's Labour's Lost*, she mistrusts the conventional words of love, and Viola's emphasis on the theatrical nature of her mission makes this mistrust greater – as it is presumably intended to:

> OLIVIA: Come to what is important in't. I forgive you the praise.
> VIOLA: Alas, I took great pains to study it, and 'tis poetical.
> OLIVIA: It is the more like to be feigned; I pray you keep it in.
>
> (I. v. 180–5)

When they are left alone the joking continues in the same vein for a while; but Viola cannot restrain her curiosity about her rival, and asks to see her face. Her first reaction is a little catty – 'Excellently done, if God did all' (I. v. 221) – but she is deeply impressed all the same. She can now see Olivia from Orsino's point of view, and with the generosity that is part of her nature she urges his suit with a new seriousness. Olivia's readiness to unveil, and her comic but touching anxiety that the result be appreciated – 'Is't not well done?' (I. iv. 220) – suggest that she is succumbing herself, but she keeps her defences up with conventional anti-Petrarchan jokes. Viola will have none of this, and persists now that she has seen it in taking Olivia's beauty seriously:

VIOLA: 'Tis beauty truly blent, whose red and white
         Nature's own sweet and cunning hand laid on.
         Lady, you are the cruell'st she alive
         If you will lead these graces to the grave,
         And leave the world no copy.

OLIVIA: O, sir, I will not be so hard-hearted; I will give out
         divers schedules of my beauty. It shall be inventoried,
         and every particle and utensil labell'd to my will: as –
         item, two lips indifferent red; item, two grey eyes with
         lids to them; item, one neck, one chin, and so forth.
         Were you sent hither to praise me?

VIOLA: I see you what you are: you are too proud;
         But, if you were the devil, you are fair.
         My lord and master loves you – O, such love
         Could but be recompens'd though you were crown'd
         The nonpareil of beauty!

OLIVIA: How does he love me?

                                               (I. v. 223–39)

The last question suggests that, for all her joking about the conventional language of love, Olivia has become fascinated by Viola's eloquence and wants to hear more.

She does indeed hear more. When Viola creates an image of yearning, unrequited love ('Make me a willow cabin at your gate . . .') she fuses her understanding of Orsino's love with her own experience of passion, and the conventional posture of

adoration expresses the truth of her own situation. As it was in
As You Like It – but this time more swiftly and directly – the
satiric view is swept aside, and we see that through convention
love can find its truest expression. Moreover, the sheer ambiguity
of the speech – does it refer to Orsino, or Viola, or both? – cuts it
loose from any specific love affair, and makes it a general image of
unrequited love, conventional, recognizable, and therefore available to anyone. It clarifies Olivia's growing interest in Cesario, for
her reaction to it is 'You might do much. / What is your parent-
age?' (I. v. 260–1). In creating this image of her own feelings,
Viola has unwittingly helped Olivia to acknowledge hers. And
like Phebe, Olivia is forced to admit the reality behind the conventions:

> Even so quickly may one catch the plague?
> Methinks I feel this youth's perfections
> With an invisible and subtle stealth
> To creep in at mine eyes.
>
> (I. v. 279–82)

Love at first sight, love coming through the eye – they are clichés,
and earlier in the scene such clichés were mocked; but here their
power is finally acknowledged. But if Viola has broken down
Olivia's inhibitions, there are obvious ironies in her achievement.
She arouses in Olivia a passion for herself, as Cesario, that she
cannot gratify. She will now have to see unrequited love from a
new, unexpected point of view: the willow cabin is at her own
gate. The scene ends with a flurry of frustration – Olivia's painful
faux pas of offering Viola money, Viola's indignant exit and
Olivia's hurried expedient of sending the ring. Some barriers have
fallen, some contact has been made, but in the end the women are
more deeply embroiled than ever in the problems of a love that
can reach out but not touch its object.[6]

Viola's reaction when she realizes what has happened is 'Dis-

---

[6] This scene is analysed from a similar point of view by Charles Tyler Prouty,
'*Twelfth Night*', *Stratford Papers 1965–67*, ed. B. A. W. Jackson (McMaster
University Press, 1969), pp. 118–22. However, he takes a different view of
Viola's 'Make me a willow cabin at your gate . . .', which he sees as more purely
artificial than I do; he views the whole scene as game-like from beginning to
end.

guise, I see thou art a wickedness / Wherein the pregnant enemy does much' (II. ii. 25–6). Disguise has allowed her the freedom to serve both her master and herself, in the way she handles her mission to Olivia; it has allowed her a freedom to comment about love, both mocking it and acknowledging its power without having to admit openly her own special interest. But disguise is also a barrier: it prevents Olivia from seeing how misdirected her love is, and it prevents Orsino from knowing how far his affection for Cesario may really go. Viola herself continually strains against the disguise, dropping broad hints: 'I am not that I play' (I. v. 173); 'I am not what I am' (III. i. 138). Orsino unwittingly looks behind the disguise to the reality:

> For they shall yet belie thy happy years
> That say thou art a man: Diana's lip
> Is not more smooth and rubious; thy small pipe
> Is as the maiden's organ, shrill and sound,
> And all is semblative a woman's part.

unusual + ironic

(I. v. 29–33)

Normally, when another character describes one of these disguised heroines, the emphasis is on the pert boyishness one imagines as a quality of the boy actor himself. This emphasis on the femininity of Cesario is unusual; it is as though Orsino is trying to wish the disguise away. In her indirect declaration of love, Viola also struggles against the barriers imposed by the disguise, depicting this time a woman in the semblance of a man:

ORSINO: What kind of woman is't?
VIOLA: Of your complexion.
ORSINO: She is not worth thee, then. What years, i'faith?
VIOLA: About your years, my lord.

(II. iv. 25–7)

The scene in which she makes this declaration is an interesting parallel to her first scene with Olivia. As Olivia's reserve is broken down, so (at first) is Orsino's self-indulgence. He begins by presenting himself as a pattern of love:

> Come hither, boy. If ever thou shalt love,
> In the sweet pangs of it remember me;

> For such as I am all true lovers are,
> Unstaid and skittish in all motions else
> Save in the constant image of the creature
> That is belov'd.
>
> (II. iv. 14–19)

But his interest in Cesario's love draws him out of himself, and shows him capable of a wry detachment from his own posturing:

> For, boy, however we do praise ourselves,
> Our fancies are more giddy and unfirm,
> More longing, wavering, sooner lost and won,
> Than women's are.
>
> (II. iv. 31–4)

The detachment, however, does not last. Feste's song, 'Come away, come away, death', establishes a mood of languid grief all too congenial for Orsino, and under its spell he returns to his old posture. When Viola asks him to imagine a woman who loves him as much as he loves Olivia, he declares,

> There is no woman's sides
> Can bide the beating of so strong a passion
> As love doth give my heart; no woman's heart
> So big to hold so much; they lack retention.
> Alas, their love may be call'd appetite –
> No motion of the liver, but the palate –
> That suffer surfeit, cloyment, and revolt;
> But mine is all as hungry as the sea,
> And can digest as much.
>
> (II. iv. 92–100)

At this point – as in the earlier scene with Olivia – attendants have been dismissed and they are alone. And once again, Viola creates a set piece on unrequited love, describing her sister, who

>   lov'd a man,
> As it might be perhaps, were I a woman,
> I should your lordship.
>
> (II. iv. 106–8)

and who, in suffering this love, 'sat like Patience on a monument, /
Smiling at grief' (II. iv. 113–14). The image, as before, is drawn
from her own experience, yet generalized. This time, she is urging
Orsino to recognize that she can feel the same passions as he does;
indeed she strives to go him one better:

> We men may say more, swear more, but indeed
> Our shows are more than will; for still we prove
> Much in our vows, but little in our love.
>
> (II. iv. 115–17)

They are virtually in competition, seeing which can outdo the
other in declarations of constancy. She is also asking him, by implication, to remember his own words about woman's constancy
and man's fickleness. He is clearly fascinated and sympathetic;
and in the ensuing dialogue we sense that they are drawing very
close to each other:

> ORSINO: But died thy sister of her love, my boy?
> VIOLA: I am all the daughters of my father's house,
> And all the brothers too – and yet I know not.
> Sir, shall I to this lady?
> ORSINO: Ay, that's the theme.
> To her in haste. Give her this jewel; say
> My love can give no place, bide no denay.
>
> (II. iv. 118–23)

Viola's riddling reply comes breathtakingly close to breaking the
disguise altogether; but still the barrier holds. With an audible
effort, they change the subject, and the feelings she has roused in
him are redirected towards Olivia. To some degree, it is the disguise that has kept them apart; but there is also something in the
images of love they have created that stands in the way of fulfilment. Orsino depicts his love as an active, selfish, insatiable
appetite; Viola portrays hers as passive, selfless, but at bottom
sterile and self-enclosed, like his own. The two are complementary
and therefore drawn to each other; but neither suggests any
capacity for sharing or for mutual sympathy. The irony is that
Orsino and Viola, in exchanging experiences as they do, demonstrate a sympathy they cannot express: the images they have
found for love belittle and even betray it, concentrating on its

privateness, but the interplay of minds that surrounds these images suggests a deeper capacity for love than either of them can make articulate. The scene ends, like the scene with Olivia, on a note of frustration.

Both scenes are lively and moving in their depiction of the efforts people make to reach each other across the barriers of situation and personality. As in *The Merchant of Venice*, characters react to a fantastic situation with behaviour that is convincingly, frustratingly human. As in *Much Ado*, more is expressed in the subtext than appears on the surface of the dialogue. And one of the basic problems of Shakespearian comedy is here explored eloquently: we see the conventions of speech, the literary images, that characters use in an attempt to make contact with each other; and we see that these conventions both help and betray them, just as Viola's disguise frees and imprisons her at the same time. There is nothing didactic in this: it is not an abstract exploration of the nature of language. Rather, it is a theatrical demonstration of language in action, of the complex dilemmas involved in the characters' efforts, spurred on by love, to break out of the privateness of the individual mind.

The comic figures operate in quite a different way, and their scenes are dramatically simpler. There is no subtext, for there are no hidden depths of feeling: the self-indulgence, the pretensions, and the mutual hostility are out in the open. And while the lovers struggle with misunderstandings they have not created and cannot solve themselves, the misunderstandings of the comic plot, centred on Malvolio, are deliberately manufactured by Maria and her cohorts. Here, the barriers that separate people are actually fortified. The hostility between Malvolio and the rest of the household has a sharpness unusual among Shakespeare's comic figures. When Malvolio threatens Sir Toby with dismissal from his comfortable position in the household, or when Sir Toby retorts 'Art any more than a steward?' (II. iii. 108), we see that each man knows, as if by instinct, the other's most sensitive spot. The air is filled with grudges and threats:

SIR TOBY: Wouldst thou not be glad to have the niggardly rascally sheep-biter come by some notable shame?

FABIAN: I would exult, man; you know he brought me out
o' favour with my lady about a bear-baiting here.

SIR TOBY: To anger him we'll have the bear again; and we will
fool him black and blue.

(II. v. 4–9)

This passage introduces Malvolio's letter scene; and Sir Toby's
last speech suggests that now Malvolio himself will be the bear.
Bear-baiting is not a bad image for the sport Malvolio's enemies
have with him – a single ungainly figure surrounded by nimble
adversaries.

Malvolio's letter scene shows how radically different are the
dramatic methods Shakespeare employs in the two plots. Instead
of the subtle mingling of sympathy and concealment in the scenes
with the lovers, we are shown two quite separate trains of thought,
operating independently. Malvolio figuratively enclosed in his
private fantasy, and the listeners literally enclosed in their box-
tree, engage in competition rather than dialogue:

MALVOLIO: To be Count Malvolio!

SIR TOBY: Ah, rogue!

SIR ANDREW: Pistol him, pistol him.

SIR TOBY: Peace, peace!

MALVOLIO: There is example for't: the Lady of the Strachy
married the yeoman of the wardrobe.

SIR ANDREW: Fie on him, Jezebel!

FABIAN: O, peace! Now he's deeply in; look how imagination blows him.

MALVOLIO: Having been three months married to her,
sitting in my state –

SIR TOBY: O, for a stone-bow to hit him in the eye!

(II. v. 32–43)

This is the Jonsonian device of putting a character on display,
while others make sardonic remarks about him[7] (a device Shakespeare uses again in Parolles's drum scene in *All's Well That Ends
Well*). The effect is not so much to provide a comic dislocation of
Malvolio – that is hardly necessary, for he is sufficiently ridiculous
on his own – as to let each party strike sparks off the other. While

[7] Cf. *Every Man in his Humour*, III. iv and *Every Man out of his Humour*, II. ii.

all the obvious laughter of the scene is against Malvolio, the fact
that he is utterly unaware of the jests hurled at him gives him,
theatrically, a comic integrity: his private world is so utterly self-
sufficient that nothing can pierce it. The number and volubility of
the interruptions emphasize the point. His listeners talk almost as
much as he does, and the fact that he hears nothing, though it is of
course a convenient theatrical convention, is also a way of drama-
tizing his complete isolation from reality.[8] He even (like Parolles)
scores a few points of his own, creating in his private world a
passive and deferential Sir Toby, against whom the real Sir Toby
can only fume indignantly, and mentioning 'a foolish knight'
whom Sir Andrew immediately recognizes as himself. Most of the
laughs are against Malvolio, but not all of them.

The scene also includes yet another set piece describing unrequited love – though this time it is not a literary convention
expressing truth, but a pure and simple sham:

> Jove knows I love,
>> But who?
> Lips, do not move;
>> No man must know. . . .
> I may command where I adore,
>> But silence, like a Lucrece knife,
> With bloodless stroke my heart doth gore;
>> M.O.A.I. doth sway my life.

(II. v. 89–99)

This reads like a parody of the attitude struck by Viola in her
'Patience on a monument' speech in the previous scene. Here the
glib rhymes and mechanical rhythm make us see the attitude as
pure cliché. And Malvolio's reaction is quite different from those
of Olivia and Orsino. Instead of moving him to sympathy with the
imagined Olivia, or even to recognizing in her plight an image of

---

[8] The point is often emphasized in production by the comic inadequacy of the
conspirators' attempts to hide. In Tyrone Guthrie's production at Stratford,
Ontario in 1957, Sir Toby, Sir Andrew and Fabian hid behind the pillars which
are part of the permanent stage, and which are considerably thinner than the
average actor. As Malvolio moved about the stage, the other actors revolved
slowly around the pillars, keeping (in theory) out of his angle of vision. At one
point, Sir Andrew actually read the letter over Malvolio's shoulder, spelling out
the words with him.

his own, the letter releases in him only another flood of egotistical self-satisfaction:

> I will be proud, I will read politic authors, I will baffle Sir Toby, I will wash off gross acquaintance, I will be point-devise the very man. I do not now fool myself to let imagination jade me; for every reason excites to this, that my lady loves me. She did commend my yellow stockings of late, she did praise my leg being cross-garter'd; and in this she manifests herself to my love, and with a kind of injunction drives me to these habits of her liking. I thank my stars I am happy.
>
> (II. v. 143–51)

I, I, I. Viola created generalized images of unrequited love, that both concealed and revealed her true situation, and struck responsive chords in her listeners. The image Maria creates is a comic fraud, and draws out of Malvolio a feeling expressed by none of the serious lovers in the play – a smug satisfaction at being the object of love. We might notice, however, that the delight of his listeners in the gulling of their victim is equally smug. The scene is splendidly funny in performance, and we do not ask awkward questions about the characters' behaviour. But like so many great comic scenes it is based on a view of humanity – in this case, of competing egotists – that is anything but sanguine. The lovers' awkward but earnest attempts at contact are thus thrown into relief. The difference between the two plots is finally not just a matter of dramatic idiom or technique, but a basic difference of vision.

We see this difference emphasized in a single long scene, III. iv, in which comic and romantic figures become embroiled with each other in a manner unusual for the play – Viola challenged by Sir Andrew and Malvolio attempting to court Olivia. Malvolio presents a comic variation on the unrequited loves of the main plot. When he addresses Olivia there is a complete breakdown of understanding, as words not only fail to communicate but cease to have any significance at all:

MALVOLIO: 'Be not afraid of greatness.' 'Twas well writ.
OLIVIA: What mean'st thou by that, Malvolio?

MALVOLIO: 'Some are born great' –
OLIVIA: Ha?
MALVOLIO: 'Some achieve greatness,' –
OLIVIA: What say'st thou?
MALVOLIO: 'And some have greatness thrust upon them.'
OLIVIA: Heaven restore thee!
MALVOLIO: 'Remember who commended thy yellow stockings' –
OLIVIA: 'Thy yellow stockings?'
MALVOLIO: 'And wish'd to see thee cross-garter'd?'
OLIVIA: 'Cross-garter'd?'
MALVOLIO: 'Go to, thou art made, if thou desir'st to be so;' –
OLIVIA: Am I made?
MALVOLIO: 'If not, let me see thee a servant still.'
OLIVIA: Why, this is very midsummer madness.

(III. iv. 37–53)

He flings what he thinks are her own words back at her, and she, so far from recognizing them, does not even understand them. To compound the joke, he does not notice her bewilderment; her interjections have no more effect than those of the eavesdroppers in the earlier scene. For all the contact they make with each other they might be speaking pure gibberish. The egotism of Malvolio's 'love' is nowhere better demonstrated, and beside him the figures of the love plot, for all their self-absorption, appear quite sensitive to each other.

Sir Andrew as the valiant duellist cuts an equally ridiculous figure, in some ways parallel to Malvolio's posture as a lover. But unlike Malvolio he cannot even imagine himself as truly valorous. When Malvolio breaks up the revels, Sir Andrew's dormouse valour can rise no higher than 'to challenge him the field, and then to break promise with him and make a fool of him' (II. iii. 120–1). However, in a world of comic deception, the appearance of valour is what matters. Sir Toby advises him:

> so soon as ever thou see'st him, draw; and as thou draw'st, swear horrible; for it comes to pass oft that a terrible oath, with a swaggering accent sharply twang'd off, gives manhood more approbation than ever proof itself would have earn'd him.

(III. iv. 168–72)

Not trusting Sir Andrew to achieve even this much, Sir Toby takes charge of the affair himself, and creates false images of both Sir Andrew and Cesario as valiant fighters. While productions usually emphasize the visual comedy of the scene, inherent in such lines as 'Fabian can scarce hold him yonder' (III. iv. 269), much of the comedy is in fact verbal. In Malvolio's courtship words become meaningless; here, they become liars, as Sir Toby creates two deadly fighters out of words alone. Viola, out of her depth in this world (as Malvolio is in the world of love) is just as much fooled as Sir Andrew. Her own deceptions – describing an imaginary sister, for example – have grains of truth in them, and she is not equipped to deal with a pure comic deception like this one.

But the final, crucial difference between the two plots lies in the manner of their respective endings. The deceptions of the love plot are partly the result of chance, and chance can take a hand in resolving them. But the deceptions of the comic plot are man-made, the result of fixed, antagonistic, personalities. And there is no easy or satisfying solution for this plot. After our initial amusement, we become aware of the inherent cruelty of the jokes against Malvolio. We have seen in earlier plays, notably *The Merchant of Venice* and *Much Ado*, that wit is not always in season, and in *Twelfth Night* the same realization grows towards the end. We are not bothered by the letter scene, whose pace and *brio* prevent any awkward emotional involvement; but when Malvolio is shut in a dark room, begging for light, we see the victim's sufferings a little too clearly, and our laughter acquires an edge of distaste. In the practical jokes against Katherina the Shrew and Christopher Sly there was in the jokers a civilized detachment, a lack of animosity towards the victim, that prevented the jokes from going too far. There is no such detachment here. The jokers' reaction when their victim is down is to hit him again:

MARIA: Nay, pursue him now, lest the device take air and taint.
FABIAN: Why, we shall make him mad indeed.
MARIA: The house will be the quieter.

(III. iv. 125–8)

No end is postulated except their own exhaustion with the jest: 'We may carry it thus, for our pleasure and his penance, till our very pastime, tired out of breath, prompt us to have mercy on him' (III. iv. 131–3). But in the end they never show mercy. The joke simply turns sour, and Sir Toby wishes to rid his hands of it, but has no idea how: 'I would we were well rid of this knavery. If he may be conveniently deliver'd, I would he were; for I am now so far in offence with my niece that I cannot pursue with any safety this sport to the upshot' (IV. ii. 65–8). Sir Toby feels no compassion for the victim; merely a weariness with the joke, and a growing fear for his own position.

Malvolio in his dark room is the play's most vivid image of the trapped, isolated self. The scene is almost an emblematic one, with Malvolio 'within', reduced to a crying voice, Sir Toby and Maria remaining aloof even from their own jest (as they have always been aloof from its victim) and Feste reducing objective reality to a mad jumble by impersonating two different characters and assuring Malvolio that the windows of his house are 'transparent as barricadoes' (IV. ii. 36). Malvolio insists that his chamber is dark 'as hell' (IV. ii. 35), and in fact it is something like a comic image of hell. The scene brings to a head references to hell and devils scattered throughout the play: Malvolio's apparent madness is of course associated with demonic possession; and Sir Toby has declared that he will follow Maria 'To the gates of Tartary, thou most excellent devil of wit' (II. v. 184–5). Even the confusions of the love plot have been attributed to devilish interference, as in Viola's 'Disguise, I see thou art a wickedness / Wherein the pregnant enemy does much' (II. ii. 25–6) and Olivia's startling cry, 'A fiend like thee might bear my soul to hell' (III. iv. 207). The dark-room scene itself ends with Feste's bizarre song of the Vice and the Devil. Egotism and loveless solitude are a kind of damnation, and the imprisoned Malvolio is our clearest image of this.

This scene of darkness and confusion is followed immediately by Sebastian's

This is the air; that is the glorious sun;
This pearl she gave me, I do feel't and see't;

And though 'tis wonder that enwraps me thus,
Yet 'tis not madness.

(IV. iii. 1–4)

The two characters are mirror-opposites.[9] Malvolio, assured of Olivia's love, is the victim of a conventional comic deception in which his senses betray him; Sebastian, actually presented with Olivia's love, wonders if it is a fantastic illusion. Malvolio insists, vainly, that he is not mad. Sebastian thinks so too, but with greater hesitation, wondering whether to trust his senses or not:

I am ready to distrust mine eyes
And wrangle with my reason, that persuades me
To any other trust but that I am mad,
Or else the lady's mad; yet if 'twere so,
She could not sway her house, command her followers,
Take and give back affairs and their dispatch
With such a smooth, discreet, and stable bearing,
As I perceive she does.

(IV. iii. 13–20)

Like Christopher Sly, like the lovers of *A Midsummer Night's Dream*, he is poised between dream and reality, unsure which is which. And, like Antipholus of Syracuse, he is prepared to surrender to a dream, and accept the happiness it holds for him: 'Let fancy still my sense in Lethe steep; / If it be thus to dream, still let me sleep!' (IV. i. 61–2).

Viola had said of Olivia, 'Poor lady, she were better love a dream' (II. ii. 24) – but now Olivia's dream is coming true. And Sebastian will find that his dream, too, is reality. The comic plot is conventionally full of false images – Maria's letter, Feste's disguise, Sir Toby's description of Sir Andrew as a dangerous swordsman. And when Malvolio adopts the external shows of love, in yellow stockings, cross-gartered and relentlessly smiling, the result is simply absurd. In this plot, images and appearances have no validity except as signs of comic confusion. But the romantic

[9] The connection between the two characters was emphasized in John Barton's production for the Royal Shakespeare Company in 1969: as Sebastian assured himself he was not mad, there were lingering cries from Malvolio in the cellarage.

plot operates by a different set of rules. In her first scene Viola is prepared to trust the Sea Captain on appearance alone:

> There is a fair behaviour in thee, Captain;
> And though that nature with a beauteous wall
> Doth oft close in pollution, yet of thee
> I will believe thou hast a mind that sits
> With this thy fair and outward character.
>
> (I. ii. 47–51)

Throughout the romantic plot, a trust in appearances, though it may lead to temporary confusion, is justified in the long run. To Orsino, Cesario looks like a woman; he is a woman. To Olivia, he looks like a man; he is a man. Antonio loves Sebastian for his appearance, and cries out against false seeming when he thinks he has been betrayed:

> And to his image, which methought did promise
> Most venerable worth, did I devotion. . . .
> Virtue is beauty; but the beauteous evil
> Are empty trunks, o'erflourished by the devil.
>
> (III. iv. 346–7; 353–4)

The charge is misdirected: Antonio has been deceived, but only in a limited, technical way; his original trust in Sebastian's appearance was sound enough. Only for the clowns is it dangerous to go by looks, as Sir Andrew finds when he strikes the wrong Cesario.

This trust in images is made possible by the special handling of the figure of Cesario, in which the extension of personality implied in disguise is taken further, and exploited in a more daring way, than in any previous comedy of Shakespeare's. When Viola and Sebastian meet at the end of the play, the reactions of the others suggest something more than the simple discovery that there are two characters who look alike. Orsino exclaims 'One face, one voice, one habit, and two persons! / A natural perspective, that is and is not' (v. i. 208–9). Antonio asks 'How have you made division of yourself?' (v. i. 214), and even Sebastian holds back for a moment the natural explanation of the seeming miracle:

Do I stand there? I never had a brother;
Nor can there be that deity in my nature
Of here and everywhere.

(v. i. 218–20)

The reunion of the twins is a moment of still, poised formality: action freezes in the contemplation of a miracle, and natural explanations emerge only slowly. Theatrically this moment counts for more than the pairing of the lovers, and so it should. The joining of the twins is the crucial action; after it has been accomplished the lovers can slip easily into couples, for the problem is already solved. But the plot significance of this moment is a clue to something deeper. The single being in a double body is an image of love to set against the opposing image of the solitary ego—Malvolio in his dark room. It recalls the fable of Aristophanes in Plato's *Symposium*: a single being, divided into two bodies, seeks reunion, and this is the source of love. The singleness of personality is broken down.[10] Orsino continues to address Viola as 'boy' and 'Cesario' (v. i. 259, 371), and the jokes have a certain resonance: unlike Rosalind, Viola keeps her male attire to the end. Sebastian's pun about his own virginity also suggests a blurring of distinctions, even a blurring of sexes:

You would have been contracted to a maid;
Nor are you therein, by my life, deceiv'd;
You are betroth'd both to a maid and man.

(v. i. 253–5)

He has, in an earlier scene, admitted something feminine in his own nature: 'My bosom is full of kindness, and I am yet so near the manners of my mother that, upon the least occasion more, mine eyes will tell tales of me' (ii. i. 35–7). Viola's almost telepathic sympathy, in taking her own escape as a guarantee of Sebastian's safety, suggests another way of breaking down the exclusiveness of personality (i. ii. 19–21). In other comedies a single personality is extended by disguise, but the extension is temporary and finally withdrawn; this is the only case in which

10 See Walter N. King, Introduction to *Twentieth Century Interpretations of Twelfth Night* (Englewood Cliffs, 1968), pp. 10–12.

the new figure created by disguise has also an objective reality, a life of its own. Viola's creation of Cesario is confirmed, as no ordinary comic pretence could be, by the existence of Sebastian. It is as though mind has actually created matter, and the distinction between spirit and body, like other distinctions, is blurred:

VIOLA: If spirits can assume both form and suit,
           You come to fright us.
SEBASTIAN: A spirit I am, indeed,
           But am in that dimension grossly clad
           Which from the womb I did participate.

                             (v. i. 227–30)

The human spirit may be bound to a particular body, or a particular mind; but that is not necessarily its permanent or natural condition. This idea is parodied in the comic plot, in Feste's exchange with Malvolio on 'the opinion of Pythagoras concerning wild fowl' (IV. ii. 48–58); but here it is one of the serious implications that surround the idea of love.

The resolution of the love plot does not depend on the will, or the knowledge, of individuals. It is an impersonal, organic process: confusion gathers to a head, and breaks.[11] Sebastian has no Prospero-like authority: he solves the lovers' problems not by what he knows, but by what he is. He provides a true version of the false, comic images of the subplot – a real lover for Olivia, a real fighter who can put the two knights in their place.[12] And he is to some degree an outsider, bringing with him (like Bassanio) the fresh air of a different world: in his second scene, we hear for the first time of a Plautine seaport town, with lodgings, markets and monuments. But his role as one half of Cesario is what matters most, and his most important action is simply to appear when

[11] As the confusion intensifies, the tone of the love plot darkens temporarily, with Antonio's painful mistake about Viola and the brief flurry of melodrama at the start of the final scene – Orsino willing to kill Viola, Viola willing to die, Olivia demanding a husband who denies her, and Orsino believing (like Antonio) that he has been betrayed. The effect of all this is to sharpen our sense of relief when the confusion is suddenly dispelled.

[12] C. L. Barber describes the sense of sheer relief when Sebastian strikes Sir Andrew: 'The particular implausibility that there should be an identical man to take Viola's place with Olivia is submerged in the general, beneficent realization that there is such a thing as a man.' See *Shakespeare's Festive Comedy* (Cleveland, 1967), p. 246.

Viola is also on stage. Viola may seem to have more will, and more initiative. But when we compare her with Rosalind we see how much she is the creature rather than the creator of the plot. We never hear the reason for her sea voyage,[13] nor is her disguise ever justified in a literal way. Other heroines offer rationalizations for their disguises, usually based on the dangers of travel. But in this case the decision is simply presented to us, justified in the most cryptically general terms:

> Conceal me what I am, and be my aid
> For such disguise as haply shall become
> The form of my intent.

(I. ii. 53–5)

In the predicaments created by her disguise Viola submits to destiny, rather than trying to solve the problem herself: 'O Time, thou must untangle this, not I; / It is too hard a knot for me t'untie!' (II. ii. 38–9). Olivia also submits to destiny in acknowledging her love for Cesario: 'Fate, show thy force: ourselves we do not owe; / What is decreed must be; and be this so!' (I. v. 294–5). The lovers in fact are in a situation beyond the control of any individual; only a benevolent fate, by bringing the twins together, can solve their problems. As in the image of love presented by Cesario, the importance of the individual is broken down – a process that disturbs initially but ultimately brings joy. As in Shakespeare's last plays, the sea is invoked throughout, and carries suggestions of a power beyond human will – frightening, destructive, yet finally benevolent – the devouring sea of Orsino's love fantasies, and the life-giving sea of Viola's 'Tempests are kind, and salt waves fresh in love' (III. iv. 368).[14] The sea has the same function here as the impersonal cycles of nature in earlier comedies: it suggests the characters' dependence on forces beyond their control.

[13] See John W. Draper, *The Twelfth Night of Shakespeare's Audience* (Stanford, 1950), p. 133.

[14] In John Barton's production the sound of the sea was heard at crucial moments; most effectively, at the reunion of the twins. Besides direct references to the sea, the play's dialogue is full of nautical jokes: 'Will you hoist sail, sir? Here lies your way' (I. v. 190); 'Then westward-ho!' (III. i. 132); 'you are now sail'd into the north of my lady's opinion; where you will hang like an icicle on a Dutchman's beard' (III. ii. 24–6).

The pairing of the lovers in the final scene is likewise beyond considerations of individual temperament. It is, like the meeting of the twins, a generalized image of love. Within that image, the pairing of Orsino and Viola carries some psychological conviction: their interest in each other is already established, and even when Olivia appears, Orsino's greeting, 'Here comes the Countess; now heaven walks on earth' (v. i. 91), is rendered perfunctory by the speed with which he goes back to what really interests him – a conversation about Cesario. His joking with Feste, and the references to the sea fight, suggest that Orsino's personality may be more balanced and complete, and his capacities wider, than mere indulgence in love melancholy. There is enough material here to make us see his match with Viola as satisfying, if we are inclined to ask for satisfaction in psychological terms. Even so, Orsino's actual transfer of affection is too swift and simple to bear much literal-minded inspection. And Olivia's marriage to Sebastian, seen literally, would be a clear case for immediate annulment. We are not, however, encouraged to take it this way. Olivia never speaks to Sebastian after she has learned the truth, and her only reference to her marriage is addressed to Orsino, stressing its formal aspect:

> My lord, so please you, these things further thought on,
> To think me as well a sister as a wife,
> One day shall crown th'alliance on't, so please you,
> Here at my house, and at my proper cost.
>
> (v. i. 303–6)

Her pairing with Sebastian is part of a formal design, and we are encouraged to think of it in those terms alone. Expecting more than this, some critics have asked, as S. C. Sen Gupta does, 'Can we call this a happy ending? Or rather shall we look upon such a conclusion to a comedy as a fitting prelude to the dark comedies and great tragedies?'[15] Clifford Leech describes the ending as 'an exposure of the triviality of human desire';[16] and Philip Edwards concludes that the union of the lovers is treated sardonically, Shakespeare having become tired of such endings.[17] Other critics

[15] *Shakespearian Comedy* (London, 1950), p. 173.
[16] *Twelfth Night and Shakespearian Comedy* (Toronto, 1968), p. 7.
[17] *Shakespeare and the Confines of Art* (London, 1968), pp. 68–9.

see the mating of the lovers as a purging of folly and a return to normality.[18] That too seems to be imposing on the ending significance of a kind that it is not designed to bear. There are no apologies or statements of forgiveness as the lovers join hands; indeed their minds are hardly examined at all.[19] The ending takes little account of the reasons for particular attachments; it is, on the contrary, a generalized image of love.

As such, its significance is limited. We can easily think of Rosalind and Orlando married and producing children, for they think of themselves that way; but the union of lovers in *Twelfth Night* is more a freezing of the moment of romantic contemplation, before the practical business of marriage: Viola is to be 'Orsino's mistress, and his fancy's queen' (v. i. 374). Feste has a few marriage jokes in his repertoire (I. v. 18; III. i. 30–3), but the lovers themselves never consider the realities of wedlock as Rosalind does. The happiness they have achieved is more stylized and conventional. It is also both miraculous and exclusive: it cannot touch the ordinary world. While Touchstone and Audrey can join the procession of couples in *As You Like It*, the comic figures of *Twelfth Night* pass through the final scene untouched by its harmony. Sebastian, the agent of release for the lovers, has given the knights nothing but a sound beating. Sir Toby's false friendship for Sir Andrew has collapsed: for the first time, the lean knight is insulted to his face. Malvolio, like Viola, has seen himself in the hands of a benevolent fate: 'Well, Jove, not I, is the doer of this, and he is to be thanked' (III. iv. 77–8). But his faith is rudely shattered. For the lovers, time is held in abeyance by a static moment of fulfilment; for the clowns, time goes relentlessly on. To Feste's 'thus the whirligig of time brings in his revenges', Malvolio replies 'I'll be reveng'd on the whole pack of you' (v. i. 364). The whirligig shows no sign of ever stopping.

In *As You Like It* time was primarily the medium of fulfilment; it was also admitted to be the medium of decay, but that view was firmly placed as secondary. In *Twelfth Night* the two views are

[18] See, for example, Larry S. Champion, *The Evolution of Shakespeare's Comedy* (Cambridge, Mass., 1970), p. 88; and Harold Jenkins, 'Shakespeare's *Twelfth Night*', *The Rice Institute Pamphlet*, XLV (January 1959), p. 21.
[19] See John Russell Brown, *Shakespeare and his Comedies* (2nd edition, revised: London, 1968), p. 33.

more closely balanced. Time brings the lovers to each other, un-tangling the knot as Viola said it would; but we are constantly reminded that time does other work as well. The two verses of 'O mistress mine' strike a balance: in the first, 'Journeys end in lovers meeting'; in the second, 'Youth's a stuff will not endure' (II. iii. 42–51). Orsino and Viola contemplate the transience of beauty: 'For women are as roses, whose fair flow'r / Being once display'd doth fall that very hour' (II. iv. 37–8). Other pleasures decay, too: Feste is warned, 'your fooling grows old, and people dislike it' (I. v. 104). Sir Toby's revels end with the cold chill of morning: 'Let's to bed, knight. Thou hadst need send for more money' (II. iii. 171–2). At the end, this sense that time finally destroys our illusions and brings us to decay is centred on the broken figures of the clowns. Time as the medium of fulfilment belongs to the lovers. And the special moment of the play's title shares this double significance: Twelfth Night celebrates the Epiphany, the showing forth of a miraculous birth; but it is also the last night of a revel, before the cold of winter closes in.

The last scene is neither a still point of harmony nor a simple dying fall: it is the busiest, most complex scene in the play, as the private, magic happiness of the lovers vies for attention with the larger, uncontrollable world of time inhabited by the clowns. The two plots affect each other slightly: Sir Toby's brisk mating with Maria is underplayed, but it may show them achieving their own kind of harmony; and when we hear that the Sea Captain who has Viola's 'woman's weeds' is 'in durance, at Malvolio's suit' (v. i. 268), there may be a suggestion that the full happiness of the. lovers is conditional on a reconciliation with Malvolio. Orsino commands, 'Pursue him, and entreat him to a peace; / He hath not told us of the captain yet' (v. i. 366–7). But for the most part Shakespeare prefers to maintain the tension by swift alternations between the happiness of the lovers and the battered condition of the clowns. Sebastian's entrance is preceded by the entrance of the bleeding knights; the vows of the lovers are interrupted by Malvolio. And while the lovers seem to have escaped from ordinary reality, it is still in the background: even the reunion of the twins is touched by a reference to their father's death (v. i. 236–40). And the ending as a whole is placed within the larger sweep of time: since Olivia and Sebastian were contracted, says the Priest, 'my watch hath told me, toward my grave, / I have travell'd but two hours' (v. i. 156–7). The twins' father 'died that day when Viola from her birth / Had numb'red thirteen years' (v. i. 236–7). The miracle of Cesario is thus played off against the uncontrollable world of time. This kind of tension is basic to Shakespearian comedy: it is at bottom a tension between stylized and realistic art. The lovers, having engaged our feelings as human beings, are now fixed in a harmony we can believe in only by trusting the power of fantasy; the clowns, stylized in their own way at first, have lost some of the immunity of comedy and now present an image of defeat that is uncomfortably real.

The tension is resolved, unexpectedly, in Feste's last song. It seems at first to belong to the vision of the comic plot. Feste sings of our decay through time, from the folly of childhood to the knavery of manhood to a drunken collapse in old age. The lovers have disappeared, and there is a solitary figure on stage. His experience, as often in the comedies, is linked to ours through the medium of nature – this time the wind and the rain. Yet before we sink too easily into melancholy, the song concludes: 'But that's all one, our play is done, / And we'll strive to please you every day' (v. i. 393–4). In *As You Like It* the play was put aside as an illusion, but its vision of humanity walking to the Ark in pairs was confirmed by the audience itself. In *Twelfth Night* the triumph of love is put at a distance, as a strange and special miracle that cannot touch everyone. But the vision of decay that opposes it is also, in the last analysis, one more illusion, part of a play. The one thing that is permanent is the work of art itself: tomorrow it will be there to entertain us again, even if we are all a day older. As in Shakespeare's sonnets, art is a means, perhaps the only means, of cheating time, of holding human experience in permanent form. Orsino says of 'Come away death',

> Mark it, Cesario; it is old and plain;
> The spinsters and the knitters in the sun,
> And the free maids that weave their thread with bones,
> Do use to chant it. . . .
>
> (II. iv. 42–5)

It has survived through time; it can entertain the simplest folk of the working-day world and the most sophisticated courtiers. We have seen in the play as a whole the power of conventional images to touch their hearers. The same may be true of the stylized image of the lovers in the final scene: the fact that it is obviously a matter of literary artifice does not make it invalid; on the contrary, its bold stylization strikes through to the heart of experience. When Feste is left alone on stage the vision of an uncontrollable world of time and decay may seem for a moment to overwhelm the happiness of the lovers. But just as, in *As You Like It*, satire fights a sudden rearguard action at the end, so in *Twelfth Night* there is, against all odds, a final rescue for artifice.

10 Conclusion: beyond Twelfth Night

The comic device of juxtaposing different styles, and ultimately different kinds of experience, has led Shakespeare increasingly to set two kinds of art against each other: an art that orders life into self-consciously formal designs, and an art that conveys an image of experience as disordered and uncontrollable. We tend to think of the latter as 'realistic', because it is hard to perceive in our own lives the finished shape we see in comedy; and if we are to see the Noah's Ark endings as reflecting one possibility in reality, we need to suspend a certain natural scepticism. The effort may be worthwhile, for the easy assumption that 'real life' has no pattern may indicate nothing more than our own failure to perceive the pattern, and part of the business of art is to keep us alert to the deeper order beneath the seemingly random surface of experience – the order that Sidney called a golden world. That, at least, was how the Renaissance regarded art; and Shakespeare, like most of his contemporaries, asks us to accept many seeming improbabilities for the sake of the truth they embody. He retains, however, a dramatist's fascination with opposing visions. In the comedies, this frequently leads to his defining the limits of the golden world by showing a disordered world outside it. The ending of *Twelfth Night* provides our clearest image of this opposition. Here, the integrity and the internal conviction of the golden world are great enough to persuade us that it is no less valid an image of life than the uncomfortable sight of the battered knights, the angry steward and the clown shut out in the wind and the rain. But the split between the two visions is more radical than before, and the balance is closer: even in *The Merchant of Venice*, Shylock was finally kept out of sight, if not out of mind; in *Twelfth Night* two different plays seem to be ending simultaneously on the same stage, and whatever the tensions of previous comedies, we have never felt this before. Shakespearian comedy as we have known it breaks apart: the device of opposing visions finally destroys the art it serves.

But while Shakespeare's attention turns increasingly to tragedy, he never loses his interest in comic form. Instead, he extends the possibilities of comedy, at first by allowing the sceptical vision freer rein. The concentration on romantic love is broken, and with it the assumption that if Jack has Jill the audience will be satisfied. The so-called 'dark comedies' owe much of their darkness to the manner in which scepticism about comic form, from being part of a piquant juxtaposition, becomes positively destructive. In *Measure for Measure* and *All's Well That Ends Well* the neat patterns of the story – and both stories are as artificial as those of previous comedies – are imposed on the awkward, intractable material of an unromantic world, where people simply will not behave.[1] Helena tries to win Bertram by the miraculous device of curing the King; everyone is impressed except Bertram. Like Bassanio, Helena has gone through the conventional process of passing a test to win love, but this time the trick will not work. Bertram is not ready for love, and the convention breaks down in the face of this intractable reality. The Duke in *Measure for Measure* similarly imposes conventional plot designs on intractable human material, and while he never meets the sort of dramatic rebuff suffered by Helena, there is a demonstrable gap between the neat, ordering patterns woven by his mind and our own sense of what the other characters are like, and what sort of world they inhabit. For example, his neat couplet, 'O, what may man within him hide, / Though angel on the outward side' (III. ii. 253–4), is too sharp a reduction of Angelo's complex nature. After the moral

---

[1] I have discussed *All's Well* from this point of view in '*All's Well That Ends Well*: the testing of romance', *Modern Language Quarterly*, XXXII (March 1971), pp. 21–41.

and emotional dilemmas of Angelo, Isabella and Claudio have been exposed in all their hopelessness, the Duke suddenly produces Mariana out of nowhere, like a rabbit from a hat. This is satisfyingly neat as a plot device, but we cannot help feeling a sudden contraction of vision, as a largely technical solution is applied to problems that were originally conceived as more than technical.

While the Duke and Helena both achieve a measure of success in the end, there is no feeling that life as a whole can be satisfactorily ordered. There will always be Pompeys and Barnardines. Angelo may repent and reform, but Pompey whipped out of one trade merely reappears in another, becoming, ironically, part of the very machinery of justice that sought to correct him. And Friar Peter, charged with bringing Barnardine to the light, has, we feel sure, an impossible task. In the final scene the heckling of Lucio distracts us from the Duke's efforts to create an ordered finale, and Lucio is the one character the Duke will not forgive: lechery and judicial murder may win his pardon, but scene-stealing is an unforgivable offence. Lucio's impertinence alerts us to something contrived and artificial in the finale, and when, out of the blue, the Duke asks Isabella to be his wife, the artificiality becomes quite blatant. The comic structure seems to be seeking its own ends, independent of the reality of the characters.

In *All's Well That Ends Well*, the marriage of the central characters is finally sealed, but with palpable hesitation on Bertram's part: 'If she, my liege, can make me know this clearly, / I'll love her dearly, ever, ever dearly' (v. iii. 309–10). It would have been so easy to express Bertram's submission another way, without that nagging 'if'; but we are reminded that Helena's victory is conditional. We are reminded also, throughout the final scene, that human nature is finally intractable. Parolles, like Pompey, is an expert survivor: he is crushed with a plot, but he springs back, not only unrepentant but exploiting his shame; and Lafeu, his old enemy, adopts him: 'Though you are a fool and a knave, you shall eat' (v. ii. 50–1). Nor is Bertram really a more hopeful subject for reform. From a realistic viewpoint, Proteus and Claudio are notoriously unattractive matches for Julia and Hero, but we are kept from thinking of them in those terms by the emphasis on formal design at the end of their respective plays. Much of the finale of *All's Well*, however, far from reconciling us to Bertram, is designed to expose him as a liar, a hypocrite, a lecher – and what is more, not very successful in any of these activities. It is not unlike the exposure of Parolles in the drum scene. There is even a painful irony in the success of Helena's bed trick: 'when I was like this maid, / I found you wondrous kind' (v. iii. 303–4). She has known him as a passionate lover only because he thought she was someone else. Yet wounded though she has been, and awkward though his repentance is Helena still claims him: she might say, as Lafeu does to Parolles, 'let thy curtsies alone, they are scurvy ones' (v. iii. 317). She does not need his repentance; she wants only him. Or as Mariana says of Angelo, 'I crave no other, nor no better man' (v. i. 424). Those who give us most pain are often those we love most deeply, for love has nothing to do with approval or self-interest, and can bind us helplessly to one whose conduct gives us great offence. This idea is implicit in *The Two Gentlemen of Verona* and *Much Ado About Nothing*, but its presentation is so lightened and conventionalized as to draw much of the sting from it. But in *All's Well* – as in the sonnets – we are forced to see this aspect of love frankly and fully, and beneath the conventional comic finale is a profounder vision of the power, and the demands, of love. The easy, technical satisfaction of seeing the lovers join hands is supplanted by something more disturbing, and in the end more moving – an awareness of how much it costs them to do so.

The formal pattern of comedy is exposed as inadequate; we are forced instead to see human character as a power stronger than the impersonal rhythms that control a purely comic world. These are the comedies of a writer whose mind is turning increasingly to tragedy. In *Troilus and Cressida* the opposing voices create a broken, discordant world, and the abstract visions of love, honour and order with which the characters try to impose meaning on their lives break down through the treacherous instability of the characters' own natures. Hector abandons his argument for peace even more quickly than Cressida her vision of eternal fidelity. Ulysses, having given definitive expression to the necessity of order and degree, reveals his own policy as a Machiavellian exploitation of men's envy of each other. *Troilus and Cressida* contains more abstract, philosophical dialogue than any other play of Shakespeare's; yet at the end war is reduced to blind fighting rage, and love to diseased exhaustion. If comic form can no longer impose a satisfying order, neither can philosophy. The major tragedies take us even further. Like the comedies, they contain broken ceremonies – Lear's love test, Macbeth's banquet, Othello's wedding night. But here the implications of the broken ceremony are far more terrible. And while there may be some suggestion of order at the end, the idea gives no real satisfaction. A striking feature of the tragedies is the inadequacy of the survivors' comments in the final scenes. Cassio may order what tortures he likes for Iago, but this will not console us for Othello's suffering; and Albany's attempts to order the state are a pitiful irrelevance. Even Malcolm's victory leaves us detached. We have seen his enemies too clearly to dismiss them, as he does, as 'this dead butcher, and his fiend-like queen' (v. viii. 69). Those are the tones of melodrama, and we have watched a tragedy. There may indeed be order in the world, but Shakespeare's tragedies force us instead to contemplate the private agonies of the soul, to align ourselves not with nature, the gods or the community, but with those who are cast out by all three.

  While the term 'comedy' has to be stretched a little if it is to include Shakespeare's final plays – since, after all, they include suffering and horror of a kind that comedy does not normally admit – we can see that, broadly speaking, they represent a return to comic form. The most important sign of this is their insistence on a total vision of order to which individual characters are subservient – thus reversing the vision of the tragedies. This, as much as the fantastic nature of the stories they tell, makes us think of them as artificial. In *Pericles* and *Cymbeline* in particular, formal design goes largely unchallenged, as though these two plays, being the earliest in the new manner, embodied the sharpest recoil from tragedy. Even the brothel in *Pericles*, though it may seem at first to revive the coarse, indestructible vitality of Pompey, is powerless against Marina's virtue. Her employers are reduced to comic exasperation as she preaches divinity to the customers, and sends them off to hear the Vestals sing. The play has a neat moral pattern unusual in Shakespeare, and Gower's final speech, surveying

the major characters, presents a self-satisfied catalogue of wickedness punished and virtue rewarded. In the words of Miss Prism,
'The good ended happily and the bad unhappily; that is what
fiction means.' Behind the moral design is the wish fulfilment
pattern of comedy: after all the loss and sorrow, the broken family
is miraculously restored. It is this kind of design, rather than any
moral issue, that dominates *Cymbeline*. The finale is an intricate,
beautifully efficient machine in which an astonishing number of
disguises are removed, misunderstandings swept away and re-
unions accomplished. The sheer scale of the achievement, as much
as the suggestion of Jupiter's intervention, identifies the final
vision of harmony as artificial. But within the play, as in *Pericles*,
there is no serious challenge to artifice: this fantastic vision is the
only kind of reality the play is prepared to show.

But in Shakespeare's last four extant plays (counting the colla-
boration with Fletcher)[2] the patterns of artifice, while still
allowed conviction of a kind, are once again challenged from
within the play by a feeling that life is not entirely controllable. In
Pericles and *Cymbeline* death strikes the wicked, and we are satisfied; in *The Winter's Tale* it strikes the innocent.[3] The plot works
itself out in the usual way, but it leaves this time a residue of unmerited suffering that cannot be neutralized. Shakespeare con-
tents himself with one miracle of rebirth: those who have loved
Mamillius and Antigonus have to make do with substitutes. And
while Autolycus may be pressed into service by the plot, he retains, like Pompey, his own indestructible life, independent and
unchastened. He sees the fortunes and misfortunes of the main
characters purely as they affect his business:

---

[2] In the following discussion, I have accepted the attribution of *The Two Noble
Kinsmen* to Shakespeare and Fletcher, and the commonly agreed division of
scenes: see Clifford Leech, introduction to the Signet edition (New York, 1966),
p. xxiv. I have kept an open mind about *Henry VIII*, but here the best evidence
appears to suggest that the play is substantially Shakespeare's: see R. A. Foakes,
introduction to the Arden edition (London, 1964), pp. xvii–xxviii. What I have
not assumed is that the presence of two writers necessarily means that a play will
be incoherent and impossible to discuss critically.

[3] The death of Simonides, announced at the end of *Pericles*, may seem to qualify
the joy of the family reunion. But Pericles's exclamation, 'Heavens make a
star of him!' (v. iii. 80) suggests a final triumph over death, and softens the
blow.

in this lethargy I pick'd and cut most of their festival purses; and had not the old man come in with a whoobub against his daughter and the King's son and scar'd my choughs from the chaff, I had not left a purse alive in the whole army.

(IV. iv. 606–9)

He represents one kind of life that no vision of magic harmony can assimilate. Prospero, in *The Tempest*, may seem at first like an all-knowing wizard controlling the plot; but in fact his world is even harder to control than Duke Vincentio's. If he does produce a final harmony, it is very hard-won indeed: we can sense the effort it costs him in his tense relations with his servants, and his own uncertain temper. He wins a satisfying repentance from Alonso, but nothing of the kind from Antonio and Sebastian; the best he can do is keep them under control by polite blackmail (v. i. 126–9). On the other hand, in his harsh treatment of Ferdinand –

> this swift business
> I must uneasy make, lest too light winning
> Make the prize light.

(I. ii. 450–2)

– the conventional narrative design seems self-consciously imposed on the lovers: so much so that it looks like needless meddling.

Henry VIII presents a vision of history in mythical terms, a grand design in which great men fall in their pride, and a miraculous vision of social order is centred on a new-born child. But there is also a constant, ironic awareness of the political and sensual motives that drive this impressive machine. It may be, as the Lord Chamberlain says of Anne Bullen: 'from this lady may proceed a gem / To lighten all this land' (II. ii. 78–9). But Henry's role in the miracle is the subject of wry comment:

CHAMBERLAIN: It seems the marriage with his brother's wife
Has crept too near his conscience.
SUFFOLK: No, his conscience
Has crept too near another lady.

(II. ii. 14–16)

Katharine's vision of the spirits who offer her a heavenly garland – as in the previous scene, we saw Anne Bullen with an earthly crown – suggests a different kind of miracle, and a glory beyond this world. But the vision ends with Katharine's cry, 'Spirits of peace, where are ye? Are ye all gone? / And leave me here in wretchedness behind ye?' (IV. ii. 83–4). We return to the misery of this world, and the harsh medical facts of Katharine's condition:

> Do you note
> How much her Grace is alter'd on the sudden?
> How long her face is drawn! How pale she looks,
> And of an earthly cold! Mark her eyes.
>
> (IV. ii. 95–8)

The heavenly comfort is real enough; but so is the earthly suffering; and the two are balanced against each other.

The Two Noble Kinsmen, the most sombre of the final plays, presents its characters as trapped unhappily in the machinery of a fantastic story. Emilia, won in a tournament of love – which she herself has refused to attend – cannot keep her mind off the defeated knight: 'Is this winning? / O all you heavenly powers, where is your mercy?' (v. iii. 138–9.)[4] And when the dispute of Palamon and Arcite reaches its neat, ironic conclusion, there is an edge of grimness in Theseus's appreciation: 'Never Fortune / Did play a subtler game' (v. iv. 111–12). The mechanical appropriateness with which happiness and misery are meted out produces not satisfaction at the justice of the gods but a stoic, even sardonic, recognition of man's littleness:

> O you heavenly charmers,
> What things you make of us! For what we lack,
> We laugh; for what we have, are sorry; still
> Are children in some kind. Let us be thankful
> For that which is, and with you leave dispute
> That are above our question. Let's go off,
> And bear us like the time.
>
> (v. iv. 130–6)

The play is nominally a romance; but its final note would not be out of place in a tragedy. As I have suggested earlier, there is often something impersonal in Shakespeare's vision of order. Here,

---

[4] References are to the Signet edition, cited in note 2, p. 260.

the final order is not so much impersonal as inhuman; and the characters submit to it with more resignation than enthusiasm. Patterned, conventional art, trusted so often, has finally turned sour.

The image of Shakespeare finishing *The Tempest*, bidding farewell, like Prospero, to his own art, and returning to Stratford to feed the swans, is as deeply satisfying as any good myth. But the existence of *Henry VIII*, and the evidence for Shakespeare's hand in *The Two Noble Kinsmen*, are embarrassing to this myth: they suggest that, unlike his readers, Shakespeare was not content with *The Tempest* as a rounding off of his career. The restlessness that kept him experimenting all along kept him writing, until – perhaps – he himself felt his art becoming laborious, and began to grow weary of it. His part in *The Two Noble Kinsmen* has at times a brocaded heaviness, and a painful slowness of movement, unlike the nimble ease of his lesser collaborator: it is as though, for the first time, he worked with reluctance. But in the three plays that precede it, the old confidence in art, even formal and patterned art, can still be detected. We saw that in *Much Ado About Nothing* and *As You Like It* Shakespeare could dissolve the distinction between conventionalized and realistic art. And these two kinds of vision, split at the end of *Twelfth Night*, are rejoined in the later plays, sometimes into a seamless whole. The vision of rebirth embodied in Hermione's statue does not, I have suggested, control the entire world of the play; but within its limits it is surprisingly comprehensive. Hermione is a piece of magic, a work of art – and a woman who has grown old (v. ii. 27–32). As in the earlier comedies. Shakespeare suggests the naturalness of magic: 'If this be magic, let it be an art / Lawful as eating' (v. iii .110–11). Prospero's magic, for all its cataclysmic power, is like Oberon's based on familiar things: 'Ye elves of hills, brooks, standing lakes, and groves' (v. i. 33). The masque he creates for the lovers, formal and emblematic though it is, embodies a concrete vision of the world we know – fields, clouds, rainbows, streams and 'sun-burnt sicklemen, of August weary' (IV. i. 135). Its splendour dissolves at a word from its creator; but so, he tells us, does the 'great globe itself' of which it was an image (IV. i. 146–58). 'Reality' is no more solid than art. And we should notice how the speech ends:

> Sir, I am vex'd;
> Bear with my weakness; my old brain is troubled;
> Be not disturb'd with my infirmity.
> If you be pleas'd, retire into my cell
> And there repose; a turn or two I'll walk
> To still my beating mind.
>
> (IV. i. 158–63)

This is not a vague romantic vision of dissolving glory, but a very precise image of a creative mind contracting, surrendering its vision of the world, descending to a wry awareness of its own infirmities. Prospero's failures and miscalculations – and he is guilty of both – are simultaneously a sign of the limits of any kind of 'art' to order the world, and a sign of the imperfections of one man. In the figure of Prospero art and reality are fused, for in seeing the strengths and limits of artifice we are constantly aware of the uncertain nature, the 'beating mind' of the artificer himself.

Henry VIII offers nothing so profound as this; but at times the ironic split between the grand design of history and the cruder facts of ordinary life is sealed up. The public triumph of Anne Bullen's coronation is connected with the Pompey-Autolycus level of existence, the coarse but indestructible vigour of sensual life. The Third Gentleman describes the crowd in the Abbey:

> Great-bellied women,
> That had not half a week to go, like rams
> In the old time of war, would shake the press,
> And make 'em reel before 'em. No man living
> Could say, 'This is my wife' there, all were woven
> So strangely in one piece.
>
> (IV. i. 76–81)

A similar crowd presses to the christening of Elizabeth, to the annoyance of the Porter:

> Is this Moorfields to muster in? Or have we some strange Indian with the great tool come to court, the women so besiege us? Bless me, what a fry of fornication is at the door! On my Christian conscience, this christening will beget a thousand: here will be father, godfather, and all together.
>
> (V. iv. 31–6)

The ceremonial triumph of the courtiers, the miraculous vision of Cranmer and the bawdy vigour of the mob fuse into a single complex image of the renewal of life – just as, a dozen years earlier, *As You Like It* had ended with mirth in heaven and fun in bed.[5]

Twelfth Night took the comedy of romantic love about as far as it could go, and in later work the range of material is much wider. We see that love can take many shapes, and that comedy itself can embody an astonishing variety of experiences. Every play is a fresh beginning, an attempt to create a new world, and to see its relation to what we understand of the old one. Even our scepticism, and Shakespeare's, about the value of art[6] becomes part of the artistic vision; but so too does our capacity for trust. At the start of *Cymbeline*, when the First Gentleman, having set up the fantastic premises of the story, declares,

> Howsoe'er 'tis strange,
> Or that the negligence may well be laugh'd at,
> Yet it is true, sir.

– the Second Gentleman replies obediently 'I do well believe you' (i. i. 65–7). We too, it seems, are required to accept the rules and to play the game. Paulina tells the watchers at Hermione's statue, 'It is requir'd/ You do awake your faith' (v. iii. 93–4). She might well be speaking to us. Yet a few minutes later, she can admit

> That she is living,
> Were it but told you, should be hooted at
> Like an old tale.
>
> (v. iii. 115–17)

– and here too our own possible responses are brought into the play. We are collaborators, in that our mixture of trust and scepticism becomes part of the drama. And as Puck appealed for our pardon, and our 'hands', Prospero goes further: an act of our imagination – not of his, which is used up – must finish the story and return him to Milan:

[5] For a fuller discussion of the robust sensual comedy in *Henry VIII*, see G. Wilson Knight, *The Crown of Life* (London, 1965), pp. 297–306.
[6] For a detailed and sensitive discussion of this aspect of Shakespeare's work, see Philip Edwards, *Shakespeare and the Confines of Art* (London, 1968).

> Let me not,
> Since I have my dukedom got,
> And pardon'd the deceiver, dwell
> In this bare island, by your spell;
> But release me from my bands
> With the help of your good hands.
> Gentle breath of yours my sails
> Must fill, or else my project fails,
> Which was to please.

(Epilogue, 5–13)

That was Feste's project too – 'We'll strive to please you every day.' The clown and the magician both seem old and tired; and the illusions of the art that created them seem used up, for they address us with an implicit acknowledgement that they are really actors. But each has a final trick up his sleeve: Feste's is to ask us to come and see the play again; Prospero's is to ask us to finish the play ourselves. The illusions of Shakespeare's comic art become, in the end, a part of our own lives.

Index

Agnew, Gates K., 74n, 77n
Alexander, Peter, 45n
Ariosto
    Orlando Furioso, 157
Auden, W. H., 165n

Bandello, Matteo
    Novelle, 157, 163
Barber, C. L., 66n, 85n, 115n, 248n
Barnet, Sylvan, 187, 188, 213n
Barton, Ann, 35, 69n, 71n, 81n, 87n
Barton, John, 55n, 86n, 245n, 249n
Berry, Ralph, 66n, 71n
Bradbrook, M. C., 55, 76n, 175n
Brook, Peter, 112n
Brooks, Charles, 12n, 61n
Brooks, Harold, 11n, 22n
Brown, John Russell, 59n, 118n, 164n, 251n
Brunvald, Jan Harold, 49n
Bullough, Geoffrey, 2n, 14n

Calderwood, James L., 71n
Carroll, Lewis, 142
Chambers, E. K., 15n, 164n, 231n
Champion, Larry S., 108n, 251n
Charlton, H. B., 14n, 39

Chesterton, G. K., 101
Coghill, Nevill, 59n, 61n, 118n
Congreve, William
    The Way of the World, 206

Danby, John F., 30
Daniels, Maurice, 55n
Dent, R. W., 99n
Doran, Madeleine, 33n
Draper, John W., 28, 249n
Duthie, George Ian, 61n

Eagleton, Terence, 228
Edwards, Philip, 87n, 101n, 250, 265n
Evans, Bertrand, 97n, 164n

Fender, Stephen, 167
Feydeau, Georges, 96
Fleischer, Jeannette, 223n
Fletcher, John, 260
    and William Shakespeare
    The Two Noble Kinsmen, 260n, 262–3
Foakes, R. A., 9n, 16n
Frye, Northrop, 17

Gascoigne, George
    Supposes, 46, 48

Gilbert, W. S.
   The Pirates of Penzance, 39
Goddard, Harold C., 118n
Godshalk, William Leigh, 30n
Gogol, Nikolai
   The Government Inspector, 218
Gower, John
   Confessio Amantis, 14n
Granville-Barker, Harley, 119
Grebanier, Bernard, 121n
Greene, Robert
   James IV, 46
Grim the Collier of Croydon, 107n
Guthrie, Tyrone, 149n, 240n

Halio, Jay L., 191n
Hamilton, A. C., 6
Hands, Terry, 147n
Heilman, Robert B., 54n
Henze, Richard, 155n
Hibbard, G. R., 42n, 46, 47n, 53
Hirsch, John, 103n
Hosley, Richard, 45n
Howarth, Herbert, 223n
Hoy, Cyrus, 88n
Hunter, G. K., 42n, 97n, 101
Hyman, Lawrence W., 119, 148n

Jenkins, Harold, 189, 195, 197, 251n
Johnson, Samuel, 169
Jonson, Ben, 46, 223, 239
   Every Man in his Humour, 239n
   Every Man out of his Humour, 239n

Kemp, Will, 24
King, Walter N., 247n
Knight, G. Wilson, 265n
Knowles, Richard, 189n

Langham, Michael, 44n, 87n, 173n
Lascelles, Mary, 195n
Leech, Clifford, 18n, 32n, 37, 39n, 137n, 250

Lewis, C. S., 118n
Lodge, Thomas,
   Rosalynde, 186, 187, 215n
Lyly, John, 156

Mack, Maynard, 42n
Mahood, M. M., 24n
Marlowe, Christopher, 191, 218
Matthews, William, 71n
McCollom, William B., 160n
Midgley, Graham, 119
Miller, Jonathan, 119n
Moody, A. D., 118n
Mucedorus, 91n
Mueschke, Paul, 223n
Muir, Kenneth, 164n
mummers' St George play, 100

Nemerov, Howard, 30
Nunn, Trevor, 44n, 55n

Olivier, Laurence, 86n
O'Loughlin, Sean, 164n
Olson, Paul A., 106n

Palmer, D. J., 200n, 219n
Palmer, John, 114n, 201n
Parrott, Thomas Marc, 138
Peele, George
   The Old Wives' Tale, 46
Pettet, E. C., 22n, 190n
Phialas, Peter G., 83n
Plato
   Symposium, 247
Plautus, 7, 16, 248
   Menaechmi, 1–3, 6, 9, 17, 18, 46
Price, Robert T., 199n
Prouty, Charles T., 155n, 234n

Quiller-Couch, Sir Arthur, 118n

Roesen, Bobbyann
   see Ann Barton
Righter, Ann
   see Ann Barton

Sanders, Norman, 21n, 28, 30n
Sen Gupta, S. C., 250
Shakespeare, William
  All's Well That Ends Well, 218,
    239, 240, 256–8
  As You Like It, xii, 3, 8, 18, 26,
    127, 136, 183, *185–219*, 221,
    222, 234, 247, 249, 251, 253,
    254, 263, 265
  The Comedy of Errors, xii, *1–19*,
    21, 23, 26, 31, 32, 39, 41, 42,
    45, 46, 47, 48, 51–2, 61, 67,
    69, 85, 90, 96n, 102, 122, 166,
    188, 197
  Coriolanus, 130
  Cymbeline, 15, 16n, 193, 259–60,
    265
  Henry IV, Part One, 100
  Henry VIII, 260n, 261–2, 263,
    264–5
  Julius Caesar, 156
  King Lear, 42, 156, 210, 259
  Love's Labour's Lost, 27, *63–88*,
    90, 91n, 94, 96n, 99, 107, 112,
    113, 117, 120n, 121, 127, 135,
    143, 145, 149, 152, 153, 166,
    167–8, 172, 179, 191, 202, 203,
    206, 207, 211n, 217, 221, 228,
    229, 230, 232
  Macbeth, 37, 259
  Measure for Measure, 9n, 71n,
    256–7, 258, 259, 260, 261
  The Merchant of Venice, 7, *117–50*,
    151, 152, 155, 156, 158, 159,
    161, 164, 181, 183, 185, 187,
    206, 216, 219, 238, 243, 248,
    256
  The Merry Wives of Windsor,
    xiiin
  A Midsummer Night's Dream, xii,
    8, 18, 41, *89–115*, 117, 119,
    120n, 130, 142, 143, 144, 147,
    149, 152, 166, 171, 192, 195,
    202, 213, 217, 218, 222, 245
    263, 265

Much Ado About Nothing, xii, 54–
  5, 71, *151–83*, 185, 186, 187,
  190, 195, 213, 215, 219, 238,
  243, 257, 258, 263
Othello, 130, 259
Pericles, 15, 16n, 259–60
Sonnets, 67, 148n, 258
The Taming of the Shrew, 41–62,
  63, 65, 66, 77, 79, 84, 112, 117,
  121, 151, 155, 165, 170, 173,
  191, 206, 218, 243, 245
The Tempest, 15, 248, 261, 263–4,
  265–6
Troilus and Cressida, 258–9
Twelfth Night, xii, 3, 8, 127, 172,
  221–54, 255–6, 263, 265, 266
The Two Gentlemen of Verona, *21–
  40*, 45, 46, 61–2, 71, 75, 77, 82,
  85, 86, 90, 117, 137, 154, 194,
  221, 257, 258
The Winter's Tale, 15, 213, 260–
  1, 263, 265
see also Fletcher
Sidney, Sir Philip, 227, 255
Smith, Marion Bodwell, 6n, 7n,
  16n
Somerset, J. A. B., 24n
Spenser, Edmund
  The Faerie Queene, 157
Sprague, Arthur Colby, 45n, 86n,
  210n
Stauffer, Donald A., 21n
Stevenson, David L., 171, 172n

The Taming of a Shrew, 44n, 45,
  59
Thompson, Karl F., 85n, 177n
Tillyard, E. M. W., 7
Tom Tyler and his Wife, 55
Traversi, Derek, 14n, 53n
Trewin, J. C., 45n, 86n, 210n

Van Doren, Mark, 104, 137n
Vickers, Brian, 41n, 216n
Vyvyan, John, 38n

Weismann, Robert, 24n
Weiss, Theodore, 137n
Wells, Stanley, 17n, 114n
Welsford, Enid, 96
Wilde, Oscar
  The Importance of Being Earnest,
  260
William, David, 227n

Wilson, John Dover, 39n, 173n
Wily Beguiled, 107n
Wood, Peter, 211n

Yeats, W. B., 222
Young, David P., 99n, 101n

Zeffirelli, Franco, 173n